Video Production

Video Production

Putting Theory into Practice

Steve Dawkins and Ian Wynd

First published 2010 by
PALGRAVE MACMILLAN

Palgrave Macmillan in the UK is an imprint of Macmillan Publishers Limited, registered in England, company number 785998, of Houndmills, Basingstoke, Hampshire RG21 6XS.

Palgrave Macmillan in the US is a division of St Martin's Press LLC, 175 Fifth Avenue, New York, NY 10010.

Palgrave Macmillan is the global academic imprint of the above companies and has companies and representatives throughout the world.

Palgrave® and Macmillan® are registered trademarks in the United States, the United Kingdom, Europe and other countries

ISBN-13: 978–1–4039–9888–0 paperback

This book is printed on paper suitable for recycling and made from fully managed and sustained forest sources. Logging, pulping and manufacturing processes are expected to conform to the environmental regulations of the country of origin.

A catalogue record for this book is available from the British Library.

A catalog record for this book is available from the Library of Congress.

10   9   8   7   6   5   4   3   2   1
19 18 17 16 15 14 13 12 11 10

Printed and bound in Great Britain by
CPI Antony Rowe, Chippenham and Eastbourne

Contents

Figures and Tables

Figures

Tables

Introduction

People working within the creative media industries often mystify the process of video production. There is a well-known saying that video production isn't as easy as it looks but isn't as difficult as it is made out to be. While it is true that professional working practices are the result of much training, our starting point is that we believe that anyone has the potential to produce excellent videos. However, there are two things which mark out good or exceptional video production, whether professional or non-professional: the ability of the video-maker to understand and effectively work through the different stages of production *systematically* and their ability to *think about* what they're actually doing at each of those stages and act upon those thoughts.

Video Production: Putting Theory into Practice is a book for students who are new to video production in further and higher education. It is a book which links the types of theory applicable to video production and encountered on a range of different communications, cultural and media courses with the practical skills of video-making. Our contention is that you need to combine the two – theory and practice – in all of your own video productions.

This book, then, seeks to do three main things:

1. to build upon the knowledge of video and moving-image production that you may already have, either from studying video on other courses or from the knowledge that comes from your experience of watching different types of video production at the cinema, on television and on the internet;
2. to provide you with the knowledge, both practical and theoretical, which will allow you both to succeed on your chosen course and to develop as a video-maker;
3. to begin to provide you with the skills and knowledge to allow you to proceed on to higher-level courses or to think about pursuing a career in one of the media industries.

Why link theory and practice?

It is often said, especially by professionals who have been working in the media industries for many years, that theory is irrelevant to film and video production as, in the real world, people don't use the concepts and issues discussed in this book. This often means that video-production students concentrate on acquiring practical skills but marginalize, or neglect altogether, theoretical skills. For Tony Schirato and Jen Webb (2004: 2), this is the distinction between those with 'tacit' ways of seeing and those who practise 'visual literacy': the former are able to describe everything that they see but really move no further; the latter are able to glean information about meaning from the smallest of clues within a text. It is this second kind of reader that you should strive to become, as it is only by being visually literate, or *knowing* about how and why existing films and videos are constructed as they are, that you will become better at *doing*. While media professionals may not *consciously* talk about the type of concepts to which you will be introduced in the book (although we know many who do!), they will definitely have, and use in their work on a daily basis, an *unconscious* awareness of all of them through their long experience of working in these industries.

As lecturers and video-makers, we understand that it is tempting for new video-makers to gloss over theory, dismissing it as unrelated to their practice, but there are immediate rewards to be had from applying theory to practice. You will find that an understanding of theory gives you the confidence to make decisions at each stage of the production process and reflect upon your actions both during and after the process. We all make decisions based on hunches or gut-feelings but often these hunches turn out to be superficial or, at worst, wrong. If you can back up your hunches with theoretical reflection, then it is much more likely that the decisions you make will be both creative and right. The difference between learning the theory and relating it to your own practice and working on hunches could well be what makes the difference between being a director and runner, especially on educational projects. That isn't to say that artistic flair isn't desirable or important, since it is what can make a good production exceptional. However, it cannot, and should not, replace a solid understanding of the process of video production, the ability to use theory to help explain that process and the ability to reflect both during and after production. It is this layered understanding and approach to video production that we hope to encourage in this book.

This is where the activities that we suggest, in conjunction with those provided by your own tutors, will prove useful, since it is only through systematic analysis and reflection that a true in-depth understanding of how and why media products are made as they are and what possibilities there are for making them in different ways.

Organization of the book

This is a book which can be read from cover to cover but can also be dipped into whenever you need information about a specific brief. With this in mind, we have split the book into two distinct sections:

1. Section I is divided into five chapters. Chapter 1 outlines the key theoretical concepts needed as a starting point when analysing existing video work and when producing your own video: these will need to be supplemented by higher-level theory, depending upon the level at which you are working. Chapters 2 to 5 introduce the key practical techniques and skills of which you need to be aware of when producing a video. It is vital that you read and understand these chapters. There is a further chapter on the accompanying website which draws on the information from these chapters and applies it to an example of an existing media product: the American sitcom, *Friends*.
2. Section II provides you with four typical student projects which allow you to experience all the different types of video production to which you may be exposed as a student – location and studio shooting, documentary and drama production, narrative and non-narrative video – while using the key theoretical concepts to explore the projects in more detail.

At various points throughout the book we will advise you to visit the book's companion website at www.palgrave.com/culturalmedia/dawkins. It is vital that you do so, as the website contains dedicated content which will enable you to proceed with the brief that you are working on. What you will also see there is a wealth of supplementary material that will provide background for your activities, downloadable resources and suggestions for supplementary reading.

This book is designed specifically for, and is relevant to, video students in education. There *are* key differences with regard to the practice of professionals within the media industries which are not relevant to students of video production and which we cannot cover in a book of this size and scope. We are aware, too, that readers of this book will be working within the limitations imposed by their own teaching institution. What this means is that there will be different ways of teaching and, more importantly, certain limitations with regard to resources. We are not saying that our approach in this book is the *only* way to learn about the process of video production. What we know, though, from over twenty years' experience of teaching video at all levels, is that the information we have included in this book, and the way we have written it, *is* useful for students. In each chapter and at each stage of production, we have attempted to provide you with ways of working which suit the ways in which students frequently learn.

If reading the book and working through the briefs has made you consider a career in the media industries more seriously, the book's companion website contains a section that provides you with useful information as to how you can achieve this. Although not exhaustive, it gives you useful strategies for improving your chances of working in one of the most competitive and rewarding industries. You might wish to read this first so that you can begin to acquaint yourself with the contents and then, when you have worked through the different briefs, revisit it with more experienced eyes.

Although there is a huge amount of information in this book to be absorbed (some of it very difficult), the reason for the subtitle of the book is that we feel that learning comes not just from academic learning but from putting this learning into practice. You must do one to do the other. The good news is that video-making *is* very hard but is also lots of fun, so there is an underlying assumption in this book that video-making is one of the most satisfying things that you can do, especially when the finished result is one that you can be proud of. We hope that you will be proud of your own productions and we feel that you will be if you *do* link theory and practice.

Producing this book has been very much like producing a video in that we have been through all the same stages but have produced a book rather than a video: pre-production, producing the words and inserting them into the first 'assembly edit' and then tuning them via 'rough cuts' and 'fine cuts' into the finished text. The book has taken an exceptionally long time and we are proud of it but we can still see flaws in it, in the same way that you will when you look at your finished videos. We have an editor friend who argues that projects are never finished, just abandoned. By that she means that it is always possible to improve a project with a little tweak here and there but that this process is never-ending: you have to know when to stop. We have made our decision about where to stop, but if you feel that there is anything in the book which is unclear, misleading or plain wrong, or you have suggestions as to how the book could be improved, we would love to hear from you.

Finally, we sincerely hope that you enjoy reading the book and surprise yourself with the videos you produce.

SECTION

I

....

Theory and Practice

In this first section of the book we will introduce you to a set of easily remembered theoretical concepts which provide a foundation for your analysis, understanding and reflection with regard to both existing media texts and your own work. However, you may need to supplement this with more developed and detailed theory depending upon the level of your course. The second thing this section of the book does is to take you through the various stages of video production in detail. This will form the basis for your own practical work.

Knowing: The Theory of Video Production

Introduction

There is something about the prevalence and simplicity of modern video cameras and camera phones which has turned many of us into non-professional video-makers, often leading us to believe that the process of making videos is simpler than it actually is. There is a tendency to think that making a video, simply involves picking up a camera, choosing the subject for the video, pointing the camera, pressing the record button and ... job done!

Although most students embarking on college and university media courses are almost certain to have made non-professional videos before, they are likely to be new to professional video production. In the following chapters, we want to show you that producing *good* video involves much more. We shall, therefore, introduce you to the theoretical concepts that you will need to consider and will outline the correct processes involved when producing a video. These discussions form the bedrock for the rest of the book in that they introduce all the relevant information which will be worked through in more detail in the remaining chapters.

The theory of video production

When starting a video production course many people are surprised or, more usually, shocked to learn that they will have to think about theory. However, this applies in other areas of life, for example when taking a driving test. Understanding how and why something happens (the theory) can inform the way in which we do something (the practice). It is exactly the same for video production.

In the introduction we looked at some of the reasons why it is important for theory and practice to be studied together, and this chapter aims to provide you with a set of key theoretical concepts from communication, cultural and media studies. They are the 'building blocks' that you need to use, both when analysing existing products and when thinking about and producing your own videos. These concepts are so fundamental that you need

```
I  Institution
C  Contexts of production
A  Audiences
R  Representation
L  Language
I  Ideology
N  Narrative
G  Genre
```

Figure 1.1 The key concepts

not only to be aware of them and understand them but also, much more importantly, to learn them and use them in all your video production work. They are not easy to remember but understanding them means that you can not only effectively analyse existing media products but also make your own productions more creative and critical.

To help you to remember the key concepts we have come up with an easily remembered mnemonic device: I CARLING (shown in Figure 1.1).

These concepts should be used as a first stage when theorizing your work but should also be supplemented by higher-level theory and further reading. We will look in much more detail at each of these concepts in subsequent chapters and will show you how they should be used to inform your own video-production work in relation to specific briefs. For now, though, let us take a brief look at each of the terms.

Institution

In everyday language, the term 'institution' may refer to something physical, often something associated with the state, such as a hospital or a prison. If we use a prison as an example, the term suggests that it is strongly built and has walls and cells and a high level of security. However, as Tim O'Sullivan *et al.*(1994: 152) note, the term 'institution' also refers to 'the underlying principles and values according to which many social and cultural practices are organized and co-ordinated': that is, the values and assumptions which lie behind these easily observable characteristics. So, if we continue with our example of a prison, in analysing the institution of a prison we would need to consider the types of values and assumptions which organize it: for example, the fact that the state controls the prison service, the idea that prisoners should be locked up in those cells and the power of the prison officers over the prisoners.

Just as we can talk about institutions of the state such as prisons, so we can talk about 'media institutions'. This term alludes to the fact that most video productions are made not by individuals but by businesses or organizations. As mentioned above, a full exploration of any media institution would need to focus both on the easily observable characteristics of what the institution is and on the values and assumptions which underpin it. So, for example, we can talk about the BBC as being a media institution. If we were to examine it in detail, we would need to look both at what the institution physically is (the buildings, studios, equipment) and, more importantly, the values and assumptions of the people working within this institution, which will affect the types and styles of programme produced. This is often related to the final aspect of interest with regard to media institutions: who actually owns and/or controls the institution.

With regard to television and video production, there are, broadly speaking, two types of media institution in the UK. They have very different values and assumptions and patterns of ownership and control:

1. *Public service institutions:* these are organizations which are often controlled, either directly or indirectly, by the government, produce media products which are generally universally available, are free from direct external control and are produced to a high standard, primarily for the 'good of the public': in the words of the founder of the BBC, Lord Reith, to 'inform, educate and entertain'. Public service broadcasters tend to be what are called major producers ('majors'). Examples of public service broadcasters include the BBC in the UK and ABC in Australia.

2. *Commercial institutions:* these are organizations which exist primarily to make a profit, either by charging for access to their products or through advertising or sponsorship. They can be split up into major commercial organizations, such as ITV in the UK or NBC in the USA, or independent organizations ('indies') such as Endemol. However, many so-called independents are, in fact, owned by the majors or, as we shall see in the next chapter, entirely dependent upon them.

It is vital to recognize that different institutions will tend to produce very different types of video (or, in media studies terminology, media text) as a result of who owns and controls them and the values and assumptions of the people working within them. In the UK, for example, the primary aim of the BBC has, historically at least, been to focus on the need to inform and educate, leaving the entertainment aspect to its rivals: ITV and, latterly, Channel 4 and Five. It is worth noting, however, that, as a result of developments in modern media such as cable, satellite and the internet, increasingly the values of the two types of institution are tending to permeate each other (Casey *et al.* 2002: 34). Both are increasingly producing programmes that they know are popular, cheap to make and capable of filling up the schedules and/or being repeated on television or, increasingly, streamed on the internet or mobile devices. This goes some way to explaining the extent of reality TV on our screens in the early part of the twenty-first century. More importantly, though, new types of media production and distribution mean that the institutional power of existing media organizations is undergoing rapid and distinct change. It is being eroded by new types of media organization such as Microsoft, Google and Yahoo, consolidated by media organizations merging into transnational corporations such as AOL-Time-Warner and possibly being subverted and made more democratic through community television, internet television and web spaces such as MySpace and YouTube. The book's website looks in more detail at these developments and the challenges and opportunities that they may offer you as a video-maker.

So, key questions that you should ask (and be able to answer!) about the institutional source of *any* text might be as follows:

- *What* is the text's institutional source: that is, is the institution a large corporation or a small independent company? Is it a public service institution or commercial institution?
- *Who* owns and controls the business or organization which produced the text?
- *How* has the institutional source of the text shaped and affected the text?

Even though your current videos are all likely to be produced within the institution of a college or university, when you are planning and carrying out research for your own videos, their likely institutional source if they were being produced 'out in the real world' is something that you need to consider carefully.

Tasks to do

1. Watch a range of different programmes on a number of different channels (both terrestrial and digital cable/satellite if possible). Make sure that you have the institution template, downloaded from the book's website, in front of you.
2. Look at the end credits of each programme to see who has produced it and keep a note of the name of the programme, the type and style of programme and the company which produced it. If you can, label each producer as a public service or commercial organization. In addition, see if you know whether the organization is a major or an independent. Go to the website of the company and look for the answer if you don't know.
3. What, if any, points can you make about types of programmes and their institutional source?

Contexts of production

No video, or indeed any other media product, is produced in a vacuum: its production will always be affected by external considerations. The term 'contexts of production' refers to the types of situation in which different media products are produced and the factors which might influence a production. These external factors will almost inevitably affect whether the text will go into production and, if it does, what it will look and sound like.

Some of the main contexts of production that you need to consider might include the following:

- *The historical context of production*: the historical conditions which exist and which allow for the production of certain types of text while excluding the possibility of others. For example, during the Second World War (1939–45), much of the film production within the USA and UK was dedicated to producing films which were, either explicitly or implicitly, propagandist: that is, they unquestioningly supported the allied war efforts and demonized the German/Japanese.
- *The technological context of production*: the emergence of affordable digital technology, both hardware and software, for example, has meant that many more people than previously can now produce media texts. Remember, though, that this context will be different for people working in different parts of the world: not everyone has the same access to technology.
- *The economic context of production*: the economic conditions which exist and which allow for the production of certain types of text. Will something be profitable? Is it possible to produce something cheaply using existing technology? This is closely related to the notion of institution that we looked at above.
- *The social context of production*: the social conditions which exist and which allow for the production of certain types of text. The women's liberation movement of the 1960s, for example, made possible certain types of cultural production which were previously unknown, as in the case of *Spare Rib*, a magazine with an avowedly feminist political agenda. In terms of moving-image production, the movement also enabled many women who had previously been excluded from cultural production to make challenging, political video. A more contemporary example might be swearing on television: in the 1970s, the Sex Pistols uttered a number of strong swear words on a UK chat show and there was a national outcry; at the beginning of the twenty-first century, the chef Gordon Ramsay can utter the same swear words more than a hundred times in ten minutes on an entertainment programme without a murmur; indeed, it is an integral

part of the entertainment. Social conditions have changed and swearing is now deemed to be more acceptable.

- *The political context of production*: the political conditions which exist and which allow for the production of certain types of text. During the 1980s, for example, the British Government decided that allowing members of the Irish Republican Army (IRA), who were at that time engaged in military activities against the British, to appear on television was 'giving terrorism the oxygen of publicity'. Members of the IRA were, therefore, expressly forbidden from appearing and speaking on UK television programmes. However, broadcasters overcame this by using actors to say their words. Following the Northern Ireland peace process of the 1990s, this was repealed. This is an old example and we are, of course, aware that there are more recent examples, but it is a very good illustration of how the political conditions of the time directly affected the shape of media texts.

Audience

The audience for any media product is simply those people at whom the text is aimed and/or those who are likely to watch it.

Historically, people have tended to talk about the 'audience' as though it were possible to categorize everyone watching into one broad group which shares the same ideas and values, both generally and with regard to what they are watching. While this might be true of audiences where people are physically together in a place such as a theatre (although we very much doubt it), it becomes very problematic when talking of the mass audience for media products such as film and television. However, this has not stopped certain ideas about the relationship between media texts and media audiences and the direct effects (more often than not *bad* effects) which powerful texts are assumed to have on a powerless audience becoming widespread. One continuing example of this might be the long-running debate about violent films and their effects on children.

The audience has increasingly been seen by both academics and producers of media texts to be much more complicated. Rather than being one homogeneous mass, the audience for any programme is likely to be split, or segmented, into different categories and to be more powerful than previously imagined. Advertisers, for example, will rarely, if ever, talk about the audience as one homogeneous group, therefore, but will talk about different audiences based on attributes such as age and gender (*demographic* categories), where people live (*geodemographic* categories) and what their tastes are (*psychographic* categories). Academic writing about audiences has also moved on in two broad ways: first, looking at the different ways in which audiences 'use' the media (what has been termed the 'uses and gratifications' model) and, secondly, looking at the different ways in which media texts can be 'read' (what has been termed the 'encoding/decoding' model). We will look at these ways of categorizing the audience, the relationship between audiences and texts and the problems of segmenting the audience in later chapters.

For the moment though, the key questions that you should ask about the audience for any text might be as follows:

- *Who* is the text addressing? Are there any specific types of audience which are implied by the text? Are there any groups of people whom the text might exclude?
- *What* is the message that the text is seeking to get over to the audience. Is there an assumption that the audience will share that message? Is there only one way of reading the text or are there various possible readings?
- *When* and *where* and *how* is the audience, or audiences, likely to see the text? At what time of day: morning, afternoon or evening? Where: at home, at school or at work? How: on television, on the internet or on a mobile phone? Will it engage their full attention or will they watch it in a distracted manner while doing something else?
- What effects might these conditions have on the way in which the text is read?

Tasks to do

1. Make a list of as many words as you can which describe people: male/female, black/white, gay/straight, young/old, etc. Don't stop until you have at least forty words and, if you are on a roll, keep going. Think, too, about whether some of the categories you have come up with can be split further: young, for example, could be split into babies, toddlers, pre-teens and teenagers.
2. Select three very different television programmes (you may include advertisements if you wish) which obviously appeal to different audience groups. For each programme, choose all the words from the list which seem to be appropriate for that programme.
3. Compare and contrast the audiences that you appear to have identified. What points and/or assumptions can you make about these audiences and the programmes made for them?

Representation

There is a general saying that the camera never lies. This is not true! The term 'representation' refers to the fact that media texts such as videos are *always* constructed artefacts. In the process of their production, certain choices about content and style are inevitably made by the people who produce them. This means that they do not necessarily show reality *as it really is* but can re-present reality in a number of very different ways (including lying!). For example, a fly-on-the-wall documentary following the exploits of a group of city-based debt collectors may alter the viewers' perceptions about these individuals simply by deciding to include, or omit, certain shots or to use certain camera angles or light in a particular way, all of which will make the reality of those debt collectors look different. The audience, of course, may only see the representation and, as such, this becomes their truth.

Much of the work on representation in media and cultural studies has tended to focus on whether or not certain representations are 'distorted' and, if they are, the extent to which they are and the possible effects. One example might be the work of the Glasgow University Media Group (GUMG) and their analysis of news from the 1970s onwards. They found that in news stories about industrial disputes, certain groups of people, such as politicians and business leaders, tended to be given more screen time during news broadcasts than, for example, union members or members of the public, and they were presented in a more positive manner. It is here that we can situate the idea of stereotyping. Stereotyping is where a particular representation of a group out of the many possible is repeatedly chosen and that representation is seen to tell the whole story about that group. It becomes the accepted way which is quickly and easily understood by both audience and producers and is a shorthand way of conveying complex debates, narratives or characters. However, the more negative aspect of the process is that this representation is repeated and repeated until it becomes established as 'the truth', even if it is not. The GUMG found that the point of view of the 'good and reasonable' business leaders tended to be given priority by the people making the news over that of the 'trouble-making' unions. In this respect, the concept of representation links very closely with that of ideology (see below).

As a media producer, which is what you will become when we begin the production activities, you are responsible for the types of representation in your videos. This is a big responsibility.

For the moment, some of the key questions that you should ask about representation within any text should be:

- *Who* or what is being represented by the text? Why are they being represented at all?
- *How* are they being represented: positively? negatively? neutrally? Why are they being represented in this particular way?
- *What* techniques have been used to create this representation?
- *What* are the effects of the types of representation on offer in the text on the way in which the audience(s) will read the text?

Tasks to do

1. Select three different types of television advertisements for differing products from television.
2. For each advertisement, work through the above questions.
3. Write a two-paragraph description of each advertisement, summarizing your key findings. What points can you make about the type of representations that you discovered?

Language

The term 'language' here refers not to the written and spoken language within a media text, but rather to media language: that is, the techniques and filmic languages used to create meaning by film and video-makers in the production of their work. Just as we can talk about written and spoken language being built up from small units of meaning into larger units of meaning, so too can we talk about the same process happening with video (see Figure 1.2).

| LETTERS | are put together to form | WORDS | are put together to form | SENTENCES | are put together to form | TEXTS |
| SHOTS | are put together to form | SEQUENCES | are put together to form | SCENES | are put together to form | TEXTS |

Figure 1.2   Letters–Words–Sentences–Texts

There are specific, accepted rules (or, in media terms, codes) which are used to organize these units of meaning. For example, the way in which lighting is used can dramatically affect the meaning of the shot and the information that the audience receive. If you look at the shots in Figure 1.3, all of which use the same subject and one lamp, you can see what we mean.

Uplighting   Downlighting   Flatlighting

Figure 1.3   Uplighting, downlighting and flatlighting

The only difference between each of these shots is that the lamp used to light the subject has been moved. The difference in meaning, though, is dramatic.

There have been various ways (or methodologies) used to examine how these media languages have been used to create certain meanings and how such meanings have been understood by audiences, and we will look at these throughout the book. For the moment, we would like to introduce (or, as is more likely the case, reintroduce) you to one of the main methodologies used: semiotics.

A brief history and résumé of semiotics

You will almost certainly have come across the term 'semiotics' already, as it is a key methodology used within communication, media and cultural studies to analyse texts. As a result, we do not intend to provide an exhaustive description of what it is and how it is used: for a more detailed description see, for example, Bignell (1997), Branston and Stafford (2006) or Gillespie and Toynbee (2006). What we want to do is to introduce the main points of semiotics which relate most directly to our current discussion around video production. As a brief definition, we can say that semiotics is 'the study of *signs* and sign *systems* and their role in the construction and organization of *meaning*' (O'Sullivan 1994: 32, emphasis added).

Semiotics is a way of analysing meaning by looking at the signs (words, for instance, but also, as we shall see in a moment, pictures, symbols and sounds) which produce and communicate meanings. The highlighted words in the definition above are central to any understanding of what semiotics is and why it is used. We shall, therefore, look in detail at each of these in the following discussion.

The term 'semiotics' was first coined by a European linguist, Ferdinand de Saussure, at the beginning of the twentieth century (although he referred to it as semiology). The word came from the Greek word *semeion*, meaning sign. It later became more generally referred to as semiotics through the work of an American philosopher, Charles Peirce (pronounced purse).

Saussure's only book was entitled *Cours de linguistique générale* or *A Course in General Linguistics* (1915*)*. It was not actually written by Saussure but was written after his death by two of his students from lecture notes made by Saussure. As the title of the book suggests, Saussure was interested in language and particularly the ways in which individual words are organized into systems of language at any one time (what is termed a *synchronic* analysis). Unlike other linguists, he was not interested in examining either the ways in which individuals use language in actual speech or writing (what he termed *parole*) *or* the history and development of individual words (the 'science' of philology or etymology) or complete languages (what is termed a *diachronic* analysis). Rather, he was interested in studying the ways in which individual words are organized into *systems* of language (what he termed *langue*) which are then used by individuals and which shape their perception of the world. In Lapsley and Westlake's elegant summation, he was 'interested in asking not how [language] developed but how it works' (1988: 33).

Central to language for Saussure was the *sign*. For him, signs were linguistic: that is, individual words. He argued that signs were composed of two distinct elements: the *signifier*, which is the 'physical' part of the sign (the word on the page, the spoken word) and the *signified* which is the mental concept associated with that sign. Following John Fiske (1990), we can represent the relationship between these two elements, as shown in Figure 1.4.

In reality, however, Saussure argued that these two components could not be separated and that they were 'indivisible'. In his own words, the sign equals the 'inseparable unity of the signifier with the signified: we never have one without the other' (de Saussure 1974: 67). He went on to make a number of key points about these signs:

1. The relationship between the signifier and signified is 'arbitrary'. For example, the signifier 'tree' has no connection, either in sound or shape,

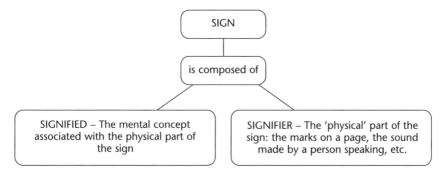

Figure 1.4   Sign: signifier and signified

with the mental concept of trees or what trees are 'really' like. This arbitrary nature of signs becomes clearer when we consider that different languages (or, to use our semiotic terminology, different sign systems) use a different signifier to communicate and explain the same thing, for example tree (English), *arbre* (French) and *Baum* (German).

That is not to say that signs have no meaning. Saussure was clear about the fact that signs are obviously meaningful to their users. Indeed, there would be no such thing as language if this were not the case. For Saussure, however, signs are meaningful only in a social context: that is, there is general agreement on the signs in use and on the conventionally accepted ways in which they can be used. There is a *system*.

It is at this stage that we need to introduce two more of Saussure's terms. The first, the *referent*, refers to the 'real thing' which is being represented by the sign: in our case, the real tree. Saussure argued that users of a language, when using that language, constantly have to relate their knowledge of the referent to their knowledge of the sign. This process of relating reality to the sign is, according to Saussure, called *signification*.

We thus need to expand our earlier diagram to include both 'reality' and this relationship between it and the signs used to represent it (see Figure 1.5).

2. As a result of the fact that signs are organized into systems with rules as to how they can and cannot be used, Saussure argued that signs obtain their meaning *not* from any inherent meaning or from external reality but from their relationship to other signs within the system. For example, the 'meaning' of the sign 'car' relies on an acknowledgement of what it is (four wheels, enclosed, has an engine, etc.) and also, equally importantly, what it is *not* (two-wheeled, open, a scooter, etc.). In Saussure's words, 'in language there are only differences' (quoted in Lapsley and Westlake 1988: 34).

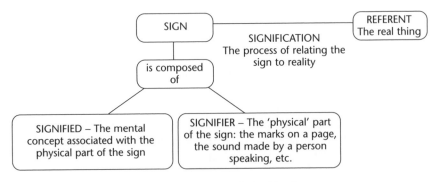

Figure 1.5 Sign and signification

3. Sign systems structure thought. Signs do not reflect a person's external reality but shape and structure that person's perception and understanding of reality. Challenging 'traditional' liberal ideas which saw (and continue to see) the human person as the centre of knowledge and meaning, Saussure argued that people do not use language in individual ways but are born into systems of language: conceptual frameworks which pre-exist them and structure their thought. One example of this which is often (erroneously) given is the idea of snow. In the UK we have a limited number of words to describe freezing weather conditions (snow, slush, ice, hail, sleet), which suggests that this is relatively unimportant in our everyday lives. In Inuit (Eskimo) culture, however, where snow is central to everyday lived experience, there are many different words for snow which reflect the types of snow in terms of the danger it represents and how it affects the ability to hunt for food or to be used for building, etc. English-speaking people's thoughts, therefore, about the same 'reality' of snow will be dramatically different to those of Inuit people.

We have seen how semiotics was used originally in the field of linguistics: that is, the study of languages. Following this, a key move was made in the 1950s by a number of European academics, most notably Roland Barthes and Claude Levi-Strauss. They used Saussure's ideas about linguistic signs but translated the findings to study *cultural* signs such as media texts (film, newspaper articles, etc.), architecture and cultural practices. What this allowed them to do was to analyse culture in as systematic a manner as Saussure had examined language in order to find the 'hidden' meanings associated with cultural artefacts and practices. Their assumption was that, as these things were the result of a process of construction, the task of semiotics was to engage in a process of deconstruction.

In one of his most famous works, *Mythologies* (first published as a series of magazine articles and then as a book in 1957), Barthes used Saussure's ideas to study aspects of contemporary French culture such as Citröen cars, steak and chips, Greta Garbo and Romans in films (to name a few) and argued that:

-   signs are not just linguistic but could be anything which communicates a meaning (clothes, media texts, food, etc.)
-   the 'meaning' of such signs is not unitary and fixed but is derived from the relationship of the signs within its sign system. So, in the example of the Citröen car mentioned above, it only obtained its meaning (stylish, elegant, graceful, etc.) because the other cars available in France at the time were none of these.
-   each sign is capable of three different levels of meaning:

1. *Denotation* was, for Barthes, the literal or obvious meaning of a sign. For example, in the car advertisements that you analysed previously, the representation of the car is the sign on a denotative level: the obvious meaning is that the representation of the car signifies a car

2. *Connotation* is a level of meaning over and above the level of denotation. It is the additional meaning(s) brought to the text by individual readers on the basis of their cultural background and social experience. So, if we continue with the example of the car in the advertisement, certain connotations will exist on the basis of what type of car it is: cheap and cheerful, tough and rugged, chic and stylish, etc. All of these are connotations.

3. Barthes's third level of meaning is *myth*. For him, myth did not mean something which was false or had never existed (as in 'a mythical beast') but referred to the way in which certain signs, or combination of signs, are used to trigger a range of connotations. For Barthes, 'myth always involves the distortion or forgetting of alternative messages so that myth appears to be exclusively true, rather than one of a number of possible messages' (Bignell 1997: 22). So, according to advertisements for 4X4 (or SUV) vehicles, if you buy such a car you are rugged, free and individual rather than, for example, someone who is hastening global warming.

The relatively detailed discussion of semiotics above is vitally important to our task of understanding how media language is used to create meaning. What should already be apparent from this discussion is the power that you have as a video producer to construct a text. If we use an analogy of a children's construction set, you have a box of parts in front of you, any of which you can choose and attach to other parts as you see fit to construct a model. The ones that you choose and the way in which you attach them is crucial to the shape of the finished model: choose certain parts and attach them in a certain way and you have a crane; choose the same parts and put them together in a different way and you have a boat. Similarly with video production, the visual and aural signs that you choose from all those available for your production and how you put them together are vital to the shape of the finished product and the meanings created by using them.

It is this power to select and include things which 'make meaning' in the final production which is described in the phrase *mise-en-scène*. At its most simple, the term, a literal translation from French meaning 'having been put into the scene', refers to those visual aspects (or signs) which have been *deliberately* chosen to appear within a single shot and, according to some definitions of the term, the manner in which they are recorded. (see Nelmes 1996:

Figure 1.6 *Mise-en-scène*

63–73 for a fuller discussion of the term). For the moment, though, we will take it to mean the former and use the term to refer to the manner in which elements of the shots have been deliberately chosen to aid the production of meaning. This includes the setting, the costumes and the props.

Imagine that the photograph shown in Figure 1.6 is a still from a video.

Each of these different elements within the frame has a semiotic significance. In the above example, key aspects of the *mise-en-scène* include the setting (informal, in a bar), the props (beer glasses, candle, etc.) and the subjects (youngish, relaxed, informal clothing). All of these elements are vital to the overall meaning. Change one and the meaning changes: for example, think of the change in meaning if the shot were in a church or the man making a face were wearing a tuxedo or the glasses on the table were mugs of tea.

The key point about *mise-en-scène* is that it requires deliberate choices and attention on the part of the video-maker. It goes without saying that the correct choice of objects in a shot and their correct placement greatly enhances the shot. More importantly, lack of attention to *mise-en-scène* and the selection of the wrong objects reduces the potential impact and, in the worse cases, the video altogether. This is why professional shoots will always have an art director/set dresser to make sure that they get it right.

If we think about our earlier discussion about audience, we can see that this is closely related to the overall meanings that the audience might take from the text. What are called *open* texts provide the opportunity to produce a range of different meanings whereas *closed* texts offer very little opportunity to do this. For the moment, though, just remember that the important thing to note about filmic grammar is that both the producers of the video and the audiences will very quickly and easily understand the rules.

So, some key questions that you should ask about media language within any text might be as follows:

- *How* are the main meanings being created through, for example, the use of soundtrack, visuals and titles?
- *What* specific techniques are being used and with what outcome with regard to lighting, composition, camera movement, editing techniques, *mise-en-scène*?
- *How* do the various elements of the text outlined above work, both individually and together, to create meaning?

Tasks to do

Watch the title sequence to *Friends*, a copy of which you will find on DVD in your local library or on the internet. Carry out a detailed semiotic analysis of it.

One of the main problems that many students face when asked to do a semiotic analysis of a media text is actually how to carry it out! If one breaks any analysis down into stages, it becomes much easier. There are three main stages to any systematic semiotic analysis:

Stage 1 – Isolating all the signs in the text at the level of denotation: you will remember from the discussion above that media texts are made up of a number of different signs. The first stage of a semiotic analysis is, therefore, to isolate all of these signs at the level of denotation: that is, the literal or obvious level that anyone with hearing or sight will be able to isolate. This means playing the text over and over again, stopping and starting the text and looking in as much detail as possible at what might appear to be the most insignificant detail. It is a good idea to use a template such as the one that you can find on the website to make the recording of your findings more systematic.

Tip: It is imperative that you try to isolate as many signs as possible. Do not think that some signs are too obvious to list: it is often the most obvious signs which carry the most meaning. Similarly, do not ignore the seemingly insignificant signs. They too will have been included deliberately to contribute to the overall meaning of the title sequence.

Stage 2 – Considering the connotations of each sign: once you have your list of signs at the level of denotation, and only then, can you move on to analysing the signs at the level of connotation. This involves you thinking about the possible meanings that each sign can have. These meanings are dependent upon the sign itself but also upon the manner in which it has been filmed and the shots around it. For example, a car can have a number of different connotations depending upon the type of car it is and how it is filmed: a stretch limousine at night in an LA 'hood' will have totally different connotations to the same limousine filmed on a dreary day on an English country road.

At this stage it is also important to think about the way in which the same signs might have different connotations for different people. For example, the Union Jack will have very different meanings for members of different ethnic groups born and living in Britain, those coming here as immigrants or asylum seekers and those who live abroad.

Stage 3: Evaluating how the signs work together at the level of myth: you are now ready to move on to the final stage of the analysis: that is, evaluating how the signs work together at the level of myth. This is often the most difficult for students but is really the stage where you look at all the signs as they are working *together* to produce meaning (which is, after all, the way in which most people – yourself included – will have read the text in the first place). More importantly, though, you are looking to isolate the way in which these signs work together to produce what Barthes called 'mythical' meanings: that is, certain preferred ways in which the text can be read.

We have included a template on the website that you might want to use to record your thoughts. We would suggest that you obtain a DVD of *Friends* and frame-grab each of the shots from the title sequence and add them into the first column.

Ideology

The term 'ideology' originally came from the work of Karl Marx, a political writer in the nineteenth century, and those who later followed his ideas (Marxists). Broadly speaking, the concept was used to show how certain institutions (such as the Church and the education system) were able physically to control and organize society by controlling the ideas, assumptions and beliefs of that society. It went further, however, in suggesting that such 'ideological' views of the world tended to be only partial and selective and actively perpetuated existing class relations: that is, the idea that it was 'natural' that the ruling class (or *bourgeoisie*) should rule over the working classes (or *proletariat*) encouraged and reinforced the continuation of this class structure. In short, ideology serves the interests of dominant groups and actively opposes those of subordinate ones.

Later Marxist writers, such as those within what was termed the Frankfurt School, related the idea to the media to argue that *all* media texts provide a partial and selective (or biased!) view of the world. Anyone making a video, for example, will have certain ideas and views about the subject, whether conscious or unconscious. For Marxists, the fact that most people who own the media and most people working within it are middle-class (or, to use Marx's term, part of the bourgeoisie) means that most of the cultural production in any society will reflect and perpetuate the middle-class view of the world rather than, say, the working-class view.

Feminist writers, too, have used the concept of ideology to argue that as cultural production is generally in the hands of men, most, if not all, media texts contain 'patriarchal ideology': that is, the ideology which states that it is 'natural' for men and women to behave in different ways and for value to be placed on the activities of men. Media texts will reflect this and represent men and women according to patriarchal ideology. These views are, almost inevitably, to the detriment of women.

So, key questions that you should ask about ideology within any text might be as follows:

- What are the major values and assumptions within the text? Why have these been chosen and others ignored?
- Are there any other values and assumptions which are 'hidden' within the text? What are they and why are they there?
- Are there other values which are simply not present?

Tasks to do

1. Watch the evening news on three different television channels and choose one news story that appears on all three news programmes for analysis. If possible, record the three examples of the story so that you can watch them over and over again.
2. After watching the three examples of the story, see if you can notice any differences in terms of:
   - what they included in the reports: locations, interviewees, the words in the script and action;
   - what they left out of the reports that others included;
   - the ways in which the reporters reported the 'facts' and the tone of voice that they used;
   - whether the report was in favour of what was being reported or critical of it;

- whether you thought that overall the stories were either balanced and unbiased or one-sided and biased.
3. Think about your findings and how they relate to the concept of ideology.

Narrative

The term 'narrative' broadly relates to the idea of telling a story. More importantly, though, it refers to the idea that the production of any media text will involve (as we have already seen in our discussion of ideology) the *construction* of a narrative through the active *selection* and *ordering* of certain elements into a coherent structure. In order to look at what they are constructed *from*, let us use a definition of narrative provided by David Jay Bordwell and Kristin Thompson (1997: 90). For them, narrative is 'a chain of events in cause–effect relationship occurring in time and space'. According to this definition, there are three main elements to narrative: causality, time and space. To understand the importance of each, let us use the example provided by Bordwell and Thompson:

1. 'A man tosses and turns in bed. A mirror breaks. The phone rings.' It is difficult to understand this as a narrative because we are unable to determine the temporal or causal elements that link the events together.
2. But a different description of the same events can allow this to happen: 'A man has a fight with his boss; he tosses and turns that night unable to sleep. In the morning, he is still so angry that he breaks the mirror while shaving. Then his telephone rings: his boss has called to apologize.

For Bordwell and Thompson, the second description is a more 'complete' narrative because it allows the audience to:

- connect the events in a cause and effect relationship: the argument causes the sleeplessness; the anger causes the rage that leads to the broken mirror, etc.
- connect the events temporally: the sleeplessness follows the argument but comes before the breaking of the mirror. We are also able to deduce that the actions occur over two days.
- connect the events spatially: he is in the office, then at home in bed, moves to the bathroom and then where the phone is.

There are a number of different ways of structuring or organizing the narrative of media texts that we will look at in more detail in later chapters. For the moment, though, to explore this idea of selecting and ordering elements to create a coherent structure, we want to concentrate on one of the most ubiquitous of narrative forms: the linear narrative.

A linear narrative is a narrative where the beginning, middle and end appear in that order: that is, the chain of cause-and-effect events and the time are in the correct order. This type of narrative structure was examined in detail by the theorist Tzetzan Todorov (1977). He was concerned with looking at the ways in which Hollywood films created meanings through the organization of their narrative structures. He argued that any linear narrative, of which most Hollywood films whatever their type were an example, moves through five main stages:

1. *Equilibrium*: everything is harmonious.
2. *Disruption*: someone or something comes along to disrupt this state of equilibrium.
3. *Recognition*: all the characters within the narrative recognize that the disruption has taken place.
4. *Attempt*: the characters within the narrative try to rectify the disruption that has occurred.
5. *Enhanced equilibrium*: a state of harmony is re-established, often a better equilibrium than the first state of equilibrium (the traditional Hollywood happy ending).

You only have to think of some recent films that you have seen to note that this structure is still one of the most popular narrative structures in mainstream film. This type of narrative is not limited to Hollywood films, but is widespread in other types of media text. Advertisements provide good examples of the linear narrative. Soap powder advertising, for example, relies heavily on them and the stages for such an advertisement might be as follows:

1. *Equilibrium*: the main character in the advertisement (usually a child) is clean and tidy.
2. *Disruption*: the character spills something on his/her clean clothes or falls into a muddy puddle.
3. *Recognition:* the character walks into the kitchen and shows someone (usually the mother – another example of patriarchal ideology) the now dirty clothes.
4. *Attempt:* the mother rectifies the disruption by washing the clothes.
5. *Enhanced equilibrium:* the clothes are returned to a state of pristine whiteness and we see them being used again.

So, key questions that you should ask about the narrative within any text might be as follows:

- *Is* a linear narrative apparent? If so, what are the different stages? If not, how might you describe the narrative?
- *What* has been included in the narrative and what left out?
- *What* specific techniques have been used to tell the story, for example the use of voice-over, the creation of suspense, the point of view of the text?
- *How* have the characters within the narrative been used?

Tasks to do

1. Watch and record a broad range of advertisements from television.
2. Select five different advertisements, preferably different types of product and different styles of advertising. Using the template that you can download from the website, see if you can isolate and record the different stages of the narrative structure. If you can't, write down what stages are missed out or why it doesn't seem to fit in with Todorov's stages. What points can you make about why it doesn't fit in?

Genre

At its most simple, the term 'genre' simply means 'type'. In relation to the media, it refers to a specific type of film, music, television programme, etc. In terms of video and television, there are many different genres to be found. These could include documentaries, soaps, science fiction, quiz shows and make-overs.

If we think about our discussion of semiotics and *mise-en-scène* above, we saw how certain signs are included within media texts to create certain meanings. The term genre refers to the manner in which these signs are organized within certain texts by *codes* which, when repeated, become *conventions*, or the accepted manner in which they are shown. So, we can talk about the genre of historical dramas, all of which will share certain characteristics: they will be set in the past, they will usually involve elaborate costumes and locations and the spoken language is likely be different to current language.

However, one of the key theorists of genre, Steve Neale (1980), argues that genres work on two, apparently paradoxical, levels: repetition and difference. At the level of repetition, certain signs will exist in most programmes within the genre and will be organized by the same codes thus marking them out as being within the genre. Crime series, for example, will tend to include cops, fast cars, villains, uniforms, etc. These elements will almost always appear but may be filmed differently. So, if we return to our earlier discussion of semiotics, each media producer has the ability to choose from a range of different signs (what is known as the paradigmatic) to create meaning.

At the same time, however, each programme within the genre will exhibit difference to keep it fresh and, on the surface at least, to identify it from the other programmes. That is, it will include different signs from all those on offer (what is known as the paradigmatic) but will put them together in different ways (what is known as the syntagmatic): *Inspector Morse* has a slow pace of editing, beautiful locations and classical music, and the narrative relies on Morse's intelligence and experience to solve crimes, whereas a US series such as *CSI* has a much faster pace of editing, grittier locations and 'urban' music, and the narrative relies upon the latest technology to solve the crimes.

We shall look in much more detail at what makes a genre when we examine an example of a sitcom in the bonus chapter on the website and apply our key concepts to it.

So, key questions that you should ask about genre might be as follows:

- Is the programme similar to other programmes that you have seen or does it appear to be unique?
- If it is similar, what is it about the programme which makes it similar: the look, the content, the types of characters, the type of story? What is different?

Tasks to do

1. Choose two different types (or genres) of television programme, for example crime series and soap operas.
2. Choose two examples of each genre and watch them carefully. While you are watching, try to make a note of the following information:
   - the types of location used;
   - the types of character;
   - the types of narrative;
   - whether there are typical props and costumes;
   - whether there are any other shared characteristics.
3. Once you have done this, see if you can begin to make certain points about each of the different genres: for example crime series tend to have goodies and baddies and it is always the goodies who win.

What you have probably realized by now is that, although we have separated out each of these key concepts, in reality they are all intertwined. It is impossible, for example, to talk about the types of representation in an advertisement without making reference to all the other concepts. To demonstrate this, in the *Friends* bonus chapter on the website we have applied all of these key concepts to a specific television programme to show how and why they are useful and how they are linked in practice. Over the course of the book, we will be returning to them constantly in order to apply them to specific briefs. What you need to remember is that these are the *fundamental* concepts that you need in your analysis but you should also aim to introduce higher levels of theory that you encounter and enjoy and which are relevant to the exact project that you are undertaking.

Before you do any of this, however, we need to take you through the correct stages of the process of video production.

2 Doing: Preparing for Video Production

If producing excellent video is your aim, then it is vital that you understand, develop, practise and use a wide range of different skills and attributes. If you don't, you may well end up with a video which is disappointing for you and unwatchable for anyone else. We subscribe to one of the most basic rules of the industry: 'garbage in, garbage out'. However, we are adamant that the converse also applies: 'quality in, quality out'. So, if you are serious about improving your professional production skills, there are six essential areas in which you can actively strive to develop throughout your video production career. These relate to:

1. *Ideas and the research process:* coming up with creative, theoretically informed ideas and, through a thorough process of research, being able to assess realistically how achievable they are and how successful the end products might be.
2. *Planning and management:* understanding and practising rigorous project management and communication and organizational skills.
3. *Process and equipment:* having an in-depth knowledge of production processes and video production equipment.
4. *Reflection:* constantly reflecting upon the creative, theoretical, technical and logistical aspects of the project, resulting in a process of on-going quality control which is sustained throughout the process of production.
5. *Flexibility:* having the capacity to react to changing circumstances in a flexible, positive and creative way throughout the process of production
6. *Drive, enthusiasm and determination:* remaining focused on the project and being able to sustain a level of constant enthusiasm, motivation and drive for the project as a whole and for the individual tasks which need to be carried out to complete the project.

This is the definitive list of what needs to be addressed if you are to be successful as a video-maker. That is why we refer to them as essential elements. So, our suggestion is that you print this list out and stick it on your wall and in your diary so that you never forget them. It is your job to make sure that you develop the necessary skills in all six areas as nobody else will do it for you. If you do this, you will almost certainly encourage everyone else in your group to do the same. Let us look in more detail at each of them so that you can see what they mean in practical terms.

Essential Element 1: Ideas and the research process

The first essential element relates to the idea of coming up with creative, achievable ideas which are informed by theory and solid research. Creativity is the skill that most employers in the media industries look for in prospective employees. The good news is that people who want to study media production tend also to be among the more creative and have a high level of enthusiasm and flair for their subject which they will continue to develop, so part of being a successful video-maker relies on you fully developing your creativity.

Creativity is a word that all of us know and being creative is generally regarded as a good thing, but what is meant by the term 'creativity'? Most dictionaries define it as a mental process which either produces original and unusual ideas or uses existing ideas in original and unusual ways. So, for the moment, we can define creativity as being an activity which results in the production of something partly or wholly new or the taking of something which already exists and looking at it from a completely different perspective: both involve imagining new possibilities which have not been considered before.

The creative idea

In terms of video production, creativity *starts* with applying imagination and originality to the brief in order to come up with a good idea. When generating ideas, you have relatively limited options: you slavishly copy an existing idea, adapt an idea or come up with something totally new and different. The second and third of these options are creative, the first isn't!

Space does not allow us to tell you everything you need to know about how to be creative, but we will offer suggestions as to how you might be so when we start looking in detail at generating ideas in later chapters. In general terms, though, in interrogating an idea for its creativity you need to ask the following simple questions:

- Is your idea different to those with which you are familiar or does it merely copy them? What would you need to change to make the idea more creative? Could you turn an existing idea on its head, for example instead of the dog biting the man, the man bites the dog?

- Is your idea ordinary or boring? If so, could it challenge accepted conventions or expectations, be made absurd or surreal, become humorous or a shocking exaggeration of the truth? If not, what would you need to do to alter it? What is its viewpoint? Could it be told from a different viewpoint?
- Is your idea a new or interesting way of representing something either technically or aesthetically, or through its content? Who does it represent and to what purpose? Could it be told through someone else's eyes?

One way in which you can begin to become *truly* creative is by becoming more generally informed. By this we mean that you should be looking at as many different types of video and moving-image work in as many different places as possible, whether it relates to a brief you have been given or not. Only by exploring in detail what is around – on television and specialist websites and in cinemas, art galleries and art centres – *with a critical eye*, will you start to come up with creative ideas and, more importantly, know whether your ideas are creative or merely derivative. Video-makers should be like sponges, soaking everything up and 'stealing' ideas and bits of ideas: types of framing, ways of lighting, types of narrative, methods of editing.

Specifically, this entails you immersing yourself in your topic or subject *before* you begin the process of generating ideas. This will take some time and effort but will pay off. The Greek philosopher Epictetus reportedly said, 'No great thing is created suddenly' and, as far as producing the moving image is concerned, he was quite correct. So, part of the process of coming up with creative ideas for a specific brief should involve:

- thoroughly researching and critically analysing similar videos or genres;
- thoroughly acquainting yourself with the relevant underpinning theories using I CARLING and academic texts;
- reading materials such as articles in newspapers, magazines and journals and on the internet;
- only stopping researching when you feel that you are in a position of knowledge and understanding.

Only once you have done all of these can you start to come up with informed, creative ideas.

Creative realization of the idea

Coming up with an original and creative video may start with an idea, but true creativity is about much more than this. Thinking creatively encompasses all aspects of the production. By that we mean that everything that you do with the idea is capable of being done in a number of different ways: from the predictable through to the truly original. It is possible to have a relatively mundane initial idea but, through reflection and hard work at every stage of the process of production, to come up with a creative finished video. So, at an early stage of the production process, you might already be thinking about the style of the video in terms of camerawork, lighting, narrative, music, sound and effects. Each of these aspects offers further opportunities to be creative if you ask the general questions about creativity detailed above.

With this in mind, we would argue that the act of creativity is not confined to coming up with the original idea but should involve thinking about every stage of the process. It is a continuous and developing activity, which should start at the beginning of a project and be sustained throughout. At each stage, you should be able to imagine new possibilities: how to come up with imaginative ideas but also how to work in different ways and how to use creatively the tools at your disposal.

For example, a group recently working on a documentary about the life of the sixteenth-century British playwright Christopher Marlowe used period costume and locations but had the characters performing a rap to camera using contemporary street language and the conventions of rap music video. While this technique was not in itself unique, it required the group of students involved to give serious thought to how to make the content creative using the research, skills and resources at their disposal.

Essential Element 2: Planning and management

Some video students may consider that creativity is all that they need to be successful. However, given the equal importance of each of the six elements for professional video production, ignoring one element is fatal. So, at the beginning of your video production career you also have to give serious consideration to how you will work within groups and how you will manage your projects and time.

Good group-working skills

During our years of teaching, we have consistently observed the same fundamental good and bad points about the group dynamics of production teams. One of the most frequent reasons why student video productions fail to achieve their goals is poor group-working skills. Group members fail to acknowledge the need for the group to work together as a professional production team. As most video production is collaborative and group-based, this can have tragic consequences. Those of you who have undertaken group work in the past may already be familiar with some of the reasons why groups fall apart. How many of you have experienced any of the following?

- Individuals are overbearing and dominate the group and the meetings.
- Individuals do not contribute to discussion and are negative or unco-operative.
- Individuals are unreliable and fail to attend meetings or are frequently late.
- The group perpetually argues, cannot agree on anything and therefore no decisions are ever made, which stops any real progress being made.
- The members of the group are unrealistic about what they can achieve with the project because they either overestimate or underestimate their skills and ability successfully to complete the project or the time it will take.
- The group is disorganized, meetings are not scheduled and there are no agendas, leaving the project to lurch forward painfully slowly and intermittently.
- The group has no leader(s) and no real delineation of workload and responsibilities.
- The group does not take into account the workload demands and deadlines of other projects or events.

Good group work comes from having a really clear structure that everyone understands and shares. So, although you may not be able to do much about some of the problems in the list above, there are certain things that you *can* do which will go some way to preventing such problems occurring. If you think about, and act upon, the following, you will save yourself and your group much time, effort and tension:

- understand every single aspect of the brief, both generally and each specific task;
- meet often, regularly and at a time convenient to all members of the group;
- carefully project-manage the video from start to finish, making sure that you discuss, agree and plan everything;
- choose your group members for their skills and levels of professionalism *not* how much you like them as people;
- exchange contact details and establish, and make sure that you use, clear lines of communication;
- allow individuals to take on production roles as early as possible so that work can be delegated effectively;

Table 2.1 Skills audit form

	Yes	No
Good organizational skills		
Good time-management skills		
Good project-management skills		
Good communication skills		
Able to plan short term and long term		
Have empathy and a sense of fair play		
Practical with plenty of common sense		
Determined		
Co-operative		
Pro-active and able to use your own initiative		
Motivated and able to motivate others		
Committed to the team and to the project		
Patient		
Reliable and dependable		
Able to listen, discuss and take on new and challenging ideas		
Able to react positively to criticism		
Able to work outside your comfort zone and under pressure		

- assess your progress by looking at the progress of other groups;
- allow anyone not pulling his/her weight to be given first support, then warnings and then asked to work with another group;
- be wary of anyone moving to your group from another group!

Remember, too, that groups are made up of separate individuals. So, as an individual you must take full responsibility for your actions and what you do or do not do within the project. At this stage, therefore, you might want to take a moment to conduct your own skills audit and consider how many of these essential skills you already have and which ones you need to develop further (see Table 2.1).

This is quite a long (but realistic) list of the many skills that you will need to make good video. Try rating your colleagues and have them rate you. If you or any of your team members have ticks in the No column, then it is evident that you are weak in those areas. Unless you do something *now* to remedy the situation, you are likely to be in for a very stormy ride!

Project management and organizational skills

Another of your main priorities at this stage should be to begin to acquire and develop excellent project-management skills. What this means is that you can organize yourself and others and effectively manage your own time.

As an individual, the best way that you can support any project in which you are involved is by organizing your own time effectively. Conversely, the surest way of not supporting a project is by being disorganized. So, as an individual, there are two key things that we would recommend you do *as a minimum*:

- Buy, and use, an academic-year diary or organizer so that you can record important dates, fitting them in with other commitments you may already have and transferring the information to your individual planner (see below).
- Keep your diary with you at all times and don't lose it. Although you can use the diary on your computer or phone, we would always suggest a paper-based diary, as the physicality of such a diary allows you to see, at a glance, what your commitments are without scrolling through numerous electronic entries.

However, you should be going further than this. One of the ways that you can actively do so is by organizing your time effectively through a process called *action planning*. This involves the production of three key documents:

- an individual planner;
- an individual weekly action plan;
- a group project planner.

The individual planner

The individual planner is a document which clearly shows all of your individual commitments for any given period of time: normally, for students, this will be termly. Producing an individual planner involves regularly transferring and updating the information about every project you are working on, deadlines, part-time work and any other commitments you may have from your diary to the planner (for a template, see Figure 2.1).

This is a vital document because it allows you to plan and control your time. It offers a far greater sense of timescale than a diary can and allows you to *visualize* what each project will require of you in terms of time. It quickly and clearly illustrates each project in terms of its start date, duration and deadlines and includes more detailed information about the tasks within each project. Because it allows you to work out, *at a glance*, the key dates in the production process for each project you are involved in and how the deadlines for each project relate to each other, it is easy to see if there are any bottlenecks or dangerously busy times and to plan around them.

	Week 7 29/10	Week 8 05/11	Week 9 12/11	Week 10 19/11	Week 11 26/11	Week 12 03/12
		Post-production		Pre-production		
Title Sequence (10 weeks)	Assembly Edit complete by 31.10 Screening lecture theatre two at 3pm Thurs 01/11 Write up feedback	Rough Edit complete by Tues 06/11 Screening 9am lecture theatre 3 wed Recording of music and voice-over	Final Cut to be completed alterations and copy Monday 12/11 Tom's b'day bash 16/11	Screening and feedback (Tues 20/11 9am, LT 3) Hand in production folder and finished DVD (22/114pm)		
Documentary (10 weeks)		Production Meeting One: Initial ideas generation 9am 07/11 Blog by Thursday 08/11 Doc visiting lecturer 09/11 2pm LT 3	Production Meeting Two: 10 ideas and research notes 4pm 12/11 Production Meeting Three: Feasibility studies 4pm 15/11 Cannons Bar 8pm 16/11	Production Meeting Four: Six of the best – pitches and feasibility 19/11 1pm Production Meeting Five: Top three ideas presentation to class – 21/11 1pm	Presentation to class of final idea – 9am wed. 28/11 Production Meeting Six: Treatment inc costing submitted and feasibility complete. 30/11 9am Detailed research starts Group tutorial Friday	Production Meeting Seven: folder check 05/12 2pm. kit list, recces, risk assessment and schedules ready. Meet health and safety rep 07/11 4pm
Dissertation (20 weeks)	Research on Bauhaus complete Visiting Speaker Lecture Theatre 2 9am 01/11	Research on modernist writers Conrad, Yeats & Kafka. See Martin Sheen re support	Write up notes on selected writers Progress Seminar wed pm 14/11	Research Modernist painter Picasso. Check out three examples of work 21/11 present	Visit to London galleries (see Jed re costs) 29/11	Dissertation Tutorials start again. Ensure research folder is ready 04/12
Drama Short (10 weeks)				Pre-Production	Launch Lecture and guest script writer 29/11 LT 2 9am Work on script Prod meeting 4pm	Script outlines 06/12 9am LT 2 Script dev Prod meeting 04/12 Prod meeting 06/12

Figure 2.1 An individual planner

There is no particular format for a planner but it must show each week for any given term. This is easy to do using a word-processing package or software easily available from the internet. It doesn't matter what format you choose so long as it makes sense to *you*. Because your planner offers a week-by-week account of your planned activities, it is able to inform and guide the production of the second key document: your individual action plan.

The individual action plan

An action plan is a written document which enables you to plan your personal work load, normally for one week. It is produced by taking the information from the corresponding week on your individual planner and transferring it on to a document which details *all* the tasks for the week which you need to complete and when they need to be completed by (see Figure 2.2).

If you are going to do this effectively, you need to make sure that your action plan contains information about all your commitments, whether academic, work-related or personal.

It is important to note that both individual planners and individual action plans are what we call *live* documents: that is, they are fluid and always subject to change. There may be a number of reasons for changes: a deadline being moved, the addition of new tasks or the reallocation of work if a member of the group leaves.

The group project planner

Given that video production is always collaborative, proper planning also involves the production of one more document: a group project planner (see Figure 2.3). This document is slightly different in that it relates *only* to the project that you are working on together and contains the details from the individual planners of every member of the group.

So, for each project, your production team will need to:

- produce a detailed project plan which realistically records and plans all stages of the project;
- ensure that every task is planned in the order in which they will need to be completed;
- take into account the information contained on each group member's individual planner as these may highlight times when group members are unavailable (external factors affecting one individual will impact on the group and could jeopardize the project, so you must make sure that you

Action Plan   Week Starting: 19/10   Name:

	Morning	Afternoon	Evening
Mon	Sound and Image Production	1pm doc prod meeting – pitches 4pm driving lesson 5pm coffee bar Meet Darryl re presentation	Start evaluation for TS Research for props and costumes Out with Sarah and Lucy 8.30pm
Tues	9am–12.00 LT 3 Screening of title Sequence Ring Mr. Dawes re: location and permission	Screen Design Workshop	Evaluation: continue with notes taken Finish cue cards for presentation and check DVD. Print off handouts E-mail cue cards to Darryl and blog eval
Wed	Contextual Studies (Essay research presentations)	R121 presentations; best three ideas 4pm drama production meeting R118 Write up minutes	Write up production diary and print Check over doc production folder – Sarah to e-mail agenda Record festival docs on TV 9pm Write up evaluation
Thurs	Media Production	Media Production hand in doc production folder and DVD office	Finish notes on Picasso and start reading chapter 4 Update contacts book and take in for prof prac
Fri	Tutorial 11am R20	Professional practice – contacts book	Meet Pete to discuss thoughts around drama and e-mail notes to Lucy
Sat	Work shift 7am !!!	Finish work 4pm – collect car	Chris's 7.30pm
Sun	SLEEP! Midday: PowerPoint final idea for presentation next week	Dissertation with Saj my house (lunch) 5pm: Swimming	Write up action plan for next week production diary update

Figure 2.2   An individual action plan

Group Project Timeline/ Planner - Documentary									
Week 1	Week 2	Week 3	Week 4	Week 5	Week 6	Week 7	Week 8	Week 9	Week 10
Pre - Production						Production	Post- Production		
Discuss brief Initial ideas generation & discussion. Basic research and feasibility on ideas	Select 3 ideas Further research & feasibility Pitch main ideas and select one for further research- group Seminar 1.30 RT 109 Thurs prepare for pitch next week	All groups final idea pitch and printed outline Thurs 1.30 RT130 Interview techniques workshop TV Studio Wed 1.30-4.00 Development based on feedback	Further research inc location searches, permissions Contributors and release Book kit Lighting & sound workshop TV Studio Wednesday 9.00 (Interview questions)	Recce & full Risk Assessment Further research inc location searches, permissions Contributors and release	Test shoot/ edit/viewing and feedback	Location recording of documentary inc all interviews and sound (Production Stills)	Assembly Edit Screening RT120 Thursday 2.30 Start on assembling production folder	Rough Cut V/O &Music ready production folder	Final Cut Screening RT120 Thursday 2.30 production folder completed and reviewed Final Edit refinements, export & test Submission inc production folder and evaluation Friday 4.30 meet 10.00
Production meeting: Tuesday 1.30 RT 109 Thursday 9.00 RT20	Production meeting: Tuesday 1.30 RT 109 Thursday 9.00 RT20	Production meeting: Tuesday 1.30 RT 109 Thursday 9.00 RT 20	Production meeting: Tuesday 1.30 RT 109 Thursday 9.00 RT 20	Production meeting: Tuesday 1.30 RT 109 Thursday 9.00 RT 20	Production meeting: Tuesday 1.30 RT 109 Thursday 9.00 RT 20	Final production meeting RT109 Monday 9.00	Assembly Edit review meeting Thursday 4.30 RT 103		

Figure 2.3   Group project planner

co-ordinate individual action plans when producing the group project plan);

- record other important events such as holidays and festivals which may affect production;
- ensure that information on the planner is transferred back on to each team member's own individual planner and, subsequently, their weekly action plan.

Remember that this is also a live document and subject to changes. As a result, it may require frequent updating.

All of the above are vital methods of organizing and planning and are accepted professional practice. They will, if carried out properly, support you through your college or university course and your later professional working life. Many students see the setting and meeting of work targets as unpleasant at first. However, if you do it properly, it does ensure that all elements of your workload are identified, allocated and completed on time. With very large projects such as the video projects in this book, this is essential. We are not saying that you should love doing all of this, but we are saying that you won't be very successful if you don't.

Essential Element 3: Process and equipment

The third essential element in producing excellent video is to follow the correct process and to understand the equipment that you will use at each of the stages within that process.

This process is one that *all* video makers will follow, whatever the size of their budget or the type of video they are producing. There are three main parts to this process:

- *Pre-production* is the stage where all the preparation work is done for the video: that is, the ideas, research and planning stage. It is everything you do prior to filming.
- *Production* is where the footage and sound for the video is obtained. It is the filming or recording stage.
- *Post-production* is the editing of all material recorded at the production stage. It is where the raw footage and sound is edited into a finished production and where titles, music, voice-overs and any special effects are added. It is everything you do after the filming.

We can represent these stages as shown in Figure 2.4 overleaf.

The key thing to recognize is that the production process is a linear process: that is, it starts with the development of a range of ideas and finishes with the presentation and distribution of the completed video. It is not possible to jump backwards and forwards between the stages of the process or to skip certain parts: you *must* complete each stage of the process before you can move on to the next.

Just as you will need to understand the process of production, you will also need to be familiar with the hardware and software you will be using. The cameras, tripods, lamps, microphones and associated accessories, as well as the computers and editing software, are the tools of your trade and, as with the production process, the more you use these tools the better you will become.

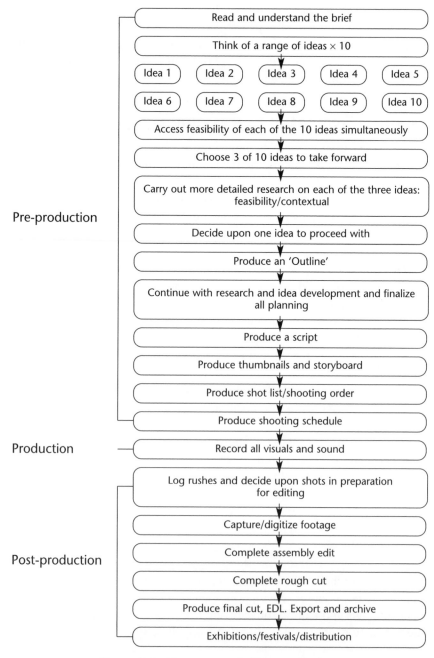

Figure 2.4 The process of video production

Essential Element 4: Reflection and quality control

In his influential book *The Reflective Practitioner* (1987: 25–26), Donald Schön argues that there are three levels of thinking about your own practice:

1. *Knowing-in-action* is 'the sort of know-how we reveal in our intelligent action – publicly observable physical performances like riding a bicycle [...]. In [such] cases the knowing is *in* the action. We reveal it by our spontaneous, skilful execution of the performance: and we are characteristically unable to make it verbally explicit.' It is the almost unconscious thinking we do when completing everyday tasks.

2. *Reflection-on-action* is the 'thinking back on what we have done in order to discover how our knowing-in-action may have contributed to an unexpected outcome'. It is the reflection that happens after a project is complete.

3. *Reflection-in-action:* this is 'thinking about what [you] are doing while [you] are doing it'. It is the reflection that allows us to change things for the better *as we're doing them* and not simply to reflect upon them after the event.

While knowing-in-action may, at first glance, look like the ideal way of working, it may be the opposite of true creativity in that such intuitive working means that people often do things the way they have always done them without really thinking about them. We would agree with Schön that it is the third type of thinking which is the hallmark of the truly reflective practitioner. By this we mean that you will need constantly to reflect upon the progress you, the team and the project are making (reflection-in-action) and critically reflect upon the project retrospectively (reflection-on-action), usually through group critiques and evaluations.

The ability to act as your own sternest critic and to identify areas for improvement throughout the production process is a form of self-imposed quality control which is fundamental in developing and improving the quality of your production work and your professionalism.

Although you may have to be very critical of your own ideas or those of others, this will result in further improvements which will contribute positively to the project. This process of reflection-in-action should be ongoing and forms an important part of 'steering' the project as it allows you to make important and workable decisions: for example, in pre-production you select a particular idea because it is simple to shoot in two days, based on the knowledge that your group can only sustain two days' filming together; you encourage a new member with very good post-production skills to join your team because, upon reflection, you feel that you do not have a strong enough editor; you decide that using lamps would greatly enhance the video, but because no one in the team has had enough practise using them, you decide to sign up to a couple of lighting workshops prior to filming in order to improve your skills. On a basic level, all of these examples represent some kind of reflection-in-action and subsequent action which will invariably improve the quality of the finished video.

Essential Element 5: Flexibility

What we mean by flexibility is the ability of the individual and the group to take on board changes and make them work.

Productions may be fraught with minor changes, often imposed from outside. These might include changes to scripts, locations, schedules, budgets and resources. There are two main choices when such problems occur: panic and let things fall apart or deal with them. The capacity to react *positively* to changing circumstances during the production process and problem-solve your way through is vital to the success of any project. Flexibility is a state of mind, as is panic! So, if your first response is to panic, by all means do so but then make sure you think flexibly.

When dealing with changes it is possible to make things work for you rather than against you. Positive or lateral thinking will enable you to do this and this is really what we mean when we use the term 'flexible'. Minor examples include a team member dropping out and other members having to pick up new roles and responsibilities on top of what they already have and the alteration of a shooting schedule so that it includes additional footage which can only be filmed in the very early morning on two consecutive days which have a full twelve hours' filming to follow.

Essential Element 6: Drive, enthusiasm and determination

These are the most fundamentally important, but indefinable, attributes that you can develop. By drive, enthusiasm and determination we mean the ability to just keep on going, whatever happens: put simply, it is about having a positive *can do* mentality. Having drive, enthusiasm and determination requires you to remain on-task and energized, it inspires others to follow suit, it can save a struggling project or make a mediocre project better, it provides the energy to solve yet another problem and to continue when others may have given up and it instils confidence in the team which sees the project through to its very end. This positivity is infectious: a team which thinks positively and works positively is likely to be rewarded with positive outcomes in terms of the overall experience and the final project. This in turn builds competence and confidence for the next project. As with all things, though, the opposite is also true and negativity breeds negativity!

All of the six essential elements are intrinsically linked and have equal standing: no single element is more important than the others and they all impact on each other. So, if you get all six right, you stand a good chance of producing a great video; get one wrong and you immediately reduce the chances of this. By thinking about the six elements before you even begin to produce video material, you have the opportunity to make them part of your work ethic before you develop bad habits.

3 The Practice of Video Production: Pre-production

Pre-production is the first stage of any video production. Although, to begin with, this is the stage that some students like least, most video professionals argue that it is the most important stage and is crucial to the success or failure of the finished product. Steve Cartwright (1996: 4), an American videomaker, has devised what he terms the '70–30–10 rule':

> As a general rule [...] we often devote as much as 70% of our time to the pre-production process and 30% to post-production with the remaining 10% (if you work at 110% as I do) devoted to the actual shooting. [...] The percentages should tell you where the real work and success of the programme lie. It's not in the 10%. It's in the 70%.

Cartwright's rule is a *vital* rule and one that we will remind you of frequently in the following chapters because, whatever type of video you are producing, it is impossible to overestimate the importance of pre-production.

As we have already seen, the pre-production stage can be broken down into a number of extremely important tasks. Remind yourself of them by looking at Figure 2.3. We will work through each of them in later chapters but, for the moment, the following points will help you to gain an overview of what is required for each of these tasks.

Understanding the brief

More often than not in education you will be provided with a brief by your lecturer. It is the place where the general theme, the specific series of tasks associated with the production process and the timescale for completing the project will be outlined. Read *very* carefully every brief that you are given.

Briefs sit somewhere on a continuum with two poles: having absolutely no parameters set or having extremely strict parameters set:

1. *Having absolutely no parameters set*: working without parameters offers total freedom of choice about what to produce and how to treat it, the only limitation being what is, or isn't, in your head. This way of working can allow for flashes of inspiration and creativity which are followed through into the production of what may be very original productions. However, this type of brief is relatively rare in education as the inherent risk is that being faced with a blank piece of paper and having to come up with good ideas from nothing is actually very difficult, especially if you are relatively inexperienced.

2. *Having very strict parameters set:* as it is really difficult to build something from nothing, it is often easier to work to a set of agreed parameters. These may be explicitly detailed within the brief: for example, for a drama, the brief may give a theme or title, the length of the production, a limit to the number of locations or number of actors and whether you have to work from an adaptation or original script. The downside for this type of brief is that, as everything is given, there is often a perceived lack of 'ownership' on the part of students.

Students new to video production or lacking in confidence often want and need some parameters, so a frequently used technique by tutors is to have just one parameter which forms the basis for generating the ideas for the video. For example, the crew are asked to:

- work from a full or partially written script provided;
- develop a story from one or more given props or locations;
- work from a quote from a source such as a poem, a speech or a line from a song;
- gain inspiration from a single word, which could be as broad as 'love' or as narrow as 'escalator';
- develop a story from a piece of music, a painting or a photograph.

Clearly, if the brief allows it or if the group are confident enough, the group can set its own parameters.

Whichever type of brief you are given, you must understand it both in terms of what it is asking you to produce (the product) and every task or element that you need to complete to achieve that end product (the process). If you are unsure about *anything*, you must have it clarified as early as possible.

At this stage, *before* you carry out any pre-production work, you should do two things which will be vital to the success or failure of your finished video:

1. Carry out your main contextual research. Thinking about how the key concepts we introduced in Chapter 1 relate to what you are being asked to produce means that all of your later discussions and actions will be informed by them. Remember that Schön's ideas about reflection-in-action suggest that the people who do this become the more effective and creative practitioners.

   This is the kind of research which is not explicitly carried out in the industry because people within the industry often feel that they 'know' the area as a result of working daily within it. However, it is our contention that this type of research, especially at the beginning of your career and within an educational setting, should underpin the practical work that you are carrying out. If it doesn't, you run the risk of making very basic errors. For example, we recently had a group of predominantly black students produce a video where the main character's bicycle was stolen. The problem was that the main character was white and all the thieves were black. This negative stereotype was picked up by all the viewers at the final screening but was something that none of the group had even considered.

2. Start thinking about who you intend to work with to complete the brief and what production roles they, and you, will fill. It is important that you consider what skills you have and what skills you need within the group. Try not to select individuals simply because you like them; choose them on the basis of their professional merits and their skills. A small production team should not have four or five people with the same skills.

Thinking of ideas

It is easy to assume that coming up with an idea is a one-stage process. However, there are four stages in the process of developing an idea *which is suitable for production*:

1. thinking of a range of ideas and narrowing it down;
2. assessing the feasibility of the best ideas;
3. carrying out some research on each of the remaining ideas;
4. deciding upon the final idea.

Thinking of ideas can be a long and difficult process and, of all the ideas which are generated, possibly only one or two will be capable of coming to fruition. That is why, at this stage, you should never think of just one idea but should think of as many ideas as possible and as broad a range of ideas as possible.

Thinking of a range of ideas and narrowing it down

If understanding the brief is the first and most important thing you can do at this stage, exploring and generating ideas or potential responses to the brief is the next. This is often one of the scariest parts of the production process. Try not to panic: it need not be scary if you realize that you do not have to come up with a great idea immediately. Creative ideas are not necessarily instantaneous but may be the result of hard work. Thomas Alva Edison once said that inventing things was 1 per cent inspiration and 99 per cent perspiration, and the same applies when generating ideas for video production. It is hard work.

So how do you actually think of ideas? Bearing in mind our earlier discussions about creativity and the three main methods – to copy, to adapt or to innovate – there are various ways of generating ideas which will allow you to have a range of good ideas to choose from as well as, it has to be said, some which are not so good. Knowing the difference between the two is often all that separates a good project from a bad one! Some of the tried and tested ways of coming up with ideas for videos are:

- adapting other material: short stories, poems, song lyrics, cartoons and art;
- using other forms of story: jokes, dreams, fables and urban myths;
- using experiences or memories from your own life or that of someone you know;
- looking in newspapers or on the internet for interesting stories especially, the short, human-interest stories: for example, dog eats remote control, baby draws work of art, man cycles around the country backwards;
- listening to conversations around you which can be remarkably fruitful and snippets of which can form the start or thread of a narrative;
- asking 'What if ...?' (for example, *What if* aliens landed in your home town? *What if* you woke up one day forty years older? *What if* you could see into the future?);
- and finally, of course, having a flash of inspiration. Often, when you least expect it, an idea for a great video will pop into your head. Make sure that you record these ideas as soon as possible so that you do not forget them.

Brainstorming is one of the best-known ways of generating as many ideas as possible, particularly in a group situation and especially if you have already begun to think about ideas using the techniques above. One way to brainstorm is for all members of the group to sit down and agree upon exactly what the brief is asking of them. Everyone in the group then calls out ideas for a given period of time (normally one or two minutes), while one person in the group writes the ideas down on a blank piece of paper. At this stage there is absolutely *no* discussion of the idea so every idea must be written down and no idea dismissed. Once the time period is up, the piece of paper should be covered with ideas.

At this stage, all the ideas on the page may be valid and should be considered but you need to whittle them down. To do so, you need to ask three main questions about each idea:

1. Do we *all* like the idea and why, or why not?
2. Is the idea capable of development and how?
3. Are there any alarm bells ringing in your head about the idea and why? What are the *immediately apparent* reasons why this idea is not valid?

As a result of asking these questions, some of the ideas can be discarded immediately: they may involve too much expense; they may be difficult to execute; they may rely too heavily on sourcing something very particular (such as permission for a location or access to a person or an object integral to the concept) which ultimately may not be possible. Be careful, though, not to dismiss potentially good ideas *too* quickly: some really basic research – a phone call or two minutes on the internet – might show that what at first seemed problematic has a solution: a flight may be much cheaper than anticipated; a relative or friend may be able to provide an old car or a property which is needed for the shoot. In going through this process of questioning every idea, you will be able to narrow down your long list of ideas into a shorter one which can go through to the next stage of the process.

Finally, a word of warning about generating ideas: this stage of the pre-production process is the one which is often lightly skipped over, and this can be a very big mistake! Every year we see many potentially good student groups perform poorly as a *direct* result of the decisions, or, more likely, lack of them, made at this stage. Many groups end this stage with only one or two ideas but, for each of the briefs in this book, we suggest that you end this stage with ten ideas *as a minimum*.

Assessing the feasibility of your ten best ideas

Once you have a broad range of ideas that you all like and that, from your very brief discussions, you think may be feasible, you need to discuss each one in more detail to find out if they actually *are* feasible. These are two completely different things. As a group, you need to spend time thinking about, and talking through, your ten ideas to find out what potential problems there might be which could stop you producing your video to the highest possible standard. At this early stage, the work around feasibility should involve relatively *detailed* discussion using the headings below and some relatively *basic* research around each area.

Whatever the brief, the potential problems that you need to discuss for each of the ten ideas are normally related to the following:

- *Finance*: approximately how much is your idea going to cost? Have you considered all likely costs: transport, stock, equipment, accommodation, the cost of the people in your video (actors, presenters or contributors), catering and props, costumes and set dressing? Are your costs relatively accurate? Do you have, or can you raise, enough money to produce the video?
- *Logistics*: this involves moving people and equipment from A to B. Does your idea involve any logistical difficulties, for example transporting large numbers of people or large quantities of equipment to a location? Do you have the ability to do that within the group or will you look outside for help, for example by borrowing a car or hiring a van? Does the time of year or the weather pose any logistical difficulties? Are any locations particularly hazardous or difficult to access?
- *Health and Safety*: is your idea safe to produce or are there any immediately apparent risks involved?
- *Technical resources*: does the production of your idea require technical resources that you or your institution do not have? If so, where will you get them from? How will you learn how to use them? Can you think of alternatives?
- *Human resources*: do you need people with greater technical knowledge than your group possesses? Do you need the help of outside organizations? Who and where are they? What actors, presenters or contributors do you need and where will you get them from? Who do you need to contact for permission to use the necessary locations?
- *Experience and ability of the crew:* do you have, among your group, the necessary technical and creative experience and ability to realize the idea properly?
- *Time*: is it possible to produce the idea in the given timescale? If not, how can you amend the idea to make it more likely that you can? What can you do to speed the process up while maintaining quality?
- *Output*: where will you output the final video: DVD? Internet? Mobile phone? Why? Is the idea technically and creatively suitable for its appropriate distribution channel and, in terms of content, suitable for a wider audience?

We often refer to these as *limiters* as they are the things which have the potential to limit the ability of the idea to be *successfully* produced as a video. A lack of consideration of each area can seriously jeopardize the project at a much later stage: for example, if a group fails to get permission to shoot at a specific location, they may well be refused entry on the day of the shoot.

That is why you will come across these limiters three times for each brief. Although they may be extremely repetitive, this is a good thing as, after a while, you will start to apply them to your ideas without even thinking. However, your reasons for revisiting them and the depth of your research will alter:

- *The first time* you use them to reveal the potential problems inherent in each of your ten ideas. Through a relatively detailed discussion of, and basic research around, each idea, you will rule out those ideas which stand little chance of being realized.
- *The second time* you will carry out a more detailed discussion of, and more in-depth research around, each of the three remaining ideas and obtain hard facts which enable you to make a decision about which idea you wish to take into production.
- *The third and final time* is when one idea has been chosen to be taken forward. It requires you to build upon the research already carried out before actioning that research. At this stage, you have committed yourself to an idea and the work now requires you to make it happen by, for example, booking travel, accommodation and equipment, finalizing contributors and locating props and costumes.

At the end of this first stage we would suggest that if you do not have *three* really strong ideas to take forward, then you should either start the process of generating more ideas or think about whether you can combine elements of one or more discarded ideas into one good idea. Never be tempted to go forward with just one idea. If *all* of your ideas are lacking something, then go through the process again with another blank piece of paper. Alva Edison also famously said, 'I haven't failed. I've just found 1000 ways that don't work!' If you still cannot come up with any good ideas, don't panic. Take some time off. It is amazing what a relaxed and refreshed brain can come up with.

Carrying out research on each of your remaining three ideas

So, once the group has agreed upon the three strongest ideas – those which are both good and, from your initial discussions, appear to be feasible – you need to develop each of them further by carrying out some systematic and detailed research.

What we mean by this is that you should use the limiters introduced above but, instead of just discussing them, you need to research each limiter in relation to each idea. By now, each idea is capable of being produced, so you need to start making phone calls, writing e-mails and letters and physically visiting people and places in order fully to understand and develop all the creative and technical aspects of each.

In carrying out your research, you essentially have two main methods of collecting your research findings:

1. *Primary research*: you go to a source and collect new information personally. This source could be a person or a place.
2. *Secondary research*: you refer to information collected by other people: in books and newspapers, on the internet, etc.

Good-quality research involves the use of an extremely broad and diverse range of resources and may be very time-consuming. Up until this stage, all of your research may well have consisted of informal conversations and information and ideas written down on various pieces of paper. Given that you are engaged in a process of serious research, you now need to compile a research folder for each of your three ideas and, as you collect accurate information on each, put your information into the appropriate folder.

In order to become an *effective* researcher, we would recommend the following:

- Carry out both primary and secondary research. Consult books and academic journals in libraries and go to archives but, as videos are normally about people, seek out individuals and special-interest groups who could make a positive contribution to your idea. You will find that the more information you amass about a subject and the more people you speak to, the more there is to know, so the list of research sources is often is as long as you choose to make it.
- Store all your research materials in *one* place. Given that this may include papers but also bulkier material such as books, DVDs and CDs, we would suggest that you use a box file or something similar. This may seem primitive but it does work.
- Clearly record exactly what each box file contains and use a logical system for indexing the material, which makes the information easy to access later on. Random pieces of paper stored in different places and files on a number of different computers or external drives leads to confusion.
- Restrict the movement of the materials. Make sure that you always know who has borrowed the box and when it will be returned, possibly by

signing the materials in and out on a sheet of paper designed for the purpose. If you have a number of individuals accessing and contributing to them, you may wish to agree a system of collation and storage so that nothing goes missing. It is very frustrating and will cost you time and energy when research material cannot be located.

- Nominate one person in the group who is responsible for looking after all of the research files.

Although your brief may not specifically ask for this, it is useful to do all of the above both as evidence of your thought processes for assessment purposes but also possibly for reference purposes at some point later in the production process. This is not uncommon!

It is at this stage that you need to look at each idea and make a decision about whether or not it can go forward and, if not, why not. Thinking about the ideas in relation to the results of your discussions about feasibility and your research will allow you to narrow your choice down in a more informed way. It also goes without saying that when discussing your ideas you should return frequently to the brief to make sure that you are still on the right track.

Deciding upon the final idea

Once you have completed all the above hard work, you have to make a decision based upon the results of that work, normally in conjunction with your tutor, about which video will go into production.

An idea should never go forward simply because it is the easiest, the best of a bad bunch or because a dominant member of the group insists upon it. It should only go forward if it is creative, feasible and inspires passion in the group. If you are lucky, all members of the group will be in agreement and the decision will be an easy one. More often than not, though, group members will have different preferences. If this is the case, there are two things that you can do:

- First, try individually writing down three things that you really like about each idea and three things that concern you or that you feel might create problems later on. Once all members of the group have done this, get together and compare notes. If all agree that some areas of an idea still have a question attached to them, you need to resolve them at this stage, otherwise it may suggest that the idea should not go any further forward.
- Secondly, you should think about asking people outside the production group to help you make the decision. In the media industries, this is referred to as *pitching* an idea. So, once you feel that you have researched

and explored each of your ideas thoroughly enough, pitch them to a wider group of people.

When pitching an idea, you should be able to articulate it in no more than twenty-five words. This is a really useful skill to foster as, in the industry, you will often be asked to outline ideas in this manner. If you cannot do this or you cannot all agree on the correct twenty-five words, then it suggests that not all members of the production group share the same vision of what the finished video will be or that the idea still needs some more work before it is ready for production. You should also back up your twenty-five words with mood boards, drafts of thumbnails and possibly existing videos which have provided your inspiration.

Although your group may have a clear favourite at this stage, do not just defend this idea but get your audience to look equally at all three ideas to see where they think the strengths and weaknesses of each idea lie. Listen carefully to what they say: they may well have thought of things that you have not considered or may come up with some really good advice about how you can improve your idea. At the end of this pitching session, you should be able to arrive at the one idea that you will actually produce.

The end result of all this work to date, work which could have taken many days or weeks of repetitive and frequently frustrating work, is that all members of the group share the same understanding of what is going to be produced and are keen and ready to move on to the next stage.

Finally, though, remember that the process of video production is an organic one and, despite your enthusiasm for an idea and all your hard work to this point, an idea can fail through no fault of your own. In these circumstances, do not be too downhearted. It is often better to abandon an idea which is not going to work and to fall back on another idea, rather than spending huge amounts of time and effort trying to recover the original idea. That is why having research folders for all three ideas is such a good idea: another basic rule of video production is *always* have a Plan B in case things go wrong.

Producing an outline

An outline is the first formal document to be produced in any video production. It provides a concise summary which allows the reader quickly and easily to see the scope of the production. It has two main functions:

- It pulls together all the important information about the production which currently exists to give it shape and focus. In writing the outline, the group is essentially agreeing the idea.

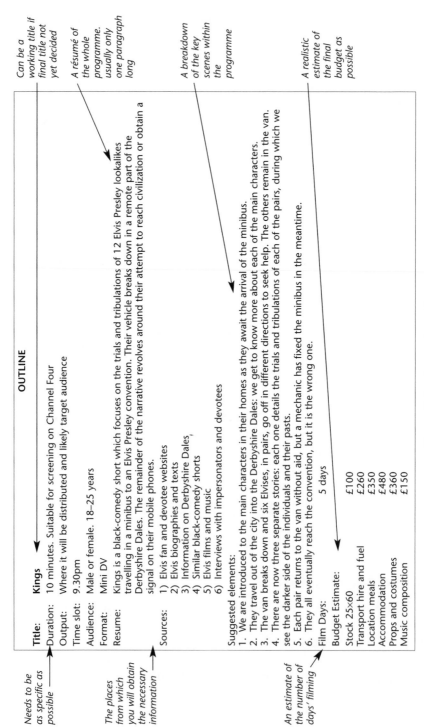

OUTLINE

Can be a working title if final title not yet decided

Title: Kings

Duration: 10 minutes. Suitable for screening on Channel Four

Output: Where it will be distributed and likely target audience

Time slot: 9.30pm

Audience: Male or female. 18–25 years

Format: Mini DV

Resume: Kings is a black-comedy short which focuses on the trials and tribulations of 12 Elvis Presley lookalikes travelling in a minibus to an Elvis Presley convention. Their vehicle breaks down in a remote part of the Derbyshire Dales. The remainder of the narrative revolves around their attempt to reach civilization or obtain a signal on their mobile phones.

Sources:
1) Elvis fan and devotee websites
2) Elvis biographies and texts
3) Information on Derbyshire Dales
4) Similar black-comedy shorts
5) Elvis films and music
6) Interviews with impersonators and devotees

Suggested elements:
1. We are introduced to the main characters in their homes as they await the arrival of the minibus.
2. They travel out of the city into the Derbyshire Dales: we get to know more about each of the main characters.
3. The van breaks down and six Elvises, in pairs, go off in different directions to seek help. The others remain in the van.
4. There are now three separate stories: each one details the trials and tribulations of each of the pairs, during which we see the darker side of the individuals and their pasts.
5. Each pair returns to the van without aid, but a mechanic has fixed the minibus in the meantime.
6. They all eventually reach the convention, but it is the wrong one.

Film Days: 5 days

Budget Estimate:

Stock 25×60	£100
Transport hire and fuel	£260
Location meals	£350
Accommodation	£480
Props and costumes	£360
Music composition	£150

Needs to be as specific as possible

The places from which you will obtain the necessary information

An estimate of the number of days' filming

A résumé of the whole programme. usually only one paragraph long

A breakdown of the key scenes within the programme

A realistic estimate of the final budget as possible

Figure 3.1 A sample outline

- It acts as a document which is used to sell the idea to those people who will make the decision as to whether or not the idea should go into production and, in the industry at least, who will provide the necessary finance to enable the production to take place.

The first of these functions is, for students, the more important, as it illustrates the means by which they will meet the requirements of the brief, although in later productions they may need to bear the second function in mind.

There is no standard format for a outline. Generally, though, in education, all outlines will abide by three main rules:

1. They will normally be no longer than one side of A4.
2. They will be written in succinct and clear prose and will normally contain no technical language.
3. They will allow the audience to visualize what it is that they will be watching.

In addition, they will all contain broadly the same information. A sample outline is shown in Figure 3.1.

Given its importance as the first key document of the production, significant time and effort should be spent on it and it should contain as much appropriate detail as necessary. In the industry an allied document would be the treatment: a much longer document which expands on each separate area shown in the outline above.

Researching the production

By now, you will be looking critically at your idea for the third time. You will now use the headings for the limiters for the final time to continue researching the idea more fully and will to start to organize the production stage. For this reason, it is often referred to as *production research*.

Kathy Chater argues that the role of production research is 'to find, assess and make available the content of a production'. For her, this 'involves any or all of the following':

- information – facts (e.g. statistics, dates and biographies) and opinions
- people – members of the public, celebrities, experts, representatives and spokespersons, contestants and audiences
- locations
- props – objects […] and prizes

- archive footage – specific events and stock footage (e.g. an aeroplane taking off)
- still pictures – photographs, slides and paintings (including engravings)
- sound – music, sound effects and the spoken word (2002: 14)

You have already done some of the work of 'finding and assessing' so now is the time to 'make it available'. This is the moment when you stop talking about your idea in the abstract and start to make it happen!

What should be apparent from this list is that some of the research relates to the technical or logistical aspects of the production and some to the content of the production. So, for the purposes of this book and while you are learning, we will refer to three types of production research: *technical and logistical research, content research* and *contextual research*. Although we will separate these three different types of research, in reality they are inextricably intertwined.

Technical and logistical research

What we are calling technical and logistical research is, not surprisingly, the research relating to the technical aspects and the logistics of the production. Much of this will already have been carried out when you had three ideas on the table but it is ongoing and will be more detailed and more focused than previously:

- *Finance:* you must now find out *exact* prices, compare quotes and then book and actually pay for transport, stock, equipment, accommodation, the people in your video (actors, presenters or contributors) and catering.
- *Logistics:* once you have finalized the list of kit and of people you need, you need to organize and schedule how you will transport them to the different locations.
- *Health and Safety:* a key element of your technical and logistical research at this stage is the carrying out of *recces*. A recce (short for reconnaissance) is a process that all film- and video-makers will go through, normally once the idea for the production has been finalized. You will already know, from the previous stage, which locations you might want to use and how to go about obtaining permission to use them, so this stage involves travelling to each of the potential locations to see if they are suitable for your purposes, both aesthetically and from the point of view of Health and Safety.

    There is a tendency among new video-makers simply to think of a location that they know and to assume that there will be no problem about using it. This might well be the case, but it might equally turn out to have very major problems which will have serious repercussions for your production. So, the more information you get at the recce stage, the less likely you are to run into problems when filming. A comprehensive recce will involve checking each location for a number of things:

- Local conditions: specifically the day and the time that you wish to carry out the shoot. For example, is the location the site of a busy market on only one day a week? Does a school finish at the time you want an empty street scene?
- Written permission: it is good professional practice to establish whether this is needed.
- Assistance: for example, do you need someone to let you into the location?
- Camera viewpoints: that is, the best place to put the camera to get the type of shots that you need. Consider who and what is likely to be in the shots. From the recce, you may realize that you need to alter the camera position or take additional equipment, such as a specific type of camera support
- Sound: are there any sounds which are likely to impinge upon the production? What additional sound equipment might you need to take?
- Lighting and power: where are the sources of power? Are there any problems with the existing lighting and power? What additional lighting equipment might you need?
- Set dressing: this is a great opportunity to see if set dressing is required and, if so, what you need to dress it properly.

It is worth making the point that you *must* do full recces for each and every location that you intend to use. In order to carry out a comprehensive recce and to adequately record your findings you should make up a recce pack which includes a notepad and pens, a tape measure, a torch, a means of recording audio and a microphone. One of the key pieces of equipment to take, though, is a digital camera. This will enable you to include pictures of each location in your recce notes. This always helps, especially if you have a large number of possible locations or if you are looking back at your notes a few weeks after the recce has taken place. To make the process more systematic, you might also want to use a sheet which allows you record all your findings quickly and easily, such as the one shown in Figure 3.2.

A more detailed risk assessment will involve a thorough identification of potential hazards (such as slipping or falling), existing control measures,

Recce Sheet

Title of production   Date of recce:

Location:

Present:

	Please indicate Yes/No for each area	Comments/Details
Local Condition: • Any known problems If yes, please detail (including source of information)	No ☐ Yes ☐	
• Aid needed If yes, please detail name, address and contact numbers for each person/organization	No ☐ Yes ☐	
• Permission needed	No ☐ Yes ☐	
• Protective clothing needed If yes, please detail	No ☐ Yes ☐	
Viewpoints: • Appropriate viewpoints isolated	No ☐ Yes ☐	
• Any obstructions	No ☐ Yes ☐	
• Easy to reach and safe If no, please detail requirements	No ☐ Yes ☐	
Requirements: • Power available If no, please detail alternative arrangements	No ☐ Yes ☐	
• Lighting appropriate If no, please detail alternative arrangements	No ☐ Yes ☐	
• Sound equipment (please detail)		
Anticipated problems: • Sound If yes, please detail	No ☐ Yes ☐	
• Picture If yes, please detail	No ☐ Yes ☐	
• People If yes, please detail	No ☐ Yes ☐	
• Other If yes, please detail	No ☐ Yes ☐	
Other considerations (please provide details for each): • Security considered		
• Welfare considered (transport, food, First Aid, etc.)		
• Set dressing required		
• Props required		
Comments:		

Please attach sketches (including power points, anticipated camera viewpoints, position of lighting etc.) and photographs of the location and its site

Figure 3.2   A sample recce sheet

people who may be at risk, the severity and likelihood of any risk and, most importantly, action to be taken to reduce the risk. Each risk can be scored numerically in order to highlight whether it can be tolerated, reduced or, as in some extreme cases, considered unacceptable, in which case the shoot cannot go ahead. You can download a sample risk-assessment sheet from the book's website.

- *Technical resources:* by now, you should have become acquainted with your media store or loan shop, its regulations and the staff within it. You should know what types of camera, lighting, microphone and supporting equipment will be available to you, how much of it there is and how long you can book it for.

   Once you know your brief, a key part of the technical and logistical research is to find out exactly how that equipment works and what its limitations are. With regard to the former, this should involve download-ing manuals from the internet and familiarizing yourself with how to use the kit properly by accessing internet user groups; with regard to the latter, you need to shoot test footage in circumstances similar to those in which the real shoot will take place.

- *Human resources:* there are certain types of video which may require you to access specific human resources from either outside your group or outside your institution: for example, experts in the production process or people with specialist knowledge such as make-up artists. Book and pay for them or, if that is not possible, book them for a training session.

- *Experience and ability of the crew:* whatever type of video you intend to produce, you should always use the research stage to make sure that all members of the group are fully informed about their roles and responsi-bilities. As mentioned above, use the test shoot to ascertain that you know how to use the kit properly but also to determine whether or not you work effectively as a crew. If not, do something about it now!

- *Time:* produce, or update, your detailed group-project planner, making sure that all the research and organization to date is now on it. Remember to allocate all the remaining tasks realistically.

- *Output:* make final decisions about how you will distribute the finished video. Consider potential publicity and marketing for your project and contacting relevant media organizations to generate interest in your video.

Content research

Clearly, some of the technical and logistical research will impinge directly upon the content of your production. For example, if you do not have a location, you do not have a production to put content into. However, some of your research is much more explicitly concerned with information about the content of a production and this is what we shall refer to as content research. This might include all the remaining items on Chater's list:

- digging up information, facts, statistics and opinions;
- sourcing the right celebrities, guests, interviewees, experts, members of the public, speakers, audiences and representatives;
- location-scouting for aesthetic purposes, rather than for technical or safety reasons;
- locating props and costumes;
- sourcing previously recorded material such as archive or stock footage;
- finding still images such as photographs;
- locating audio recordings such as sound effects and music.

As a general rule of thumb, the more wide-ranging your research and the more information you obtain about a subject, the more likely it is that the information will be useful and interesting and will allow you to have an unusual or innovative take on a subject. So, we would also add that your research at this stage should continue to involve theoretical and contextual consideration of the idea.

As there is an element of risk in all video production, the final stage of your research process should be to isolate any anticipated problems – or, as we call them, the 'what-ifs' – and to consider likely solutions: what if it rains and we need to carry on filming? What if our flight is delayed? What if the camera breaks? As we saw in Chapter 2, this ability to reflect in action, in the form of contingency planning, is a key skill in video production.

Contextual research

Contextual research is the type of research which you carry out when you first receive a brief. It is the research which allows you to find out about the broad area in which you are going to be working and involves reading around that area and watching as many programmes as possible within the genre and about the genre.

Producing a script

The script is one of the key documents for most productions. It describes in detail each individual scene and the shots which make up that scene and it contains information about where the individual shots take place and,

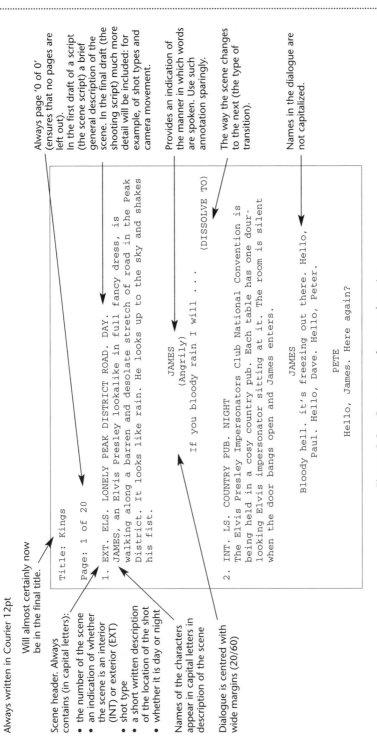

Always written in Courier 12pt

Will almost certainly now be in the final title.

Scene header. Always contains (in capital letters):
- the number of the scene
- an indication of whether the scene is an interior (INT) or exterior (EXT)
- shot type
- a short written description of the location of the shot
- whether it is day or night

Names of the characters appear in capital letters in description of the scene

Dialogue is centred with wide margins (20/60)

Always page '0 of 0' (ensures that no pages are left out).
In the first draft of a script (the scene script) a brief general description of the scene. In the final draft (the shooting script) much more detail will be included: for example, of shot types and camera movement.

Provides an indication of the manner in which words are spoken. Use such annotation sparingly.

The way the scene changes to the next (the type of transition).

Names in the dialogue are not capitalized.

Title: Kings

Page: 1 of 20

1. EXT. ELS. LONELY PEAK DISTRICT ROAD. DAY.
JAMES, an Elvis Presley lookalike in full fancy dress, is walking along a barren and desolate stretch of road in the Peak District. It looks like rain. He looks up to the sky and shakes his fist.

JAMES
(Angrily)
If you bloody rain I will . . .

(DISSOLVE TO)

2. INT. LS. COUNTRY PUB. NIGHT
The Elvis Presley Impersonators Club National Convention is being held in a cosy country pub. Each table has one dour-looking Elvis impersonator sitting at it. The room is silent when the door bangs open and James enters.

JAMES
Bloody hell. it's freezing out there. Hello, Paul. Hello, Dave. Hello, Peter.

PETE
Hello, James. Here again?

Figure 3.3 One page of a sample script

crucially, all the dialogue within that scene. There are specific formats for a script depending upon the type of video and whether it is being produced on location or in a studio, and these *must* be followed. We will look at some of the different formats for producing scripts and at scriptwriting techniques in later chapters. For the moment, though, an example of what is called a fictional or drama script is shown in Figure 3.3 so that you can see exactly what information you need to include.

On no account should any filming take place until the script is complete. By that we mean that you have produced numerous drafts, each one better than the previous one, and that all members of the production group are happy with the final draft. The script can then be 'locked'. If you start shooting from an unlocked draft and it subsequently changes, you may be left with, at best, continuity problems and, at worst, completely useless footage. So, you *must* have a system for recognizing the latest draft. In the writing of this book, we had so many versions of each chapter that we had to devise a simple system for identifying the latest draft and dating it. In our case, this involved having a large silver bulldog clip on a print-out, with the date of printing, of the latest draft and filing each previous version when a new draft was produced. If you don't know what the latest draft is you will find that people are working from different drafts: this can be frustrating as it wastes time and it looks extremely unprofessional.

Producing a storyboard

Prior to storyboarding, you need to produce 'thumbnails'. These are initial outline sketches which are usually no larger than a thumbnail (hence the name) but are relatively detailed. Usually produced on A4 plain paper, they are quicker and easier to produce than full storyboards but are produced in the first flush of creativity and, as such, are useful for exploring a number of different possible narratives, styles, shot compositions and camera techniques (see Figure 3.4).

The storyboard develops the thumbnails into a form which represents what the video will look like after it has been edited. It can be produced at the same time as the script or, as is more usual, after the script has been completed. It contains much of the same information as the script, but the major difference is that it includes a visual representation of each shot in the production. This can be hand-drawn, made up of stills from a digital camera or a moving storyboard (known as an *animatic*). Like much of the documentation in video production, there is no one correct format for a storyboard, but any storyboard will contain the information shown in Figure 3.5. A page of a sample storyboard is shown in Figure 3.6.

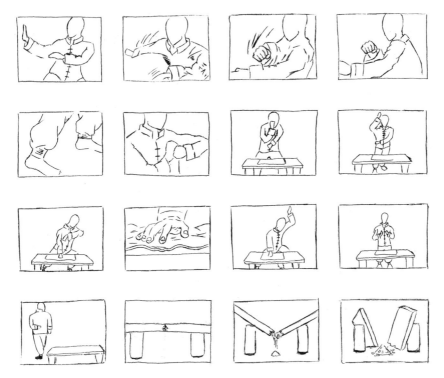

Figure 3.4   One page of sample thumbnails

It is at the stage of producing a storyboard that you need to give much more careful consideration to the types of shot that you, as a video-maker, have at your disposal. Remember our discussion about the children's construction set in the media language section of Chapter 1? Well, the shots are the most fundamental of the building blocks available to video- and film-makers. There are three main decisions that you can make with regard to the shots that you include on your storyboard and, by implication, in your final production:

- the type of framing;
- the point of view;
- the movement.

The type of framing

Before considering the types of framing of individual shots, it is at this stage that you need to make a decision about what your frame will be: that is, what *aspect ratio* you intend to shoot your video in (see Figure 3.7). Historically,

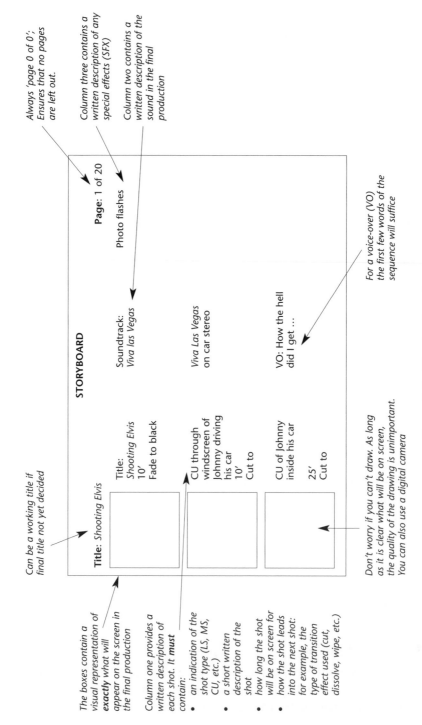

Can be a working title if
final title not yet decided

Always 'page 0 of 0'.
Ensures that no pages
are left out.

Column three contains a
written description of any
special effects (SFX)

Column two contains a
written description of the
sound in the final
production

The boxes contain a
visual representation of
exactly what will
appear on the screen in
the final production

Column one provides a
written description of
each shot. It **must**
contain:

• an indication of the
  shot type (LS, MS,
  CU, etc.)
• a short written
  description of the
  shot
• how long the shot
  will be on screen for
• how the shot leads
  into the next shot:
  for example, the
  type of transition
  effect used (cut,
  dissolve, wipe, etc.)

STORYBOARD

Page: 1 of 20

Title: *Shooting Elvis*

Title:
Shooting Elvis
10'
Fade to black

Soundtrack:
Viva las Vegas

Photo flashes

CU through
windscreen of
Johnny driving
his car
10'
Cut to

Viva Las Vegas
on car stereo

CU of Johnny
inside his car

25'
Cut to

VO: How the hell
did I get …

For a voice-over (VO)
the first few words of the
sequence will suffice

Don't worry if you can't draw. As long
as it is clear what will be on screen,
the quality of the drawing is unimportant.
You can also use a digital camera

Figure 3.5 The storyboard

Figure 3.6   One page of a sample storyboard

video was shot in 4:3 ratio: that is, the picture was four units wide to three high. Now, though, most video is shot in 16:9 or widescreen. If you decide to shoot in widescreen, you need to make sure that your storyboard is laid out in 16:9 and that you compose your shots with this ratio in mind. To complicate things slightly, however, many people still view video material on 4:3 televisions or monitors and so, when composing your shots, you need to compose them with a 14:9 ratio. This allows people viewing on older 4:3 televisions or monitors to see most of the action in a form which does not look out of place and badly composed. The easiest way to do this is to compose a shot in a 16:9 rectangle but to ignore the first and last unit of width.

Any type of camera is capable of producing a range of different types of shot (see Figure 3.8). These types of shot are fundamental to every film or television programme, from cinema epics to local television news programmes. They all follow the same rules of framing. They are generally called *simple shots* as they contain no camera movement, just the movement of the subject within the shot (Thompson 1998: 56).

If you have a shot with more than one person in the frame, then it is known as a *two-shot* (two people in the frame), *three-shot* (three people in the frame), and so on. Normally, when editing a conversation between two

Figure 3.7 Aspect ratios

Extreme long shot (ELS)
This type of shot is used to establish where the action is taking place. The first shot in a scene is normally an ELS.

Long shot (LS)
Normally places a subject in the frame. A person occupies one-third to two-thirds of the frame.

Mid (or medium) shot (MS)
Retains some of the background detail while focusing mainly on the subject. Cuts at the waist.

Medium close-up (MCU)
Cuts just below the chest. Used to show more detail about the subjects and their actions.

Close-up (CU)
A head and shoulders shot. Good for showing emotion.

Big close-up (BCU)
Removes all the background and focuses on one part of the subject. Rarely used for people as it is very unflattering.

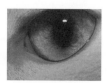

Extreme close-up (ECU)
Used for showing very close detail.

Figure 3.8 Shot types for video production

people, there is a technique known as shot/reverse shot. This is where the first shot is of the first person while the second shot is of the second person, normally in the same type of shot (CU etc.)

Within simple shots, there are three generally accepted rules of composition of which you need to be aware:

1. the headroom rule;
2. the looking-into-shot rule;
3. the rule of thirds.

The headroom rule

When framing a subject, ensure that there is room in the frame above his/her head so that it does not look as though the top of the head has been cut off. Conversely, avoid having so much space above the head that it looks as though the person is falling out of the bottom of the frame (see Figure 3.9).

Too much headroom   Correct   Too little headroom

Figure 3.9   The headroom rule

The looking-into-shot rule

When framing a subject, ensure that he/she has enough of the frame to 'look into' and that his/her face is not squashed into the edge of the frame (see Figure 3.10).

Correct   Incorrect

Figure 3.10   Looking into/out of shot

The rule of thirds

One of the main rules of composition within film and television is one which is common in fine art and is known as the *rule of thirds*. This rule is based on the assumption that good composition requires the main subject of interest within a shot to be placed *not* in the centre of the frame (as many novice video-makers will do) but, rather, at any of the intersections of the lines of an imaginary noughts and crosses grid placed over the frame (see Figure 3.11).

This rule is so widely used that audiences are now able readily to anticipate where the interest in a shot will occur. However, some commentators such as Ward make the point that the overuse of the technique in art and the media means that as a compositional technique it has possibly become 'stale and static' (Ward 2003: 124)

These three compositional rules have grown up over a long period of time and are accepted by both producers and the audiences for film and video. However, these rules are being broken in a whole range of contemporary television and film productions. You should break these rules *only* if there is a good reason and you can provide the justification for doing so.

Figure 3.11 The rule of thirds

The point of view

In most types of video production, the camera acts as a non-participating bystander. There are certain decisions which can be made as to where to view the action from. You can decide:

- *from which point of view the shot will be taken*: an *objective* shot will provide an onlooker's view of the scene and will show *all* the characters and action in any scene. In film theory, this is known as an *omniscient* view. A *subjective* shot will show the action from the point of view of one of the characters. This is known in the industry as a POV shot.
- *the angle of the shot*: having the camera low and shooting up at an angle makes things appear larger and more imposing than they really are, whereas having the camera higher and looking down at an angle makes things appear relatively small and insignificant (see Figure 3.12).

There is a general rule of shooting that you should always 'cover' a scene using simple shots: that is, you should film enough footage with simple shots to be able to edit it together properly. To cover a scene, always shoot what is known as a *master shot* – that is, a complete take of the whole scene in a 'loose' shot such as an LS – and then shoot a number of takes of each different section of the scene in increasingly 'tighter' shots (from an LS to an MCU to a CU, etc.).

Figure 3.12   The use of angles

The movement

It is good professional practice to ensure that the camera remains as still as possible by mounting it on a tripod and you should *always* plan to do this as a matter of course. There will be occasions, though, when you want some movement in your shots. This can be either for aesthetic reasons (it looks better than a still shot) or for reasons of necessity (you are following movement, such as a chase). Whichever is the case, there are a number of movements that the camera can successfully make. These types of shot are called *complex shots* (Thompson 1998: 56) and involve movement of the subject of the shot, the tripod's pan and tilt head and/or the focal length of lens: that is, from wide to telephoto or vice versa:

- *Pan*: the camera moves on its horizontal axis: that is, from left to right or right to left. This can be a *surveying* pan, where the observer is surveying a landscape, or a *following* pan, where action within a scene is being followed.
- *Tilt*: the camera moves on its vertical axis: that is, up and down.

As well as simple and complex shots, there are also *developing shots*. This is where the subject of the shot, the tripod's pan and tilt head and the camera mount move and/or the focal length of lens is altered:

- *Crab shot:* the camera remains motionless, but the tripod upon which it is mounted moves from left to right or vice versa using a piece of equipment known as a track and dolly. This provides a very smooth movement.
- *Track shot:* this is similar to a crab, but the camera moves towards or away from the subject
- *Crane shot:* the camera remains motionless, but the tripod upon which it is mounted is moved up or down using a crane or a jib

There is one final type of shot that we sometimes encourage students to think about: what we call *imaginative* shots. These are shots where none of the above movements are what you are looking for and you have to improvise, for example by putting your camera in a basket tied to the ceiling and swinging it 360 degrees. With these kinds of shots you are limited only by your imagination and what your camera, your tutor and Health and Safety considerations will allow!

There is one other rule of shooting of which you need to be aware, especially if you intend to use such movements in your video. This is known as either the *180° rule* or, more commonly, *crossing the line*.

This rule relies on the idea that, in any shot, there is an imaginary line

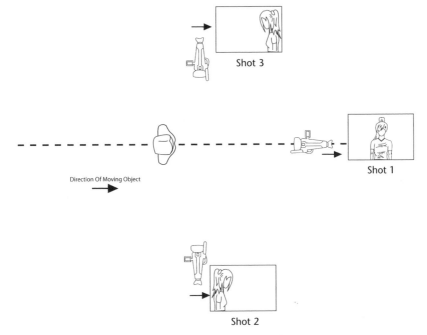

Shot 3

Direction Of Moving Object

Shot 1

Shot 2

Figure 3.13   Crossing the line

between the points of action which the camera must not cross. In Figure 3.13, the line would be between where the woman is and where she will end up (Shot 1). The reason that the line should not be crossed is that if a camera takes a shot from one side of the line (Shot 2), she appears to be walking left to right, but if the camera is moved over the imaginary line she appears to be walking in the opposite direction (Shot 3). This means that it would not be possible to edit the shots together and maintain visual continuity. The only way that you can move across the line is if you shoot a linking shot along the line.

The key point we are making here is that the decisions about the type of framing, POV and movement are made by you as a direct result of *conscious decisions* about what you want the finished video to look like. This is an integral part of your pre-production planning: you must *never* leave it until the production stage.

Producing a shot list and shooting order

When the storyboard is complete you should produce a written description for every shot you have storyboarded. This is called a shot list and is simply a list of all the shots which are needed within the finished video, following the order of the shots on the storyboard and providing additional information. It

Shot 1: (long shot/establishing shot: 3 sec) Camera tilts down from moon to cottage at night. Upstairs bedroom light is on and the remainder of the house is in darkness. Cut to …

Shot 2: (Close up 4 sec) of owl perched on branch in tree in front garden, as it turns toward the house camera pans right to cottage and slowly zooms toward bedroom window. 1 sec cross fade to …

Shot 3: (long shot: 3 sec) of bedroom where a young woman sits up in bed alone reading by the light of a bedside table lamp. Cut to …

Shot 4: (Extreme close up: 2 sec) of clock which shows midnight. Cut to …

Shot 5: (close up: 4 sec) of book entitled Ghost Stories at Midnight. Camera vertically cranes upwards from horror story book cover to face of woman who hears the owl screech outside and looks startled, toward the bedroom window. Cut to …

Shot 6: (woman's POV) shadows of trees move eerily across the window and curtains move with breeze from open window. Cut to …

Shot 7: (long shot: 3 sec) from floor level under the bed showing woman's feet as they slip into her shoes and walks toward the window. Cut to …

Shot 8: (Exterior long shot: 3 sec) of bedroom window as woman opens curtain and then closes the window. Cut to …

Figure 3.14 A sample shot list

is useful in terms of explaining shots, camera and action, particularly for shots which are very complicated or difficult to illustrate on a storyboard. There are a number of different ways of laying out a shot list but we have found the lay-out shown in Figure 3.14 to be of the greatest practical use to our students, owing to its simplicity.

This example offers sufficient information for all members of the crew to understand each shot but provides additional information which enables the director and camera operator to realize the shot in terms of action, camera position, movement and intention. It does not, however, take into account additional shots that the director may wish to obtain on the shoot.

Once all the shots have been listed, it is possible to take the shot list a stage further. This is called the *shooting order* and is produced simply by grouping shots which can be recorded at the same time and at the same location. So, for the above shot list we would group all of the night-time exterior shots together and all the night-time interior shots together. This practice can be extremely useful when shooting drama where there may be hundreds of individual shots which would need to be carefully and logically scheduled.

Producing a shooting schedule

Central to the success of the production stage is organization, communication and planning. This primarily involves making sure that all members of

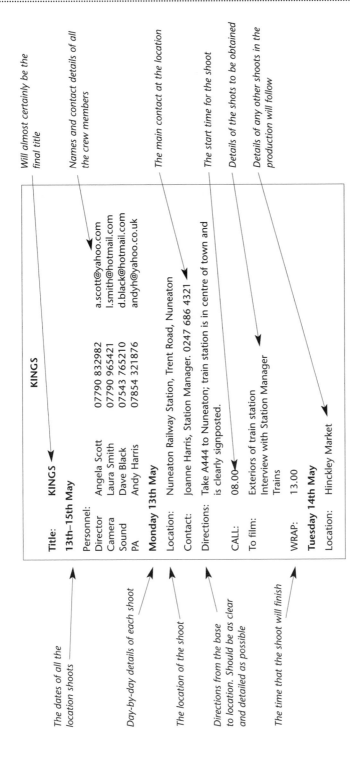

The dates of all the location shoots

Day-by-day details of each shoot

The location of the shoot

Directions from the base to location. Should be as clear and detailed as possible

The time that the shoot will finish

Will almost certainly be the final title

Names and contact details of all the crew members

The main contact at the location

The start time for the shoot

Details of the shots to be obtained

Details of any other shoots in the production will follow

KINGS

Title:	KINGS
13th–15th May	
Personnel:	
Director	Angela Scott	07790 832982	a.scott@yahoo.com
Camera	Laura Smith	07790 965421	l.smith@hotmail.com
Sound	Dave Black	07543 765210	d.black@hotmail.com
PA	Andy Harris	07854 321876	andyh@yahoo.co.uk

Monday 13th May

Location:	Nuneaton Railway Station, Trent Road, Nuneaton
Contact:	Joanne Harris, Station Manager. 0247 686 4321
Directions:	Take A444 to Nuneaton; train station is in centre of town and is clearly signposted.
CALL:	08.00
To film:	Exteriors of train station
	Interview with Station Manager
	Trains
WRAP:	13.00

Tuesday 14th May

Location:	Hinckley Market

Figure 3.15 The shooting schedule

the production team (the crew) are certain about the dates and times of each shoot (or occasion when filming takes place), the location of the shoot, which members of the crew or 'talent' are needed, what technical resources are needed and which shots from the script are being shot. All of this information is recorded on to one document: the *shooting schedule*. The production of the shooting schedule is the final element of the pre-production stage. Again, there is no single accepted format for a shooting schedule, but all will contain the same information (see Figure 3.15).

A full shooting schedule will contain all the information needed for each shoot and, as a result, can run to many pages in length.

In scheduling, be realistic about what you have to do on each shoot: allow for travel time, kit set-up, set dressing, lighting, rehearsal and filming. Allow plenty of time for each shoot as it is likely to take much longer than you initially expect.

So, to recap pre-production, the key skills that you need to develop are the ability to be creative, practical, well organized and systematic in approach, to carry out all the tasks diligently and thoroughly, to reflect constantly upon and review progress and to communicate effectively throughout each of the different stages. This is why, if it is done correctly, it takes up 70 per cent of your time!

The Practice of Video Production: Production

Only once you have completed all the necessary pre-production planning and research can you move on to the production stage. This stage involves you using the materials that you generated and developed in pre-production as the basis for filming your production, either in the studio and/or out on location. Cartwright's rule says that only 10 per cent of your time should be spent on this stage, as much of the imaginative and creative work has already been done. However, especially at the beginning of your production career, *preparing* for it will take much longer and requires you to understand in detail what this stage involves.

In this section, therefore, we want to look at five main areas:

1. the types of equipment you will use to produce your video;
2. the production roles that you should adopt and the responsibilities which go with each role;
3. the organization of the shoot and set etiquette;
4. the Health and Safety issues that you need to consider on a shoot;
5. what needs to be done after the shoot.

You might notice that this information straddles the pre-production and production stages. You will already have begun to research much of the information in this section during the pre-production stage but now you will be required to understand it properly and to apply it. This is where knowing and doing meet.

Equipment

At the beginning of your career, it is likely that you will be using relatively inexpensive, low-end kit and will work up to more sophisticated, broadcast-quality kit as you progress. In this chapter, therefore, we want to introduce you to the basic equipment that you will use. It is probably a good idea to have a camera, tripod and microphone with you while you are reading through the following sections.

Camera

All video cameras essentially have the same parts and work in the same way: light enters the camera through the lens, is focused on to a part of the camera called either a charge-coupled device (CCD) or other type of chip and is then converted into an electronic signal which is in turn recorded on to the recording medium such as tape, DVD or, increasingly, a hard disk drive. As one of the keys to making good video is the ability to be able to control each aspect of this process, the difference between the most basic and the most sophisticated cameras is the quality of the different parts of the camera and the extent to which you can control them manually.

Modern video cameras are extremely sophisticated tools which are designed to be as user-friendly as possible. This is fine for everyday domestic use as you can rely on the camera to do everything for you. However, as far as using a camera for serious video production is concerned, we want to make three really important points that you must always remember:

1. No matter how advanced the camera is, it remains just a tool for you to use.
2. You will *never* use the camera's auto setting but will *always* work with the manual controls. Only by doing so will you be able to control every aspect of what the camera records and ensure that your footage is exactly as you want it and not how the camera thinks it should be.
3. You need to know how to use this tool properly. Camerawork is one of the key areas where you can explore and develop your creative skills, but only if your technical skills permit you to make the very best use of your camera.

Knowledge of equipment and processes is one of the six key skills that you need to master to become a professional video-maker, so fully understanding your camera is fundamental to your success. We are aware that students reading this book will be working in very different circumstances: from the institution with only one or two lower-end cameras to the most highly-equipped department. Whichever camera you have access to, you should download a copy of the instruction manual from the manufacturer's website and read it carefully until you understand the functions of the different buttons, switches and menu commands. We would argue that it is possible, even with lower-end equipment, to make good video if you understand the limitations and possibilities of your equipment. That is the craft of video-making.

Using the camera

So, what are the things that you need to know about using and making the most of the camera?

One of the first things to know is very obvious to experienced video-makers but is something that almost all new video-makers fail to think about: checking their kit prior to leaving for a shoot. Make sure that you develop the habit of checking *all* your equipment, not just your camera, to ensure that you have everything and that it all works. At best, it can be really annoying to start a shoot and find that you are missing equipment or it does not work; at worst, it can mean the end of the day's shoot or even the end of your film.

Another obvious point is that once you have the kit, you need to take good care of it. Given that you are likely to be sharing the kit with all the other students on your course, it is important that everyone should look after it. Most camera kits come in bags or cases: keep them in there whenever you are not using them, particularly when travelling or when moving from one location to another. Always know what the bag should contain and always check that it still contains everything when you return it.

You will learn how to use the camera effectively and creatively on your course and, with practice, your knowledge of the camera and your camera-work will improve. Here, though, are some basic technical pointers to get you started.

Viewfinder

Many cameras come with two types of monitor: first, a small viewfinder with eyepiece, which is used by professional camera operators to check the contrast levels and focus within the shot; secondly, an LCD screen which is very good for checking the overall composition of the shot. All professional cameras will give you the option of using an even larger external monitor and you should do so whenever possible.

White balance

Setting the white balance on a camera is a way of telling the camera whether you are filming in natural light or artificial light. Although, to our eyes, all light looks white, it is, in fact, made up of different colours: natural light tends to look predominantly blue on camera; professional studio lighting is predominantly orange; strip lighting tends to be green. The reason for this is that different types of light have different colour temperatures. Colour temperature is usually measured in degrees Kelvin (or °K): sunlight is usually 54°K while professional studio lighting is normally 32°K.

Most cameras have an auto white-balance setting. As with most camera controls, however, we would advise that you ignore this button and always set the white balance manually. This must be done each time you move the camera from one light source to another (for example, from indoor, artificial light to outdoor, natural light) or when you move the camera within the same setting. Otherwise, your shots may not have the correct continuity of colour.

Iris

The function of the iris control is to allow you to alter the amount of light entering the camera. You will see some printed numbers, known as *f numbers*, either around the ring behind the lens on professional cameras or, on some smaller cameras, on a control wheel near the lens. Moving this ring or wheel opens or closes the iris to compensate for too much light or too little light. The basic rule is: the larger the number, the smaller the aperture and the less light entering, thus making your picture darker (in professional terms this is called *stopping up*); the smaller the number, the larger the aperture and the more light entering, thus making your picture lighter (*stopping down*). When looking at your shot, in the viewfinder, on the LCD screen or on a professional field monitor, you will be able to see if your image is too light or too dark.

Focus

In automatic focus mode, movement and different light sources will cause the camera constantly to adjust and readjust the focus. So, again, only ever use the manual control to control focus.

In general, the aim should be to get the subject of your video in focus. A shot where the subject is not in sharp focus but should be is known as a *soft* shot. If you want everything in your shot to be in sharp focus, you need to:

1. zoom in fully and focus on an object behind the subject you want to shoot;
2. zoom back out.

Everything between the object on which you focused and the camera will be in focus, including your subject. If you were to focus just on the subject, that subject might move back slightly and thus be out of focus.

Focus is not just about achieving a clear and crisp image. There may be occasions, especially when you become more confident as a video-maker, where you want to use focus more creatively and play around with how much of what is in shot is in focus. This is called *depth of field* and there are two main ways of referring to this: *deep focus* and *shallow focus* (see Figure 4.1).

Deep focus
Most of the picture is in focus

Shallow focus
Only the subject is in focus: background and
foreground are out of focus

Figure 4.1 Depth of field

Increased DOF (deep focus)   *Decreased DOF (shallow focus)*

◄───►

Iris:
Larger *f* number, smaller aperture   Smaller *f* number, larger aperture

Distance:
Camera further away from subject   Camera nearer subject

Focal length:
Decreased focal length   Increased focal length
(wide angle used)   (telephoto used)

Figure 4.2 Changing the focus of a shot

There are three main ways of changing the focus or depth of field in a shot:
the iris setting, the distance between the camera and the subject and the focal
length of the lens being used (see Figure 4.2).

Shutter speed
The basic rule of shutter speed is: the lower the shutter speed, the more
blurred the image; the faster the shutter speed, the crisper the image. Slower
shutter speeds, below 1/50th of a second, offer a more filmic quality to your

material while those over 1/1000th of a second are good for filming fast action and allow you to freeze that action.

Problems to avoid when using a camera

There are a number of warnings that we would give about the use of your camera:

- *Zoom:* the basic rule of zooming is 'don't'. This is one of the few functions that your eyes cannot perform but your camera can and that is why it looks unnatural in most videos. If you do have to use a zoom, and there are a few occasions where you *might*, always use it sparingly, practise using the rocker switch or zoom ring before going for the shot and always go for a smooth, continuous zoom. Never zoom in a bit, stop, and zoom in a bit more: it looks awful and means that you almost certainly won't be able to use that footage in your final video.
- *Effects controls:* some cameras, especially consumer models, have buttons on them which allow you to add effects to your footage in order to 'improve' your video. Never, *ever* use them! The reason for this is that if you have 'clean' footage, it is easy to add effects and, crucially, take them off again in the edit. If you have added effects on your camera, it is impossible to do so. Remember the first rule of video production: garbage in, garbage out. Professional video-makers, of whom you are one from this point onwards, will always add effects at the post-production stage, as any of the effects that you find on a camera can be found on even the most basic edit software.
- *Sound:* most cameras have their own microphone mounted on board the camera. The basic rule with on-board microphones, no matter how good, is only to use them in an emergency. One of the main reasons for this is that they tend to record the sound of the camera's motor and the camera operator. Another problem is that, although the quality of these microphones has improved dramatically in recent years, especially on higher-end cameras, they are generally not sophisticated enough to record sound in a professional manner. You should, therefore, develop the habit of using a professional external microphone plugged directly into the camera or into a sound mixer.

  One more point about sound: *always* monitor your sound both by looking at the camera's sound-level meters (normally on the LCD monitor) occasionally and by *always* listening using good-quality professional headphones, not earphones from an MP3 player that happens to be lying around. Only by doing this will you know that you have the correct microphone, that it is working and that you are recording the correct sound.

- *Stock:* your tapes are known as 'stock' and you must treat them with care as they are easily damaged. Always ensure that you:
  - *use new, branded stock.* Never be tempted to use cheap, unbranded stock: it may be tempting when you are paying for it but when you come to view what you have recorded, you may regret it. Equally, never record over a tape which has already been used.
  - *keep tapes safe.* Keep them away from magnets (TVs and speakers), damp and extremes of temperatures. If you move a tape from a cold to a warm environment, wait ten minutes for it to warm up to the temperature of the room to avoid the tape being chewed up by the camera.
  - *treat tapes with care.* Treat your stock with kid gloves at all times. Do not drop them or knock them about, especially once you have recorded on them as they may be liable to signal damage or *dropout*. This will ruin your footage and make it unusable.
  - *label tapes properly.* Always make sure that each used tape has, as a minimum, a tape number, a contact name and a mobile phone number clearly visible. Make sure that you always know where they are: we have a desk drawer at work which is full of used tapes that students have forgotten to label!

  Increasingly, with the introduction of hard-drive and card media storage, some of the comments we make in this book about stock will become redundant. Labelling and looking after your recording medium carefully, however, will remain exactly the same:

- *Recording:* when inserting a tape, check that the tab on the tape is in/closed and push the tape very carefully into the tape cradle. Never force any part of the camera here, as it is very easily damaged. On a new tape, always record thirty seconds of colour bars, as generated by the camera itself, for two reasons: first, it means that you record over the first thirty seconds of tape with some non-crucial video, as the beginning of the tape is more subject to damage through creasing; secondly, it allows you to colour-correct footage from different cameras in the edit suite. If your camera does not generate colour bars, leave your lens cap on and record thirty seconds of black. When shooting, always record a little more than necessary at the beginning and end of each shot – known as a head and tail – each time you record. This extra six seconds can make capturing the footage easier in the edit, as there is more of a timecoded lead in/out for each take.

Camera operation tips

When using a camera:

- **Always** check your camera kit as soon as you collect it.
- **Always** make sure that whenever you put something down for a minute – for example, the camera plate found on top of the tripod – that you pick it up again and put it back where it belongs.
- **Always** use a tripod and set the camera up properly:
  - level the tripod. Attach the plate from the tripod to the camera first and then click it into place on the tripod. Do not overtighten the plate screw as it will break the camera casing: fingertight and then a quarter-turn with a coin is fine.
  - turn on the camera. Remember there are often three 'on' positions for the camera:
    1. switches the VTR 'on' for playback;
    2. switches the camera 'on' for recording;
    3. switches to the camera "memory" or recording of still images

  So, before contacting your media technician because the camera is apparently not recording, check to see whether you have accidentally set the camera to 'VTR' or 'memory'.
  - insert a new tape. If the camera will not record, eject the tape and check to see whether the tab has been removed.
  - check that all the camera settings are correct. Look at how the camera is currently set up by checking the icons on the LCD screen. One common mistake is to have the time and date on the LCD. No other information represented by the icons on screen is recorded on to the tape, but the time and date are and cannot be removed in the edit.
  - stay manual at all times.
  - make sure the lens cap is off (We receive three or four phone calls a year from panicking students telling us that they cannot see a picture even though the camera is on and recording!) and put it back on when you have finished shooting.
- **Always** white-balance whenever setting up the camera or moving the camera from one location to another.
- **Always** protect the camera from excessive temperatures and humidity. Cold, damp mornings cut battery life, affect tapes and can cause cameras to switch off. Keep them dry and they will love you for it!
- **Always** let your media technician or tutor know if you damage anything or notice that something is not working properly. Only then can the kit be taken out of use and repaired. Otherwise, someone else gets the tripod with the head which is far from fluid or the camera which does not work!

Camera supports

Good professional practice requires you always to use some form of camera support unless you specifically wish to obtain a jerky, more 'edgy' feel to your shots. The reason for this is that shots taken without a support may look steady in the viewfinder, but on a full-size monitor they will look terrible. There are a range of supports available to you which will enable you to get the full range of simple, complex and developing shots that we outlined in Chapter 3:

- *Tripods:* there are a whole range of camera supports available, from a one-legged monopod to the more usual three-legged tripod. They vary greatly in quality and their ability to do their job. Cheap, lightweight tripods are normally only good for static shots but good-quality tripods have fluid heads which allow for beautifully smooth, controlled pans and tilts. Most will also have a spirit level to enable you to get the head, and therefore the camera, completely level. Some students tell us that they can't be bothered to carry heavy tripods around. However, it really is worth it, as the resulting shots will be far superior! In the industry, you will often hear tripods referred to as 'sticks' or 'legs'.
- *Track and dolly:* the combination of a camera on a dolly (little truck) running on wheels on a track offers the opportunity to produce controlled horizontal movement such as crabbing.
- *Jib/crane:* just as track and dolly shots allow for horizontal camera movement, a crane or a jib will permit vertical movement.
- *Magic arm:* this handy device allows you to clamp a metal arm to a solid object, such as a tree or part of a building, and then fix the camera to the other end of the arm. It is best for static shots in places where setting up a tripod would be difficult.
- *Car mount:* this consists of suckers, a cross bar and a camera mount and allows you to attach most medium-sized cameras to moving vehicles. They are very good for car interior shots, for tracking shots using a slow-moving vehicle. The suckers attach to any flat surface such as glass or metal and stay there, so they can be used in situations where using a tripod is simply not possible.
- *Steadicam:* the format and price of a Steadicam varies, but basically it consists of a cradle worn by (or a device held by) the camera operator on to which the camera is attached. The idea is that the camera operator can move in any way and in any direction and the shot will remain steady and free from shake or other unwanted movement. It can be quite difficult to use and does take some practice. Professional Steadicams require the operator to complete an accredited training course.

Don't worry if you do not have access to all of these camera supports: amazing camera movement can be created without expensive specialist equipment. Using your imagination and your creativity costs nothing and so long as you carry out a proper risk-assessment of your ideas, there are a variety of interesting and creative shots that you can produce. Using a wheelchair with an operator, for example, allows you to produce good tracking shots, especially on a smooth floor.

Sound equipment

Although you are on a video production course, you also need to have a really good understanding of sound and the equipment used to record it, as video is made up of both images *and* sound. This is something that students often forget but that professionals never do: Gerald Millerson (1992: 87), for example, calls sound 'the essential component' of video.

There are two distinct types of sound which need to be recorded in video production: *synchronized (sync) sound* and *non-synchronized (non-sync) sound*:

- *Sync sound:* this is sound, mainly dialogue, recorded at the time of filming. It includes interviews, actors talking, presenters or reporters talking to camera and the sound of any action which is in shot. Just about anything which requires syncing should have sound and vision recorded simultaneously, ideally on to the same recording medium.
- *Non-sync sound*: this is all the other production sound recording where sync is not required. It includes all the sounds identified by the sound designer for a scene, such as the background ambience of a location, location sound effects and off-camera sounds. Other examples of non-sync sound include post-production sound recording such as *Foley* sound, sound effects created in a recording studio rather than on location, voice-over and narration.

Given the fundamental importance of sound for good video production, we will look at it in more detail in each of the later chapters. For the moment, though, we just want to introduce you to the basic sound kit that you are likely to use: microphones, sound mixer, boom and headphones.

Microphones

As mentioned above, you should never normally use the on-board camera microphone except in dire emergencies. Always use a professional microphone. You can normally recognize these as they have an XLR connector. Make sure that you use a cable of the appropriate length for the task because linking them can cause sound distortion or interference.

All microphones have a particular pick-up pattern. This pattern relates to where the microphone will pick sound up from:

- *Omnidirectional* microphones pick up sound from all around the microphone. This is very useful for recording ambient sound but not so good if you need to isolate a particular sound, such as someone talking.
- *Unidirectional* microphones only pick up sound in front of or to the side of the microphone.

For video production there are basically three types of microphone that you might use, each with a characteristic pick-up pattern:

- *Hand-held microphones:* these tend to be *cardioid* microphones (they have a heart-shaped pick-up pattern). This means that they will pick up sound from in front of and to the side of the microphone but will record little sound coming from behind the microphone. They are, therefore, useful for *vox pops*, studio interviews and presenting to camera.
- *Rifle microphones:* rifle microphones, also known as shotgun microphones, are usually unidirectional, have a very narrow pick-up pattern and are useful for picking out specific sounds. Usually mounted on a *fishpole* or *boom*, they allow the sound recordist to get close to the source of sound. As the name implies, they must be accurately aimed at the source of the sound, as close as is possible, but need to be kept out of camera shot. Ideally they should be housed in a shock mount: a rubber mount which cuts down on sounds generated by the pole itself and the noise generated by the operator's hands on the pole. Where air flow or wind might be a problem, a windshield, sometimes called a *softie* or *dougal*, can be used. This encases the microphone and reduces the buffeting noise that the wind will make when it blows across the microphone. Rifle microphones are particularly useful if your set-up time is limited or if your subject does not wish to wear a tie-clip microphone.
- *Tie-clip microphones:* tie-clip microphones, also known as *Lavalier* or *lapel* microphones, are usually omnidirectional in their pick-up pattern and come in two distinct types: cabled and wireless. They pick up sound from a limited area: namely, from around the speaker's mouth and chest area. For that reason, they should be attached to clothing within eight inches of the subject's mouth. Cabled tie-clip microphones need to have their cable concealed under the clothing of the speaker to the camera, ensuring that the cable is not in shot.

  The advantage of tie-clip microphones is that they exclude almost all background noise, which is important when someone is presenting to camera on a busy street. However, they also lose any sense of sound perspective, so ambient or background sound may need to be recorded separately and mixed later. Be aware, too, that they may pick up the rustle of clothing, static from synthetic material and the head and neck movements of the subject, especially if those movements are significant.

This type of microphone is very reliable when used properly but the cable limits the movements of the speaker and the distance of the subject from the camera. Radio tie-clip microphones offer much more freedom of movement because they send their signal, not via a cable but through a transmitter worn by the speaker to a receiver attached to the camera. They also allow the camera to be placed at some distance from the speaker. Their only drawback is that the less expensive models tend to suffer from signal interference and have a limited battery life.

Whichever type of microphone you use, the basic aim when recording sound is to have your microphone as close to the action as possible, while making sure that it is out of shot and keeping the sound as clean as possible.

Sound mixer

When using more than one microphone, it is useful to be able to balance or mix the incoming sounds before they reach the recording device. This is done using a sound mixer. The microphones connect directly into the different channels of the mixer and, using headphones and monitoring via the mixer's sound meters, the sound recordist can adjust the individual sound levels for each microphone so that they balance. The balanced signal is then fed to the main camera via an XLR cable where it is recorded.

Boom

The boom is a pole upon which a microphone is mounted and which allows the sound recordist to get a microphone as close to the action as possible. It is sometimes known as a *fishpole*.

Headphones

Most cameras, especially professional ones, will allow the sound recordist to listen to the sound which is being recorded. Headphones of the highest possible quality should always be used because, in normal circumstances, the ears and brain will be quite selective and will filter out 'unwanted' noise, focusing only on those sounds which are important. Microphones (the ears) and cameras (the brain) do not do this: they record *exactly* what they hear. Only by using headphones, or, in industry terminology, *cans*, will you be able to listen to exactly what is being recorded and, if the sound is poor, ask for another take.

Sound recording tips:

When recording sound:

- **Always** plan ahead with sound and decide what you are going to record, where, when and how.
- **Always** practise using the different types of microphone and associated kit prior to recording.
- **Always** check your sound-recording kit as soon as you collect it.
- **Always** choose the right microphone for the situation.
- **Always** keep a watchful eye when shooting to ensure that you know what the visuals are and therefore what sound should be recorded.
- **Always** monitor the sound using a good quality or professional set of headphones to ensure that you record clean, undistorted sound at a consistent level from shot to shot.
- **Never** lose concentration. Even though you may only be holding a boom above the scene, if you do it incorrectly the sound will either not record correctly or the microphone will be in shot. Both can ruin the video!
- **Always** think about the edit. Make sure that you record all the different sounds that the editor might need to use in post-production.

Lighting

Harris Watts (1997: 207)makes a useful point about light:

If you had to choose the single most important thing about pictures you would be well advised to choose light. Pictures are records of the way light falls on a subject; cameras are devices for capturing light; transmitters, cables and cassettes distribute particulars about light; television sets reproduce light. So as a programme maker you have to be aware of light because it is the raw material of your craft.

Lighting design

What Harris Watts is suggesting above is that lighting can be used for both technical and creative purposes. Lighting can be used for the following technical reasons:

- Normally there will be ambient light at a location: that is, daylight or normal room lighting. This will allow filming to take place with few problems. However, on some occasions, the use of additional lighting allows filming where it was previously not possible: for example, if there is not enough light for the camera to record or if the light is coming from the wrong direction.

- The 'accidental' light at a particular location will change: for example, the sun moves through the sky and becomes more intense at midday. Given that shots for any production may be taken on different days, the use of additional lighting allows for changes in ambient light and provides continuity between shots.

The creative elements of lighting might include the following:

- It can direct the audience's attention to a particular subject or object within the shot.
- It sets the mood.
- It brings out the colours and contrast within the shot.
- It gives depth to the shots: that is, it provides a sense of three-dimensionality to a two-dimensional screen image.

As with sound, attention to lighting is often overlooked in the production of a student video. While certain types of video project, such as a documentary, can work well without using additional lighting, as your work progresses and your projects become more sophisticated, you should seriously consider using more creative lighting in your work. It significantly improves overall production values and offers the opportunity to create a distinct sense of style.

Types of light

There are two main types of light: *hard* light and *soft* light (see Figure 4.3).

It is possible to produce both types of light with professional *lamps*. Note that they are *never* referred to as lights: light is what is produced by lamps.

There are a wide range of location lamps for film and video work and most video students will have access to some form of additional lighting. Normally, for location work, this will be one of two industry-standard lamps, both of which produce hard light:

- *redheads* produce 800W of light, which is approximately 8–10 times more powerful than a household light bulb;
- *blondes* produce 2KW of light, which is approximately 20 times more powerful.

In addition, there are other types of lower-wattage lamps which may be used, especially in smaller locations or for lighting specific parts of a location, such as *Dedolights*, which are increasingly being used in education.

Hard light comes from a single source such as a lamp or the sun. It creates deep shadows and bright highlights and is useful for expressionistic lighting.

Soft light is diffused: for example, sunlight on a cloudy day. It provides an overall illumination and leads to shadows with diffuse edges. It is useful for realistic lighting. It is possible to make hard lighting soft either by using diffusion gel (*frost*) or a softbox or by bouncing the light off a reflective surface.

Figure 4.3   Hard and soft light

Whichever lamp you chose, it will normally be made up of the same parts (see Figure 4.4):

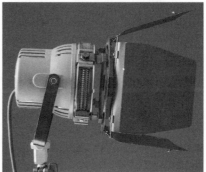

Figure 4.4   A professional redhead lamp

A basic lighting kit to cover most of the situations in which you might find yourself would normally be:

- three lamps;
- a portable lighting controller, or *dimmer*, to control the intensity of the light;
- colour-correction gels to alter the colour temperature of the light;
- *frost* – a sheet of fireproof material which is used for diffusing hard light;
- reflectors to bounce the light.

Using three lamps allows for a wide range of lighting situations. It permits you to use them as the three main elements of lighting, which are as follows:

1. *Key light:* this is the main or predominant light on the subject. It is the light which gives shape and form to the subject. If there is only one lamp being used, this is by definition the key light.
2. *Fill light:* this balances the key light and reduces the sharp shadows created by the key light.
3. *Backlight:* this is any light which comes from behind the subject. When it comes from above it is referred to as toplight.

So, the standard ways of using these elements, each with different effects, are as follows:

1. *Single-point lighting:* also known as *one-point* lighting, this uses one lamp only: the key light. The light from the single lamp is used to focus the audience's attention within a shot. Even if the light source is not shown in the finished programme, the question to be asked when using single-point lighting is 'Where is the light supposed to be coming from?'. This is where, as a starting point, you should place the lamp. The position can be altered along the horizontal plane (frontal, side or three-quarters) or on the vertical plane (see Figure 4.5).
2. *Two-point lighting:* not surprisingly, this uses two lamps:
   - The *key (light)* produces the main hard light which provides shape to the subject and produces the necessary hard shadows. It is normally placed at 45° to the camera and relatively high to light the eyes of the subject.
   - The *fill (light)* provides a softer, more diffuse light, normally half the intensity of the key light. The softness comes from using a sheet of frost or a softbox or, where these are not available, from bouncing the light off another surface. The fill light is normally placed at 45° to the camera on the other side from the key light and lower down (see Figure 4.6).

Figure 4.5 Single-point lighting

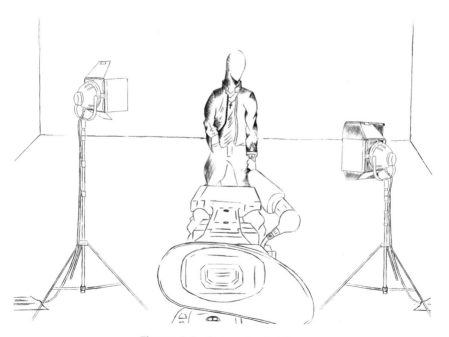

Figure 4.6 Two-point lighting

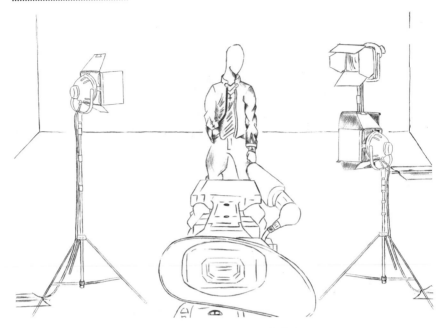

Figure 4.7   Three-point lighting

3.   *Three-point lighting*: this uses all three lamps: the *key*, the *fill* and a *backlight*. This is the usual set-up when interviewing: for example, in documentary production. It uses the same set-up as two-point lighting but with the addition of a backlight to provide a sense of depth to the image. The backlight is normally half the intensity of the key light (see Figure 4.7).

If you decide to use additional lighting in your productions, you need seriously to consider the Health and Safety issues surrounding their use. The two main rules when using additional lighting are:

1.   Use your common sense at all times.
2.   Always take your time to do things correctly.

However, in addition to these general rules, there are certain specific Health and Safety considerations to which you must adhere when using additional lighting:

1.   The lamps become very hot, so always use heat-resistant gloves when handling lamps, especially the barn doors.
2.   The lamps you will be using are fragile, especially the bulbs, which sometimes explode. Always make sure that the lamps have glass or wire-mesh protection screens (known as *scrims*) in them. Do not use them without

scrims. It is good practice also to ensure that lamps are turned away from everyone when first switched on.

3. Position leads away from people, especially where they are walking.
4. Tape all leads to the floor with gaffer tape or use cable runs. Secure lamp stands with heavy objects. If this is not possible, or is unsafe, assign someone the job of holding the stands.
5. Do not turn the lamps on and off in quick succession. It will break the element in the bulb.
6. *Never* move the lamps until they have had time to cool down. If you do, the element may break and the lamp will either stop working immediately or will not work the next time it is turned on.
7. *Never* touch the bulb in a lamp with your bare fingers: oil from your fingers will remain on the bulb and next time the light is used this may cause the bulb to explode.

This is dangerous equipment if used incorrectly. Even though you may see yourselves as 'only' a student production team, you are legally liable for any accidents or injuries caused by your failure to adhere to the above rules.

There are essentially two kinds of lighting situations with which you will need to become familiar: interior and exterior.

Interior lighting

The main advantage with using lamps inside is their controllability. You can decide:

*   **where** the light is coming from;
*   **how much** light to use by using a lighting dimmer rack, by adjusting the lamp's barn doors or by bouncing light off reflectors or walls;
*   **what** light the audience will see;
*   **which** lamps to use – you can use the professional lighting mentioned above or you can use lighting such as table lamps which act as both essential props and sources of light (such lamps are known as *practicals*);
*   **how** to use light creatively to enhance the shot through the use of coloured gels. One example of where you might want to use single-point lighting might be to replicate, for example, moonlight through a window. This could be achieved by using a single lamp, placed at a high vantage point with a blue gel.

Exterior lighting

Exterior lighting is likely to be much more of a problem for student crews owing to its uncontrollability. The main problem when shooting outdoors is the biggest lamp of all, the sun, which has a tendency to disappear behind a cloud just when you are ready to roll. Professional crews use huge lamps called HMIs to work around this and to allow them the full range of shots.

As you are unable to control the sun and unlikely to be able to access HMIs, you can improve your shots with additional lighting, but this will generally only work with CUs and MSs, as lamps will be in shot if used for LSs. Both natural and artificial light can be bounced on to subjects to offer essential additional illumination using reflectors, but again these will be of no use for LSs. It is also worth remembering that if you are using lighting on exterior shots, you may need to access an appropriate power source: normally, on location, a silent power generator.

Lighting tips:

When using lighting:

- **Never** rely on your eyes to check the effects of lighting. Your eyes are *much* more sophisticated than the camera you will be using so *always* use the camera's viewfinder or an external monitor, as it gives a truer representation.
- **Always** remember the main rule of lighting: 'Do whatever works!' If all the above information sounds much too complicated, note at this point that there is no single correct way of using lighting: it is a matter of trial and error. Play around with light until you achieve the shot you require. If this does not work, turn off all your lighting and start again, or use the ambient light.
- **Always** consider the lighting quality for *all* the shots in your video. It is no good having additional lighting in one shot which looks superb if all the other shots around it use existing lighting and look poor in comparison.
- **Always** consider Health and Safety. Lighting is the one thing which could really injure you or others.
- **Always** make sure that you have thought about all this at the pre-production stage!

Roles and responsibilities

One of the best ways of ensuring a successful shoot is to make certain that everyone involved is clear about what they are shooting, when and where they are shooting it and what their roles and responsibilities will be during the shoot.

When students begin their video production careers, they quite often work in what we term a *democratic* manner: that is, everyone in the group does everything together. We understand why this happens: it is comforting, as it means that nobody has to take sole responsibility for specific aspects of the production process. For the first few videos that you produce, you may well carry out all the pre-production in this democratic manner, as it allows everyone to make a contribution to, and have a level of ownership of, the finished video.

However, as you probably already know, professional media practice does not involve such a democratic way of working and does not allow all those involved to turn their hand to whatever job they fancy, when they fancy it. Instead, it relies upon a rigidly *hierarchical* structure: different jobs are carried out by individuals who have expertise in a particular field and there is a rigid adherence to specific production roles with their own distinct responsibilities. In our experience, many student productions which fail do so because students are not given the role that they want and become disengaged, they do not want to carry out all the responsibilities of their role, they do not have the skills needed to carry out their role or they are not really clear about what the role actually entails.

For the purpose of most student productions, where you are likely to be working in small groups, the main production roles are usually:

- director
- camera operator
- sound recordist
- PA.

You can find detailed descriptions of each of these roles in many of the resources in the bibliography and, for the specific briefs in later chapters, on the book's website. One of the best resources that we have found is the website of Skillset, the UK's industry training body. The discussions below are based on their descriptions of the different roles.

Director

In 'the industry', the director is the person with the responsibility of managing the making of the production. The duties are many and varied, depending upon the type of video being made, but for student productions, the director's main responsibilities are:

- overseeing the project by delegating and assigning tasks to other members of the production team;
- deciding upon the aesthetic and artistic direction (the 'look') of each shot and, therefore, of the production as a whole;

- directing actors;
- ensuring that each shot on the script and storyboard is filmed as required.

When on a shoot, the director is the person ultimately responsible for the success of the shoot. *The director must be obeyed without question by everyone in the crew.*

The skills needed to be a good director are:

- the ability to understand all aspects of the production process;
- the ability to lead and inspire others to realize the project's purpose and vision;
- the ability to communicate effectively with all members of the crew and the 'talent' (the people in the video);
- the ability to solve problems;
- the ability to work under pressure, sometimes intense pressure;
- the ability to support the project through all stages to the very end.

Many student groups fail to work well together because some members of the crew find it difficult being told what to do by another student (especially if they feel that *they* should have been the director!). They feel that the production should be a democratic process and that, when filming under a director, this democracy is being challenged. Democracy is appropriate at the pre-production stage; it is most definitely not so at the production stage! If you accept this simple rule now, you will undoubtedly save many hours of argument, frustration and dispute within your group.

Camera operator

As the name suggests, the camera operator is the person responsible for setting up and operating the camera. The main responsibilities are:

- deciding upon and booking the appropriate camera equipment;
- checking that the camera equipment works before setting out on a shoot;
- ensuring the that correct tape stock or recording medium is packed;
- setting up the camera safely and ensuring that it is working properly at each location;
- composing each shot *to the requirements of the director;*
- informing the director if there are any problems, either with the equipment or the composition of individual shots;
- ensuring that all the equipment is packed properly and returned clean and in working order.

A good camera operator needs to:

- have a good understanding of how cameras work and the functions of each of the camera controls;
- be visually orientated;
- have the ability to anticipate what the director might want;
- be immensely patient (there is a *lot* of waiting around) coupled with the ability to be focused at a moment's notice.

Note that in the media industries, this person is still referred to as a camera-*man* regardless of the gender of the person fulfilling the role (a very good example of patriarchal ideology in practice!)

Sound recordist

The sound recordist is the person responsible for recording the sound. The main responsibilities are:

- deciding upon and booking the appropriate audio equipment;
- checking that the sound equipment works before setting out on a shoot;
- setting up the sound equipment safely and ensuring that it is working properly at each location;
- positioning any microphones effectively;
- ensuring that clean sound is being recorded by monitoring the sound through headphones while shooting is in process;
- ensuring that all the equipment is packed properly and returned clean and in working order.

The skills needed to be a good sound recordist are:

- a good understanding of how all the sound equipment works and how to use it effectively;
- the ability to *really* listen and not be distracted by watching the action on set;
- the ability to respond quickly and professionally to requests;
- immense patience (there is a *lot* of waiting around) coupled with the ability to be focused at a moment's notice.

Production assistant

The production assistant (PA) is responsible for supporting the director. The main responsibilities are:

- keeping a log of each shot as it is being taken: the shot number, the time-code at the start of the shot, the subject of the shot, the take number and any comments about the shot (doing this job now will save hours at the post-production stage) (See Figure 4.8);
- ensuring continuity (flow of shots/action, props, costumes, settings, characters, etc.);
- acting as the director's assistant and carrying out whatever tasks the director requires;
- labelling and carefully storing all the recorded media in preparation for the editor.

Log Sheet

Project					Page of Pages	
DATE	TAKE	SHOT	TAKE	TIMECODE	COMMENT

Figure 4.8   A sample log sheet (1)

A good PA needs to:

- have good time-management;
- be organized and systematic;
- have excellent communication skills and the ability to deal professionally with anyone and everyone both inside and outside the production;
- have immense patience (there is a *lot* of waiting around) coupled with the ability to be able to be focused at a moment's notice.

Remember that when you take on one of these roles, you also take on the responsibilities (and constraints) that the role dictates. We would also add that it is vital that you understand the functions and overall responsibilities of each role, as you may take each of these roles at different stages of your course and, in a small production, may take on more than one role.

Organizing the shoot and set etiquette

Now that you know what each person within the team does on an individual level, you need to be aware of how you will work *as a team*. There are accepted practices for organizing a shoot:

1. *Setting up for a shoot:* the director will oversee the set-up, giving instructions to the crew. The director will also review the shooting scripts, such as the storyboard and shot list, and start work with the actors or talent. Circumstances such as a change in weather or lighting conditions may mean that the director has to amend the scripts. Those changes would be annotated on the shooting documentation and clearly communicated to the crew.

   The PA will assist the director and ensure that the crew have all the necessary paperwork, such as the log sheets, storyboard and shot list. The PA will hold the main working paperwork for the director.

   The camera operator should set up the camera correctly, including setting the white balance. To white-balance a camera:
   - Hold up a professional white-balance card in front of the camera but far enough away to reflect the ambient light. If there is no white-balance card, it may be necessary to improvise with a sheet of white, preferably bleached, A4 paper.
   - Zoom into the card so that the card fills the viewfinder and focus in on the card.
   - Press the white-balance button on the camera.
   - Zoom back out.

   The white balance has now been set.

If using a new tape, the camera operator should also manually set the timecode and record 30 seconds of bars (with accompanying tone) by either switching the 'Cam/Bars' switch to 'Bars' or, as on many cameras, setting it to 'Bars' in the menu to indicate the beginning of a new tape. On newer camcorders and DV models, the timecode is often done automatically when a new tape is inserted, but the bars will still need to be done manually.

The sound recordist, if not using a portable sound mixer, will ensure that the microphone is plugged into the correct input on the camera and that sound is being picked up by monitoring the sound on both the level meters and through headphones. If a sound mixer is being used, the sound recordist should ensure that the camcorder and the mixer are 'lined up' by using the line-up tone created by the mixer to set the camcorder level to –20dB and should also generate a tone to record to tape along with the bars.

Everyone on set will make sure that his/her mobile phone has been turned off.

2. *Going for a take:* when the shot has been set up by the director, the actors (or 'talent') have been rehearsed and all the other members of the crew are happy, the director will inform everyone that they are 'going for a take': that is, that they are going to start shooting. When hearing this, everyone on set should immediately:
   - be totally silent;
   - ensure that they are ready to carry out their duties as detailed above.
   In addition:
   - The sound recordist will finally position the microphone(s) and will indicate that the sound is either satisfactory or that there is a problem.
   - The PA will ask each camera person for a timecode and note this on a separate log sheet for each camera.
   - The director will say, in a voice loud enough for everyone on set to hear, 'Quiet on set' and, when all is quiet, 'Camera!'
   - The camera person will press the 'Record' or, on professional cameras, 'VTR' button and, when the camera is running at full speed (normally after about three seconds), shout 'Speed!'
   - The director will hear the shout of 'Speed!' and will then shout 'Action!'
   - The 'talent' will begin doing what they have rehearsed.
   - As the director is concerned with what the shot will look like, he/she will always look at the monitors, *never* at the action on set.
   - When the action has finished, the director will shout 'Cut!'

- The camera person will carry on recording for about five seconds. This gives the editor more scope for manoeuvre at the post-production stage.
- The director will let everyone know whether the shot has gone well or whether it needs to be done again.

3. *It's a wrap:* when all the shooting at a particular location has been completed, the director will call out 'It's a wrap!' and everything will then be packed away and moved to the next location.

   Before doing this, however, the sound recordist should record any specific sound effects not already obtained and should *always* record *wild-track*: that is, two to three minutes of ambient sound from the location which can later be looped and used in the edit to fill in sound gaps or cover discrepancies at the point of an edit.

Health and Safety

Location and studio filming has many potential hazards. However, if you carried out a proper recce at the pre-production stage, you will have completed a risk assessment which allows you to know what potential hazards there might be at the location and to have done something about overcoming them. The most basic rule of Health and Safety for a student crew is that *each* member of the crew is ultimately responsible for identifying and guarding against such hazards and ensuring the wellbeing of themselves and others at all times.

There are certain Health and Safety rules that you should develop the habit of following on *all* shoots. The most obvious of these are:

- Make sure that all boxes and leads are tidy and out of the way of the shoot and of other people who may be using the area so that they do not cause injury. You are the people who will be sued if anyone is injured.
- Make sure that all cables are secured to the floor with either professional gaffer tape (*not* any other form of tape such as duck tape) or with cable ramps.
- Make sure that anything which is unstable, such as a lamp, is securely fastened down or, if that is not possible, held by one member of the crew at all times.
- Pay special attention to electrics. Locations are often wet so if, when carrying out a recce, you think that this might be the case, make arrangements to deal with the problem. For example, take a raincover to protect the cameras and monitors and do not put electrical equipment near wet areas.

- Always aim to predict other potential hazards and deal with them before they become a problem. We once had a student injured when he was shooting someone walking towards camera and he had to walk backwards. Nobody within the group foresaw that he would fall down a kerb and break his leg and be off university for nearly six months, but he did and he was!

After the shoot

Successful professional location shooting is not just about successful preproduction and successful filming and then forgetting about the location. When you wrap, make sure that you do the following as soon as possible, even if you really don't feel like it:

- Pack the kit away carefully and properly.
- Make sure that the PA has *all* the tapes and associated log sheets, and that they are all clearly labelled, and also all the working master copies – the ones which include all the handwritten amendments and comments – of the production documentation.
- Ensure that everything is left as you found it: tidy up and put anything you have moved back in its original place. If there is any damage make sure that you let the owner of the location know and arrange for it to be made good.
- Write a letter of thanks to the person responsible for each location. From the point of view of pure self-interest, this means that if you need to go back and film there again for any reason (and there are many reasons why you might), you will hopefully receive a positive response. It should also mean that future productions will be able to film there.
- Put everything related to the production safely in a box file and store it prior to editing. That way, you know that everything is in one place and you know where to find it!

The Practice of Video Production: Post-Production **5**

Once you have completed the production stage, you will move on to the editing, or post-production, stage.

Editing is, very simply, the process of selecting certain shots from all the footage taken and using an edit suite to put them together, with reference to your storyboard, into a coherent structure in order to produce a completed video. More accurately, this should be called post-production, as it includes everything which is done after production: editing but also compositing, grading and sound design.

Up until the 1990s, the only type of editing equipment which was readily available, even within the media industries, was analogue equipment where the video signal was electronically transferred from one tape to another in a linear fashion: that is, one shot, followed by the next and then the next, and so on. This meant that there were two stages in the editing process: the *off-line* edit and the *on-line* edit. The reason for these two stages was primarily economic and related to the limitations of the equipment. The off-line edit was where the editor would put together a very rough version of the video – namely a version with few, if any, transitions or effects, no music and no graphics – in order to work out the correct order and timing of the individual shots and their relationship with the other shots in the production. This would be carried out on a relatively basic (and, therefore, relatively cheap) edit suite in order that the editor could 'play around' with the order and timing of the shots without making a lot of mistakes on expensive equipment and thus driving up costs. Once this rough cut was accepted, the editor would move on to the most sophisticated and most expensive edit suite available and complete the production by adding effects, soundtrack and titles.

The advent in the 1990s of digital, non-linear editing facilities which were relatively cheap and simple to use meant that, increasingly, editors within the film and video industries (and, when the price of such equipment started dropping dramatically, educational establishments and freelancers) could work without the need for an on-line and off-line edit, as any mistakes made could be rectified instantly. If you are using digital equipment, it is likely that you will not need to do an off-line edit.

There are a number of digital edit systems currently available and widely used within education: Avid Express DV, Final Cut Pro, Adobe Premiere, iMovie and Windows Moviemaker. Although there are differences, both in how they look and what they can do, on a technical level they all work in a similar way. All require you to follow the same basic process: transferring shot material to the computer, editing it and then exporting it to another medium such as DVD.

Ken Dancyger (1997a: xiv) argues that there are three different levels to editing:

- The 'technical' level refers to the ability to use the appropriate technology to join two clips together to 'create a sequence that has a particular meaning'. It primarily refers to learning about how the edit suite functions.
- The level of 'craft' refers to the ability to select clips which lead to what are termed 'second order' meanings: that is, the joining of two shots 'to yield a meaning that isn't apparent from one or the other shot'.
- The level of 'art' refers to the ability of the editor to create certain emotions within the audience, when 'the combination of two or more shots takes meaning to the next level – excitement, insight, shock, or the epiphany of discovery'.

It is relatively easy to teach and learn the skills needed to work at the technical level, even for those new to editing. During your video-production course you will almost certainly learn these skills in relation to the specific equipment that you are using. The only way to do this is to edit as much as possible, as often as possible and on as many projects as possible.

Learning which shots can be combined into *watchable* material with the kinds of meaning you want to create is the craft and art of the editor. In composing your shots for production, you thought carefully about the *mise-en-scène* of each shot, but in editing you have the same power to create the desired meanings in the minds of your potential audience. These skills are more difficult to teach. This is why contextual research plays such a vital part in your learning: by reading appropriate books, watching as many media products as possible and then applying what you have seen to your own productions, you start to take responsibility for how you learn. In doing so, you will also realize that effective post-production provides you with the opportunity to work on the things which polish and 'finish off' the video, taking it to another level. As this is a process of working, reflecting, carrying out more work, and so on, it requires you to think in depth about our Essential Element 1 – creativity. The start of the process, though, is a technical one: logging.

Logging your rushes and deciding upon shots

Logging simply refers to the process of looking at your footage and making a note of each shot and its suitability for the finished production. This is done on a log sheet (see Figure 5.1).

Log Sheet						
Title: *Alas Poor Yorick!*		**Reel No:** 2		**Sheet:** 1 of 13		
Shot	**Take In**	**Timecode Out**	**Description**	**Comments**	**In**	**Out**
–	–	00.00.00 00.30.06	Bars			
6	1	00.30.07 00.48.14	LS church	NG: out of focus	✓	
6	2	00.48.15 00.57.04	LS church	NG: person walking	✓	
6	3	0.57.05 01.26.00	LS church	Excellent	✓	
3	1	01.26.01 02.34.09	CU bell tower			

Figure 5.1   A sample log sheet (2)

The process of logging your rushes is time-consuming, but, if completed properly, will save you hours at the editing stage. It will also have been made easier if, as suggested earlier, the group's PA has carried out his/her responsibilities correctly and logged each shot as it was taken during shooting. This means that, potentially, the first three columns of the log sheet have already been completed before you sit down to edit and all you need to do now is decide upon the suitability of your shots for the final production. This is often known as a paper edit.

Capturing and digitizing

What you need to do now is transfer only the shots that you selected at the logging stage from your recording media to your editing package. This process is called *capturing* or *digitizing*. The process is similar for all editing software packages: the clips are played and, using a mouse and referring to the time-codes on your log sheet, the beginning (or, in editing terminology, the *in-point*) and end (the *out-point*) of each clip that you wish to capture is selected and the clip is then digitally transferred, via the software, to the computer's hard drive for storage, viewing and editing. Label each clip as you digitize it. When digitizing you should remember the following:

- Digitize only the material that you need; use your storyboard as your guide but do not be afraid to deviate from the storyboard if it improves the video.
- Make sure that you save your clips to your assigned folder and that they are always saved to the same folder.
- Ensure that your clips are slightly longer than you need by setting an earlier in-point and later out-point: it allows for much more flexibility in the editing process.
- Clearly and logically label each clip. You can use your storyboard as a guide. Do not just let them default to 'Untitled 1', 'Untitled 2', 'Untitled 3', etc. If you do, it means that you have to open up each clip to view it before placing it on the timeline, which is unnecessarily time-consuming.
- Ensure that you save your project periodically, in case the software crashes.
- Do not forget that your video will be made up of other elements and so this may include sound and music clips, graphics and other imported materials.
- Save the entire project again before shutting down the computer.
- Keep your source media safe. You may, at any point in the editing process, need it again.

The digital edit

There are three distinct stages to the edit:

1. *The assembly:* individual clips are quickly and roughly put together by dragging clips from the clip store or bin on to the timeline in the same order as they appear on the storyboard to determine the basic structure of the video.
2. *The rough cut:* the basic structure from the assembly is tightened up by trimming each clip on the timeline and the continuity, pace, effects, and dialogue are more fully developed
3. *The final cut:* this is where, as the name suggests, all the elements of the video are crafted into the final video. Colour-correction, sound design and credits are completed.

Although this is accepted professional practice, many students do not go through this process; they go almost immediately to the final-cut stage. This will work but only in a limited way. There are three main reasons that you should work through the three stages:

1. They are the accepted industry process.
2. The reason why these three stages are the accepted industry process is because it becomes a developmental process: that is, it allows for work, reflection, work, reflection, work, reflection and, as a result, well-informed decisions to be made. Remember, that reflection is the fifth of our essential elements!
3. In an educational context, it forces you to learn the value of the balance between work and reflection. For smaller projects, you may get away without doing this but for larger projects this is inconceivable.

The assembly

Once you have your clips digitized, you need to place them on to your timeline in the correct order. Technically, there are two main ways of doing this:

1. Take each clip, in order, and place it in the viewer window where it can be trimmed to the exact length that you require prior to placing it on the timeline.
2. Cllick and drag clips on to the timeline and trim them there: trimming is done simply by placing the cursor over the beginning or end of each clip and then clicking and dragging the clip.

At the assembly stage, you will simply put the clips on the timeline in the order that, from the storyboard, you think that they should be in and will use only straight cuts, as the aim is to make sense of your overall story or sequence. This initial edit will be much longer than your agreed running time but there is no need to worry about this at this stage.

One vital tip is that you should make sure that you save your work regularly while editing, after carrying out any major amendments and at the end of each editing session. At the end of each session, it is also good professional practice to produce an edit decision list (EDL). An EDL is an electronic list of the in-points and out-points of all of the clips in your bin and on the timeline and any effects that have been applied to them. You should develop the habit of producing an EDL because it is very useful if, for whatever reason, you lose your project, or it corrupts or fails, as it allows you quickly to reimport all the necessary information needed to rebuild – or, in industry terminology, *autoconform* – the project.

Once all the clips have been placed on to the timeline in order and they have been roughly trimmed to size, it is time to arrange your first critical viewing of the video to an audience which, at this point, is likely to consist of your crew and tutors. The purpose of this screening is twofold: first, to see if you have a video worth taking through to the next stage of editing (and it may be, even at this late stage, that you don't!) and, secondly, to gain some input into what you need to do to develop it further. You will need to look at your audience while they watch the video, in order to gauge their reactions to your work, and you should write down all the comments made. For most video projects you need to ask and answer the following questions:

- Does it work to the brief? Is it doing what the brief requires and, if not, why not? For example, is it too long or generically incorrect?
- Is it coherent and understandable?
- Which parts are boring, entertaining or exciting?
- Is there any material which should not be there? Is there any material which needs moving? Is there any material which should be there but is not, and, if so, where can you get it from?
- Are there any technical or aesthetic issues: for example, poor composition, soft shots, poor sound?
- What do you need to do now to progress to the next stage?

The rough cut

We mentioned above that turning material into *watchable* material is the craft and art of the editor. So, this is the opportunity to make amendments based on the feedback you received at the viewing and to work on the continuity of action within scenes and the narrative as a whole. For Ken Dancyger (1997a: 296), narrative clarity (and therefore *watchability*) is accomplished when:

> a film doesn't confuse viewers. It requires matching action from shot to shot and maintaining a clear sense of direction between shots. It means providing a visual explanation if a new idea or a cutaway is introduced. To provide narrative clarity, visual clues are necessary, and here, the editor's skill is the critical factor.

What you are trying to achieve in your rough cut is continuity of action and sound by editing both within sequences and scenes and overall to smooth out the rough edges of the assembly. At this stage, you should:

- *Trim shots and sequences.* Sequences are often too long and so need to be reduced by trimming individual clips or by removing unnecessary material. There is an editing adage worth remembering: enter late and leave early. Shots which start too early have the audience waiting for the scene to start or will slow the pace down. Conversely, shots which end too late draw out the shot longer than is necessary. The same is true of sequences, so any material which does not contribute anything to the sequence should be removed. Be careful, though, not to be too brutal: some shots, sequences or videos need 'space'.

- *Work within sequences by inserting transition effects, insert shots and cutaways to aid this continuity*: A basic rule is that if you can see or hear the edit, it is not working. With this in mind, our recommendation is that the techniques of continuity editing usually rely on straight cuts and dissolves.
- *Alter the order of sequences and shots if necessary*. You should always be clear about the reason for the inclusion and placing of a shot. Move shots and sequences around to see if this improves the unfolding of the story or the continuity of the action. Consider the introduction of new clips, if necessary.

All three of the above contribute to the real craft and art of the editor: the ability to create appropriate rhythm, pace and emotion. Each type of video has a different rhythm and pace: title sequences are different to documentaries, which are different to dramas. Within these, too, there will be differences. Knowing the appropriate rhythm and pace for what you are producing, and then achieving it, is vital. This can be done by always returning to the *purpose* of a shot, sequence or scene in order to assess whether or not the appropriate pace is being achieved. For example, if the scene involves a married couple's leisurely walk through the woods, an appropriately slow pace can be achieved by using shots which last for a couple of seconds. In a later scene involving an argument between the couple in, for example, a restaurant, you might start the sequence and the argument with relatively lengthy shots and then quicken the number of shots, and consequently the pace, as the argument develops. Inserting CUs of the couple's faces and the faces of other diners will reveal the emotional states of the characters and heighten the emotional tension for the viewer. Knowing what emotions you wish to arouse in the viewer is another important task for the editor.

You are constantly engaged in a process of technical and aesthetic quality control: if shots are poor, lose them. If there are still holes in your video, you need to think about how to fill them: either by reshooting material, shooting new material or obtaining material from another source, such as an archive.

Once you have done as much as you feel that you can, it is time to have another, wider screening of your video in what, in education, is referred to as a *crit* (short for critique). Whereas the reason for the assembly screening was to see whether you had enough for a video, the reason for a crit at this point is critically to assess the technical and creative quality of the video. You can use the same questions that you used at the assembly stage to guide discussion, but now they move up a level: the answers now revolve around the craft and art of the piece and its overall quality and polish, *not* its technical merits as previously. At the end of the screening there will be more for you to reflect upon and work upon in the final stage.

The final (or fine) cut

Hopefully, you will by now have arrived at a coherent piece which fulfils the purpose of the brief. It is time to produce the final, polished video by carrying out the following:

- *Grading* is the process of colour-correcting each shot in a video both to ensure colour continuity between shots and to produce a noticeable aesthetic look to the video. In the industry, it is often the last job to be completed before the visuals are 'locked' and is normally done by specialist graders, not by the editor. Whichever edit package you are using, there will be a means of colour-correcting your shots. As this can be quite a complex procedure and it comes at the end of what may be a sustained period of editing, you may not feel like grading your video, but it really is worth it. Poor colour continuity is one of the many things which marks a student video out from a professional video.
- Once you are completely happy with the visuals, you can lock them and start work on *titles, text, graphics and credits*. Most non-linear edit packages will include a fairly comprehensive graphics or text package which allows you to create professional titles and credits. They offer a range of fonts, sizes, colours and motion effects which are usually created in a separate window, tested and then placed on to a separate graphics channel on the timeline. As with video clips, these titles can be trimmed to suit, and effects, such as dissolves, can be added.
- As with the visual elements of video, *sound design* requires planning and organizing, so a design for sound needs to be planned for in pre-production. Using the storyboard and scripts, it is possible to produce a sound script which clearly shows location sound and any further sound requirements which could be produced in post-production, such as Foley sound effects and music.

    As your video production skills develop, you will inevitably gain a much more sophisticated understanding of the important role that sound plays within video. To understand this importance, watch your favourite film with the sound turned off, play it with both visuals and sound on and then just listen to the sound. In doing this, you will start to hear the different layers of sound which have been used to support and enhance the visuals: that is sound design.

It is at the final-cut stage that the audio mix is completed. Now that you are satisfied with the production in terms of its visuals, you can turn your attention to the balance between the dialogue, sound effects and music. The dialogue should have been edited at the assembly and rough-cut stages, so now those sounds recorded on location, such as wildtrack and sound effects, can be added. Many of these sound effects can be downloaded for a small fee or can be created in a studio through what is known as the *Foley process*. This is where essential sound which was not successfully picked up on location during shooting can be replicated in post-production.

Music is the very last sound to be edited. Again, this will have been chosen in pre-production but, in certain circumstances, may be acquired right up to the point of editing the final cut. Adding audio transitions will allow you to fade sound in and out and cross-fade between different audio tracks. Once all the sound is present, it needs to be carefully balanced to ensure that the layering of sound is correct, that all of the audio tracks balance with each other and that they all work with the visuals. This is often known as *sweetening*.

By paying careful attention to the levels of all the different sounds, a coherent sound design is produced where all is in balance and sound edits or gaps cannot be heard.

Once you have completed your final cut, it is a good idea to save your entire project, not just the final edited video, on to an external hard drive. This will enable you to re-edit it at a later date should you wish to, as, in saving the project, you are saving all the clips and effects as well as the video itself.

Mastering

Once you have completed the three stages of editing – producing an assembly, rough cut and final cut – you will need to export your video from the edit suite on to the medium that you will use to distribute your video. Depending upon what medium you are going to use, it will need to be either a straight digital cut on to tape or will need to undergo a process of compression for DVD or screening on the internet.

Each non-linear editing system will allow your video to be easily and simply output, or *mastered*, on to tape. This tape is known in the industry as the *master tape*. It is the tape containing the highest-quality recording possible which will be used to broadcast from or copy from. Make sure that you have colour bars and a countdown clock at the beginning of your video.

On the video or DVD, and on its case, you should clearly record the following information:

- the title of the production;
- the duration of the production;
- the main crew credits;
- the fact that it is a master and the date of mastering;
- the recording format, for example *MiniDV, DV CAM, Betacam SP, HDV,* and its aspect ratio;
- a contact name and number.

Always make sure that *every member of the group* receives a copy of the final cut on DV tape, even if you will only ever screen it from another format such as DVD, as it will allow you quickly and easily to import your production back on to your edit suite. If every member has their own copy, it could possibly save a great deal of time and effort at a later date when the tape needs to be retrieved.

In addition, you should always produce DVD copies of your videos as they are more easily screened than professional tapes and can be sent out to, for example, film festivals. To burn your video on to CD or DVD involves a process of *compressing* your video so that the large file sizes inherent in video production can be squeezed on to DVDs with a limited storage capacity and *authoring* so that the DVD has a menu. Again, the course you are on should teach you how to carry out both of these processes with the technology at your disposal.

You should develop the habit of making your work look as professional as possible by designing a label for your disc, purchasing a plastic case and designing an insert for the DVD. Depending upon your skills, this can be done using a basic word-processing package or, given that you should be trying to improve your professionalism across the board, a more specialized general DTP package or a specific application designed for the purpose. Image-manipulation software will allow you to frame-grab images from the video and incorporate them on to the DVD label and case cover. Make sure that the name of the production and your name and contact details are clearly visible on both the disc and the cover. Given the amount of time and effort that you will have spent on your video, it is a shame to neglect this aspect and, as it is the first thing anyone will see of your video, you neglect it at your peril.

Conclusion

The first section of this book has provided you with a large quantity of potentially new information to absorb. Before you move on to the next section, therefore, you need to ask yourself two key questions:

- *Do I understand all the key concepts?* Could I describe what each of the terms means without referring back to the book? If the answer is no, go back and read Chapter 1 again.
- *Do I understand the process of video production fully?* Could I describe what each of the three main stages of the production process requires of me without referring back to the book? If the answer is no, go back and read the relevant chapter(s) again.

For those of you whose interest has been whetted by the previous chapters, there is a bonus chapter on the book's website which uses the discussions around theory and the process of production to analyse a media product: the American sitcom *Friends*.

You should also develop the habit of rereading Chapters 1–6 whenever you undertake a new brief. The reason we suggest this is that each time you do this your increased experience of video production will give you new insight into what you are reading.

Our ten top tips for video production

1. Exchange contact details for everyone in the group – e-mail addresses and mobile phone numbers as a minimum – at the very start of a production. This will save you no end of frustration later on.
2. Practise the art of effective communication: that is, develop the habit of listening to the people in your group as well as talking to them.
3. Always seek to defuse tension within the group rather than causing it or encouraging it. Nobody benefits from the group falling apart, even if one person wins an argument.
4. Make sure that you are organized and reliable. If group work is to succeed, group members need to be able to depend on each other at all times. Manage your project properly, rather than letting it drift along.
5. Spend time on your work. Don't rush into an idea: explore, discuss and spend time properly researching and developing it. Don't leave your work until the last minute: not only is it unsatisfactory but the end result is likely to be poor. Be as imaginative as possible. Never be happy with the easiest or most basic idea. Always aim high. If you aim for the stars, you might reach the top of a tree but if you only aim for the top of a tree …
6. Don't always work in the same group. Most people tend to work with friends who share similar opinions, as there is comfort and security in doing so. However, this means that you are never exposed to other opinions. Look around your class, see who is producing work that you rate

highly and find out whether they would like to work with you. They may feel stifled by the people they are already working with.

7. Spend time learning how to use the equipment properly *prior* to shooting. Take kit home, download manuals and advice from bulletin boards on the internet for that piece of kit and play around with it. Only then will you use it to its full potential and be able to do so when under pressure.

8. Make sure that you have *all* the equipment you need before setting off and check that it all works. There is nothing more frustrating than arriving at a location and finding that you haven't brought a tape or a spare battery for the camera or that one of your key pieces of kit doesn't work!

9. Always overestimate how long something will take. If you think it will take one week, allow for two. You may still find that you are pushed for time.

10. Enjoy yourself. Video-making is fun and, even if you are under no end of pressure, remember that you could be doing something really horrible and boring instead.

11. OK ... we know we said ten, but the last one is really important too. Make sure that you show your work at screenings or festivals outside of your college or university. Not only will it introduce you to many more local film-makers but it will also give you the opportunity to see other people's work (and to realize how good yours is in the process!)

SECTION

II

···

The Briefs

In this second section of the book we shall use the insights you have gained about both theory and practice to work through a series of typical student projects. Each chapter will take you, step by step, through the stages of pre-production, production and post-production while simultaneously signposting and highlighting appropriate theoretical considerations specific to that brief. These briefs, although separate, become progressively more sophisticated but build upon each other in order to enable you gradually to develop your theoretical and practical skills and more fully to understand the way in which theory informs practice.

The Television Title Sequence

6

Introduction

A title sequence is the short piece of video at or near the beginning of most television programmes. It generally remains the same for each episode in a series and is normally separate from the content of the programme, although, as we shall see in a moment, it often provides important information to help the viewers make sense of the programme they are about to watch. Despite the fact that title sequences are so commonly used and that there are so many different types of title sequence, there is little academic writing about them. This chapter will, therefore, aim to encourage you to think about some of the theoretical issues around title sequences, as well as providing you with information about the types of creative and technical issues involved in their production.

The production of a title sequence has the capacity to be one of the easiest of briefs in that it can simply involve watching a wide range of television programmes, taking notes on how the title sequences within different genres are constructed and then copying what you have seen. However, student title sequences also offer you more opportunity than many other types of video to be creative in your video-making. This may be your first video and you may be more concerned about getting the process right and using the technology correctly, but it is the creative title sequence that we wish to encourage you to produce as a result of working through this chapter.

Before you begin the process of pre-production, though, we want to provide a more sophisticated definition of what we mean when we talk about title sequences: *a title sequence is a short production of between 15 and 45 seconds (but more normally about 30 seconds) which contains the creative use of a combination of visuals, sound and graphics and which is produced by a media organization to introduce a programme to the audience and to differentiate it from other, similar programmes.*

You will remember that in Chapter 1 we stressed the need to consider theory at all stages of the production process, especially at the initial stage of pre-production. Before you reach the ideas stage, therefore, you must carry out your contextual research so that your ideas are informed by theoretical considerations or, at the least, that you are aware of how those theoretical considerations relate to your ideas.

To encourage you to explore this definition and examine what each part of the definition means, we suggest that you tackle the following activity.

Tasks to do

1. On a blank piece of paper, write down as many television genres as you can. You should have a *minimum* of ten.
2. Look at the weekly television schedules and, from *six* of the genres you isolated, choose programmes scheduled at different times of the day and on different channels, preferably both terrestrial and cable/satellite. Watch the title sequence for each programme and record the following information: the name and genre of programme, the channel it was screened on, how long the title sequence lasted, what the content and style of the sequence was (animated, real actors, etc.), where any action took place, the types of character in the programme, how the music/sound and graphics were used and, finally, who produced it. Prepare a single-paragraph description of each of the title sequences. What are the similarities and differences?
3. As you did with the title sequence for *Friends* in Chapter 1, carry out a shot-by-shot semiotic analysis of *one* of the title sequences (but not *Friends!*)

From this activity, you should have noticed the different ways in which existing title sequences are constructed from three main building blocks: the visual elements, such as filmed footage or animation, the sound and the graphics. You may also have noticed that many of your title sequences share certain characteristics. Writing in 1983, Roy Twitchen and Julian Birkett (1983: iii–iv) argued that all television title sequences have eight 'functions' which are related to these shared characteristics:

1. They identify the programme and mark it off from others, therefore helping to break up television into manageable, self-contained chunks.
2. They can act as a 'taster' of the kind of programme that is to follow, persuading us to keep watching.
3. They can rehearse, for the regular viewer, the pleasures of the programme to come. Note they are made to be seen many times.
4. They can indicate the kind of story it is, sometimes by reference to other programmes.

5.   They allow an opportunity for important credits to be shown: titles, stars' names, writer etc. These may also be an enticement to keep watching.
6.   They can locate the events of the programme in time and space.
7.   They allow the signature tune to be played, which both heralds the programme and, as the name implies, further establishes its identity.
8.   Sound and image combined announce, simply, 'the show's about to begin'.

Using the I CARLING key concepts will enable you to go further.

Institution

From the activity above, you may have noticed that different types of media institution tend to produce different types of title sequence. MTV, for example, a cable/satellite commercial broadcaster, will produce a specific type of title sequence: fast-paced and with a heavy reliance on graphics and music/sound, it often has no obvious relationship to the subsequent programme, other than the fact that it is, in its broadest sense, music-based and youth-orientated. This is closely related to the type of image that the institution wants to project to its audience: in MTV's case, a contemporary, rebellious, youthful, non-mainstream image. As Michael Barry, Senior Vice-President, Music for MTV, noted when introducing MTV's new interactive services in 2006: 'It's really important that we don't become so mainstream that we are irrelevant to our target demographic.'

When thinking about your own title sequence, you need to have a clear idea of the type of institution which would be producing the programme and of the channel it would be seen on. You will need this information for your outline.

Contexts of production

Title sequences, like any other media product, are not created in a vacuum. They will always reflect the things which are happening around them. If you look at title sequences from the 1970s, they are the product of a world with different politics, social rules and conventions. This is what we mean by contexts of production. For example, if we look at title sequences for police dramas from the 1970s, such as those for *The Sweeney* or *Starsky and Hutch*, we can see that there is a certain type of police officer being represented: one who is rough, tough and does not abide by the rules. While this may have been representative of the behaviour of some members of the police in the 1970s, political initiatives both within and outside the police force have made it much less likely that such behaviour would be tolerated in today's police force. Title sequences have reflected this change in the socio-political context.

One of the key contexts of production for title sequences is the technological context. The relatively recent developments in media technology and software capability have meant that title sequences on television are immeasurably more sophisticated than they were even ten years ago, especially in relation to the quality and sophistication of the graphics. In addition, as a direct result of the number of digital channels and the range of programming, the demand for the production of title sequences has increased. The sheer diversity of programming across all these channels and the increasing range of genres and subgenres has lead to a massive growth in output. Finally, the growth of distribution channels such as the internet, which are currently largely outside the legal and regulatory constraints of mainstream television, has also contributed to the dramatic increase in the number of title sequences. Equally importantly, the title sequences now being produced are much less generic and much more imaginative.

Audience

Given that most of the television programmes we see are introduced by a title sequence, it is almost impossible to make specific points about title sequences and audience. However, it is possible to make some very general points. The first relates to the institutional origin of title sequences. Some channels, such as MTV, have a relatively homogeneous audience: that is, the audience members tend to be of a similar age and have similar interests. As a result, the producers of programmes for that channel can be reasonably certain that the type of title sequence they are producing will appeal to that audience. Other channels, such as BBC1, have a much more heterogeneous audience: that is, an audience of very different ages and different interests. So, even though we mentioned above that each institution tends to produce a specific type of title sequence, the producers of each programme have to give serious consideration to the type of programme that they are producing and the demographics of the audience for whom they are producing the programme when deciding what the title sequence should look like. It seems obvious to state that it would be a huge mistake to produce an MTV-type title sequence for a more sedate programme such as the British sitcom *Keeping up Appearances* but we have in the past had students wanting to do this!

A number of Twitchen and Birkett's functions for title sequences that we introduced at the beginning of the chapter should alert us to the importance of the title sequence in attracting and retaining a specific audience: it alerts viewers to the fact that a programme which they may or may not like is about to start; it may persuade viewers to keep watching, in which case the familiarity of the sound and visuals will prepare them for the pleasure and enjoyment of the programme or, if they don't like the programme, it allows them to switch over or do something else.

You *must* gain a clear idea of the audience for your title sequence. You will be able to do this if you answer all the questions about audience that we provided in Chapter 1.

Representation

All media texts are constructed: they are the result of *conscious* choices about what should and should not be in them. The person or persons constructing them have the power to create certain meanings – the *preferred reading* – by including certain things and leaving others out.

Whatever genre of title sequence you choose to produce, questions about *who* or *what* is represented, *how* they are represented and *why* they are represented in such a manner should be at the forefront of your mind. To provide a concrete example, we will focus our discussion at this point on police drama series.

If we think about who is being represented in police drama series we can see that there are certain types of character who reappear on numerous occasions (see Table 6.1).

It is very easy, given the speed at which the title sequence has to convey its information about the characters or the situation, for students to fall into the trap of stereotyping certain people or groups for dramatic or comic effect. This very often suggests that they have not fully considered representation at the pre-production stage. While it *is* possible and acceptable to produce a title sequence which utilizes stereotypes, it is unacceptable to do this without first carefully considering the meanings and their likely effects.

Language

We mentioned in Chapter 1 that the term 'media language' relates not to the written and spoken language in a text but to the visual language used: that is, the rules of filmic 'grammar' that the producers of the text use to create meaning. We also saw how this relates to elements such as composition, movement and *mise-en-scène* and, more importantly, how each of these is combined into a coherent whole.

So, in relation to title sequences, if we pick a television genre and briefly examine what appear to be the main characteristics of many of the title

Table 6.1 Character types in a police drama

Police types	Criminal types	Others
Mavericks/risk-takers: it is unclear whether they are good or bad. They have decided to work for the law but could have been criminals and often use the techniques of criminals	Unintentional criminals: those who do not intend to break the law	The public
		Victims of crime
	Good criminals: those fighting for good or justice even though against the law	Accidental heroes
		People who stop the police doing their job: rigorous lawyers, civil servants, the higher reaches of the police force
Rule bound cop: those who do things by the book	Terrorists	
	Psychos	
Desk-bound older cops	Career criminals	
Slick professionals: the know-alls	Hard men	
	Gang members: part of a larger group	
Duffers: the butt of jokes		
The odd: those who should not have become cops		
Unofficial crime fighters		

sequences, we can begin to see how such sequences use the rules of media language to create their meaning. If we take the contemporary urban police drama as an example:

- The title sequences tend to use a positive, upbeat, contemporary, possibly electronic soundtrack with a fast pace. This is designed to create certain preferred connotations in the mind of the audience: energy, enthusiasm for the job and professionalism.
- There tends to be a lot of camera movement, some of it very rapid. This creates a dynamic sense of constantly being on the move and, by implication, conveys the dynamic nature of policing.
- The title sequence will always include the name of the series and, especially in American police dramas, the names of key members of the cast and crew.
- Lighting is often expressionistic rather than realistic, especially in those series with 'darker' narratives. This is often used to signify the darker side of life that the police have to combat.

- The shot composition tends to focus on tighter shots: MCU and CU tends to be the norm. The shots are often of the main characters in their working environment (both in the police station and out on the streets) and, as with the title sequence for *Friends* that we looked at earlier, provide some clues about the characters and their backstory.
- The title sequences are edited using a very fast pace, with lots of short shots which supplement the speed of the camera movements. For further elaboration of this point, we will return to this in the section on the pace of editing later in this chapter.
- The *mise-en-scène* is carefully crafted to create the necessary overall sense of the specifics of the programme: for example, the inclusion of electronic equipment signifies that the narrative will involve a high-tech approach to policing, whereas the inclusion of feet walking the beat indicates a programme which will feature more traditional methods of policing.

All these individual elements combine to create what, you will remember, is called the *mythic* meaning of a text. With regard to police dramas, this mythic meaning is an overall impression of the police being in control and on the case, and using their wits and technology to rid the streets of those who threaten the law-abiding majority.

Ideology

As we have seen in the previous chapters, the concept of ideology is closely related to that of representation in that it relates to the types of representation which are provided by media texts: necessarily partial and selective and serving the interests of dominant groups within society. Even though title sequences are very short, this does not mean that they do not contain ideological positions.

We mentioned above the types of representation found in certain police drama series. It is possible that, within such representations, an overall preferred reading is being delivered, perhaps not overtly. At its most basic level, the ideological position of most police series is that the police are good and 'on our side'. In narratives in different police series from different countries, criminals are tracked down and corrupt police officers are identified; the honest, conscientious police officers may struggle for much of the programme but, in the end, they are successful. This is an ideological position. Recent police series have shown an awareness of the ideological position of previous series and have, within their narratives, attempted to work through some of the issues. The patriarchal ideology, for example, which states that women are not good enough to be 'real cops' is an issue that many police series have confronted. However, that is not to say that there are not other ideological positions in the programmes which remain unchallenged and unchanged.

Narrative

As we saw in Chapter 1, the term 'narrative' broadly relates to the idea of telling a story but, more specifically, refers to the selection and ordering of elements into a coherent structure. We also saw that Tzvetzan Todorov argued that one of the most ubiquitous of narrative structures, the linear narrative, moved through five main stages: equilibrium, disruption, recognition, attempt and enhanced equilibrium.

Although this linear narrative structure is present in many mainstream television programmes and *may* be replicated in title sequences, what characterizes the majority of title sequences is their playfulness with the elements from which they are constructed and, therefore, their lack of any linear narrative structure. Collins notes that television as a medium contains and works through what he terms 'a semiotics of excess' (1992: 331): namely, that the audience is bombarded with signs which, while linked, have no clear or necessary relation with the signs which precede or follow them. Title sequences are the television product which embodies such a semiotics of excess *par excellence*.

It is here that we can begin to talk about the specific codes which are used to organize narrative within title sequences. There are, for the purposes of our current brief, two main narrative codes which are used in the production of video texts and that we need to consider:

- The *action code* is a way of organizing the text so that, as the name suggests, actions within the narrative move that narrative forward. For example, in a wartime drama we may have a CU shot of a bomb which, in the next shot, explodes. This action (the bomb exploding) signifies that the narrative has moved forward and that everyone both within the narrative and outside it knows that it has moved forward.
- The *enigma code* is another common device used within video texts. Rather than moving the action forward, as does the action code, the enigma code 'holds up' the narrative by not giving us the whole story, thus providing a pleasurable sense of mystery (or enigma) for the audience. For example, why is that man waiting in the street? How is that woman going to get out of that predicament?

Using our brief discussion of action and enigma codes, we can say that there are three main types of title sequence, which can broadly be characterized in terms of their narrative 'fullness':

- Title sequences which use both action and enigma codes to create some sort of linear narrative within the title sequence which does not carry over into the programme. These are relatively rare. One example might be the title sequence for *The Simpsons*. The narrative starts with each member of the family in a separate place (beginning) and, through a series of actions (middle), they end up back in the home (end). However, it also includes shots such as Bart writing on the blackboard, producing the necessary enigma: why is he being kept in after school? Why is he writing *that*?

- Title sequences which provide us with the necessary narrative clues that we need to make sense of the programme to follow, without articulating a whole narrative. These may work through some of the stages of a linear narrative but, more usually, provide the backstory for the programme or, in Todorov's terminology, establish the initial equilibrium of the narrative. They may contain a mixture of action and/or enigma codes: for example, in the 1970s UK sitcom *Porridge*, an example of which can be found on YouTube, the prison door slamming (an example of the action code) gives us a clue about where the narrative will take place and what will happen to the character, but the shots of Norman Stanley Fletcher and the accompanying voice-over (an example of the enigma code) provide few clues about the character and why he is in prison.

- Title sequences which are totally empty of narrative and rely instead on a collision of signs for their meaning. These are used, for example, for most talk shows and, in the UK, *Question Time*. This type of title sequence is increasingly common across a range of different genres.

What this should suggest to you is that, as video-makers, you have a huge degree of freedom when constructing your title sequence. If you wish, you can produce a title sequence with a narrative, but the fact that many title sequences are generally not constrained by having to fit into a rigid narrative structure means that your ideas can be much more imaginative than in some other types of video.

Genre

A number of Twitchen and Birkett's characteristics of title sequences relate directly to the notion of genre. If you think of the different television genres that you analysed in the activity at the beginning of the chapter, we can start with an obvious statement: the title sequences of different genres of programme include different signs within them and, using specific technical and aesthetic codes, construct the sequence in such a way that it is normally quite apparent what the genre of programme is: cookery programmes are different to sports programmes, which are different to children's programmes, and so on. We already know that one of the characteristics of genres is that, on the one hand, they rely not only on *repetition* (of signs and the manner in which those signs are organized by codes) across programmes within the genre but also on *differences* between programmes. For this brief, therefore, what you need to do is both isolate which signs are repeated over different programmes within the genre and also look at how they are organized differently within specific programmes.

Twitchen and Birkett were writing in 1983, before most of the readers of this book were born, and, in the intervening period, there have been huge changes in the media landscape. One of the things that you, as a group, need to establish, therefore, is what the generic conventions of title sequences are *now*.

A key part of your initial research for each of your ideas should involve you carrying out some more detailed media analysis using *content analysis*. This is a methodology which looks for, records and analyses easily observable, measurable and 'objective' characteristics. With regard to title sequences, this might include their length, how many characters are included and the locations used. Whereas semiotics is what is called a *qualitative* form of research in that it gives us data which is 'rich' in quality but cannot be quantified as, for example, percentages or in graphs and pie charts, content analysis is a *quantitative* methodology in that the findings *can* be presented in such a form, but those findings are less rich.

Tasks to do

Carrying out a content analysis study of title sequences involves watching as many title sequences as possible and from as wide a range of television programmes as possible and *systematically* recording your findings on a grid (we have done the first one for you as shown in Table 6.2).

Table 6.2 Content analysis study of title sequences

Programme	Genre	Channel	Time	Locations/ characters	Music	Graphics	Production Company
Friends	Sitcom	Channel 4	9 pm daily	New York. White: 3 male, 3 female. All different personalities	Upbeat, Incidental	Young, quirky	Bright, Kauffman, Crane

Once you have completed your grid, you are then in a position to analyse your results: if 100 per cent of the title sequences have music, then you can say that it is a generic convention of all genres that they contain music; if you find that only 10 per cent of the title sequences for police series show the characters in the programme, you can say that it does not appear to be a generic convention. This is extremely useful for you as a group in that it means that you know, albeit from very limited research, the ways in which the different elements are put together in the construction of contemporary title sequences.

When carrying out such a content analysis study, students often limit their attention to those programmes that they would usually watch anyway or, when doing it for this brief, select programmes only from their chosen genres. The reason that you should be watching as many different programmes on as many different channels as possible is that it will allow you to develop a better understanding of the types of techniques that the producers of different types of title sequence have used to convey their meanings.

Finally, however, we would remind you that the fact that different title sequences within a genre may well share certain conventions does not mean that you have to copy them slavishly in the production of your own title sequence. You can adopt such conventions but equally you can defy them. For example, soap opera title sequences tend to concentrate on providing the audience with a sense of geographical location, whereas sitcoms tend to focus on providing the audience with information about the characters within the series, but there is nothing to stop you producing a title sequence for a sitcom which focuses solely on the location, such as that produced, for example, for the UK version of *The Office*. Remember that this type of creativity is one of the essential elements for good video production that we outlined in Chapter 2.

Drawing all of the above information together, you should now have some understanding of what title sequences are, how they are constructed and the functions that they perform. You are now ready to start working through the three main stages of video production: pre-production, production and post-production.

Pre-production

The aim of your pre-production for this video, along with every other video that you ever make, is to maintain the highest production values possible. The best way of explaining what is meant by the term 'production values' is to think about a time when you have been watching an advertisement in the cinema and thought, 'Wow! That's amazing!' That is what is meant by high production values: it comes from the attention to detail paid to everything that the audience sees and hears. You also know when those values are absent:

normally in the advertisements for local carpet shops or restaurants. The advertisements with high production values, along with most of the films and programmes you see at the cinema or on television, benefit from a large budget, use sophisticated equipment and have very experienced professionals working on them. However, this should not discourage you from always aiming to achieve the highest-quality production values possible using the resources available to you.

We are mentioning this here both because it is something you should strive for from the beginning of your career but also because title sequences rely absolutely on having high production values, often higher than the programmes they introduce. It would be very rewarding if the viewers of your title sequence thought, 'Wow! That's amazing!' when they watched it. Well, they are much more likely to if you follow the correct process and give your full attention to all the stages of production.

You will remember that Cartwright's 70–30–10 rule states that, of the time spent on any production, 70 per cent should be on pre-production, 10 per cent on production and 30 per cent on post-production (because he always works at 110 per cent!). We stressed the importance of working through the different stages of production in as systematic a manner as possible. The pre-production stage involves working through each of the different elements: coming up with a range of ideas, researching and evaluating the feasibility of each of the ideas, choosing an idea, producing a outline, carrying out the research process, recceing possible locations for their suitability, producing the necessary documentation such as the script and the storyboard and producing a shooting schedule – *in that order*. In general terms, we have seen how to do all of these things in previous chapters, so in this chapter we will focus on each of these areas with specific relation to producing a title sequence. Keeping our earlier definition, the results of your research, the eight functions of title sequences and the idea of high production values at the front of your mind, you are now in a position to begin working through the first element of the pre-production stage: thinking of ideas.

We will, from this moment on, take it for granted that whenever you receive a brief you have read and fully understood it before going on to the next stage. Do not go any further forward unless you really do understand what is required of you.

Thinking of ideas

Thinking of a range of ideas and narrowing it down

Not spending enough time and effort on thinking of an idea is one of the main reasons why most student title sequences are weaker than they might have been. One reason for this is that students often do not have a good enough understanding of what title sequences are and the broad range of title sequences within each genre. The result is that they often simply produce an almost frame-by-frame copy of an existing title sequence.

There is often a good reason for this, to which we alluded in the introduction to this chapter: namely, that some people will choose to work within their comfort zone by producing something very similar to what they already know. Every time we set this brief, we see adaptations of the title sequence to *Friends*, where its main features – a good idea of the characters, less idea of the location and even less idea of the narrative – have been adapted to the students' own environment. As a result, their title sequence will contain a range of student characters – such as the bookish one, the drunken one, the athletic one, the dizzy one and the sexually promiscuous one – who will be filmed at a range of university locations, all set to upbeat music. However, while some of these adaptations are good, the majority are merely ordinary and unimaginative. Another favourite is the spoof, often the 1970s-style police series, complete with ludicrous false moustaches and 1970s costumes. Fall into the trap of producing a spoof at your peril: unless you fully understand the genre you are borrowing from and the finished video is of a really high quality, they simply do not work. One of the reasons for this is alluded to by Frederic Jameson in his seminal article 'Postmodernism or the Logic of Late Capitalism' (1991). In it, he argues that there are two types of what he calls a 'retro' text: parody and pastiche. Parody is where a text draws upon a previous text and has some form of understanding and respect for it. Pastiche, on the other hand, is where a text uses the conventions or features of a previous text but for merely stylistic reasons: it is, in Jameson's words, a 'blank parody'. So, in trying to produce a spoof, what should be a parody often turns into pastiche.

We do sometimes encourage students who are completely new to media production to consider adaptations of existing title sequences. The reason for this is that, in producing a formulaic video, they already have a structure to work to and can, therefore, concentrate on learning the technical process. We would nearly always discourage the production of a spoof because, while it looks on the surface as though it would be fun to produce and amusing for the audience, in reality it is incredibly difficult to do well but incredibly easy to do badly. If you have more video production experience, we would discourage you from doing either: instead you should concentrate on being more creative and producing a title sequence which is more challenging.

Tasks to do

At this point, we would suggest that you visit the book's website and look at the examples of student title sequences. While you are watching them, think about the following for each:

— Whether or not it fulfils the functions of title sequences as outlined by Twitchen and Birkett and, if not, why not?
— How it uses the three main elements of title sequences: visuals, sound and graphics.
— Whether it fall into the categories of adaptation, spoof or creative title sequence that we mentioned above?
— Whether it is any good or not and why.

If you want to avoid making a poor title sequence, one of the skills that you can develop at this stage is the ability to think of ideas in terms of quantity and quality. It is vital that you think of as many ideas as possible. In Chapter 3 we saw some of the ways in which you can, as a group, generate a wide range of good ideas and you should get used to using as many of these as possible. In addition, in completing the activity at the beginning of this chapter, you have already gone a long way towards thinking about how existing title sequences are constructed and you should have a much better idea of the range of title sequences upon which you can draw in the production of your own.

When thinking of ideas for title sequences, you have three main options:

1. Use a specific existing title sequence as a basis for your production and essentially copy the style, and possibly the content, of this title sequence. However, as we saw above, this is the easiest way of coming up with an idea but it will, by definition, not be a particularly original idea.
2. Adapt the conventions of existing title sequences, maybe playing around with them to make something a little fresher. One of the ways in which a more creative take on an existing idea might be produced is to integrate the conventions of two existing genres to produce what is known as a *hybrid*. The original title sequence for *House Invaders* (BBC1, 1997–present), for example, used the conventions of both DIY programmes (shots of drills and other DIY tools) and secret agent programmes (the type of music, the colourful graphics and the poses of the presenters) to produce an original and fresh title sequence for what is a fairly generic programme. Although this has some of the elements of 'spoof' that we warned against above, the difference here is that the quality of the title sequence is very high.

3. Come up with a completely new idea. This may involve taking an existing genre or subgenre and offering a completely different take on it by deliberately going against the existing conventions and playing with the audience's expectations of the programme that they are about to see. Such examples are rare as, in the real world, title sequences have historically needed to inform the audience clearly about the type of programme to follow. If you have the confidence to attempt the type of title sequence which has no clear-cut rules, you need to ensure that it works as a title sequence: that is, the sequence must support the following programme and not work against it, in terms of either style or content. The risk is high but if you get it right, you are likely to have a superbly original title sequence.

All of these approaches are valid but the key thing to remember is that, whichever approach you choose, you should think of as many different ideas as possible. For each of your ideas, you should also think about the potentially different ways of presenting that idea. For example, the idea of a title sequence for a ghost story might be presented in a number of different ways: as a horror story, as a children's story, as a musical. If you don't think of presenting ideas in a number of different ways, you risk merely using the signs and codes of your chosen genre in a typically conventional manner. This is acceptable but it is much more exciting to play around with the idea and produce something which is slightly more unusual or stimulating.

It also seems very obvious that when you are thinking of ideas, you must first consider the programme for which you are attempting to create the title sequence. This is because, as we saw in Twitchen and Birkett's functions, the title sequence has an inherent link with the programme itself. It characterizes the programme which follows, and the items which are selected and included in the title sequence gain increased significance in the programme.

Remember, too, that you need to give *equal* consideration to all three of the main elements of title sequences from our definition above – visuals, sound and graphics.

Assessing the feasibility of your ten best ideas

Once you have come up with your ten ideas, you need to assess the feasibility of each in order to whittle them down to the three ideas that you will take forward for more detailed consideration. The good news in relation to feasibility is that one of the reasons that we often give this brief out to students who are relatively new to video-making is that title sequences are comparatively short and many of the potential problems around feasibility that you will face with larger productions are either less of a problem here or are absent altogether.

You do, however, still need to talk through each idea fully in relation to each of the potential limiters that we introduced in Chapter 3: finance, logistics, Health and Safety, technical resources, human resources, the experience and ability of the crew, time and output. Remember that at this stage you are simply using the limiters to reveal potential problems with each idea which could stop it going any further forward.

Carrying out research on each of your remaining ideas

Once you have selected your three most promising ideas, you will immediately need to revisit these ideas in relation to the limiters. Although this may seem repetitive, the reason for this is that you now need to use them as a guide for conducting much more detailed research on each in order to develop each idea and acquire more specific detail. By that we mean that you need to get *definites,* rather than *possibles*: for example, definite costings, definite locations and definite information on transport.

Don't forget that you need to produce a research folder for each idea.

Deciding upon your final idea

By now, you should have a much clearer idea of which of your three ideas you would like to take forward into production. There are a number of things that you can consider to help you make the decision:

- Which of the ideas meets the requirements of the brief most closely?
- Which idea is the most technically and creatively challenging?
- Which idea will be most successful in introducing the subsequent programme (rather than the one you will most enjoy making)?
- Which idea can you produce with the highest production values?
- Which will allow you to show your skills at their best *and* allow you to develop them further?

One final thing to remember when you are deciding is that, as a general rule, simple is good: that is, it is much better to do a simple idea excellently than to do a complex idea badly. That is not to say that you should aim low, merely that, at this stage in your production career, you need to be aware of what you can and cannot do.

Once all the ideas have been discussed and you are clear as to which you can and cannot do and why, you can make a final decision about which idea you are going to use and how the idea will be presented. Only then, will you produce your outline and move on to the research process.

Title of programme: Cooking Students
Duration: 30-second title sequence
Time Slot: 11.00 p.m.
Audience: Male/female 18–25 years
Format: MiniDV
Resume: The title sequence is for a series of light-hearted and humorous cookery programmes for students. The entire sequence is filmed in a student kitchen in a hall of residence and depicts four students who cannot cook. A presenter/chef comes to their rescue by preparing a fabulous meal with their assistance and the sequence finishes with them sitting down to supper.

Suggested elements:

1. Four hungry students in the kitchen at their hall of residence.
2. Each student displays his/her inability to prepare or cook food.
3. All four sit around the table looking forlorn, staring at a pan of burnt baked beans.
4. Enter the presenter chef, armed with ingredients for a delicious, nutritious and economical meal.
5. Scenes of expert preparation follow, with the students looking on and assisting.
6. Cut to table as the students tuck in and the chef looks on proudly.

Film days: 1 day

Estimated budget:	Transport	£8.00
	Stock	£7.00
	Props and costumes	£7.00
Total		**£22.00**

Figure 6.1   A sample outline for a television title sequence

Producing an outline

In Chapter 3, we discussed the reasons for producing an outline and how to construct one. For this brief, you should see the production of the outline as the opportunity to clarify your group's thinking about the idea as it currently stands. You need to remember that, while you are not writing an outline for a programme but merely for its title sequence, you will still need to consider the type of programme you are making it for. This should be clearly articulated in the outline (see Figure 6.1).

Carrying out the necessary research

Now that your group has one idea that it intends to proceed with, you need to carry out more detailed and systematic *technical and logistical research* and *content research* around that idea. This research is exactly the same as detailed in Chapter 3 so we are not going to go through it again in detail here but will assume that you have undertaken it.

Specifically for this brief, the most important aspects of the research, both technically and creatively, are likely to revolve around locations, actors, and props, costumes and dressing:

- *Locations:* we saw earlier that, sometimes, students choose completely the wrong location for their video because it is the first one they looked at, nearby, free or convenient to use. All of these are the wrong reasons to use a location. The *right* reasons for using a location are because it looks exactly as you want it to look on screen and because it is safe to use for your purposes.

  Given the importance of location as a key signifier of meaning in what is such a short piece of video where *every* sign matters, one of the key aspects of the title sequence that you have at your disposal is the choice of location. Choose the right one and your job will be much easier; choose the wrong one and it may make your job impossible. Remember that the location you choose has to provide the preferred reading that you want to convey to your audience. This is not easy: professional location scouts may look at hundreds of locations before finding the right one. While, as a student, you do not have the time or resources to do this, you should develop the habit of looking further than the obvious. If you need a pub, look at four pubs and choose the best of the four, even if it is not exactly right: you can improve it by dressing the set. In recceing each location, therefore, you are filling in your recce sheet not just with logistical considerations (although you must do that for each and every location you plan to use) but also with creative ones.

  For example, look at the two pictures shown in Figure 6.2 and try to describe the person whose bedroom it is in one sentence.

  It is instantly clear to the audience that the two bedrooms belong to people of different ages and with different lifestyles, attitudes and values. If you remember, this is related to the term *mise-en-scène*. You can make

Figure 6.2   Choosing a location

the audience think whatever you want about the person whose bedroom it is by 'putting into the scene' certain items which quickly and clearly steer the audience in the direction *you* want: walls covered with carefully chosen posters, a child's teddy bear, dirty washing on the floor, piles of unopened text books on the table, an unmade bed. All this material needs to be considered at the recce stage, storyboarded, sourced and, at the production stage, used to dress the set correctly. At the recce, you can use the tools in your recce pack to measure up the location for props and dressing and take digital stills from all angles so that anyone given the job of dressing the set can quickly and easily see what needs doing.

- *Actors*

  No member of the crew should consider acting in the sequence: you are learning video production, not acting, and so, for some of you, this will be the first time that you will be required to use actors properly. As this is likely to be physical acting with no dialogue and because the shots are so short (potentially only 2–3 seconds each), it is possible to use actors who have limited experience of acting. It may be that you have friends who will agree to act for you but, if they do, try to use ones who have some experience in drama. Failing this, try contacting your institution's drama department, if it has one, or a department at another local institution.

- *Props, costumes and dressing*

  As with the comments about location, each sign within the limited and very short shots has to convey the correct meaning immediately. This requires you to think very carefully about each prop, costume and element of the set dressing and then source the correct ones. It is no good having a title sequence for a 1960s cop show if the car in it is from the 1980s.

Content research

There is a very good possibility that you are basing your title sequence on bits and pieces borrowed from existing title sequences from your chosen genre. Watching title sequences for these programmes will influence your decisions about the content for your own title sequence. This is known as content research, because it is directly relevant to the content of your video. If one of your ideas is a title sequence for a student cookery programme, for example, you will need to look at as many cookery programmes, student cookery books and general cookery publications as possible, all of which will provide important information. That is only part of the process though. Other areas which may be worth looking at are television cookery competitions, programmes about chefs, food or catering, healthy eating, vegetarianism, cooking on a low budget, websites and other publications devoted to cookery and student cookery, in fact, anything associated with cooking and young people, food and the preparation and eating of food. Consider also the music and text used for programmes of this kind. Do they have anything in common?

Our point here is that you need to gather a lot of information at this stage simply because it will give shape and direction to your idea. For example, if we continue with our example of a student cookery programme, without good-quality content research which further explores the topic, you may not discover that many students become vegetarian because of the cost of meat and the limited amount of money they have to spend on food. This important fact picked up by you as part of your content research might change the concept for the title sequence, which could then focus on healthy eating for students, not just cookery for students. You never really know where your content research may take you or your ideas, but without the research, the exploration of your idea will remain where it started, with little chance of really developing.

In carrying out the activity at the beginning of the chapter and in your earlier stage of research, you carried out a *content analysis* study of title sequences in general. At this stage in your research, you might want to start looking in much more detail at a range of specific title sequences, but this time using detailed and systematic *qualitative* analyses of a number of different title sequences within your chosen genre: that is, the type of semiotic analysis that we outlined in Chapter 1. To recap, you will remember that this involved three main stages:

1. isolating *all* the signs in the text at the level of denotation;
2. considering the connotations of *each* sign;
3. evaluating how the signs work *together* at the level of myth.

So, before you begin to storyboard your own title sequence, you need to remind yourself about what you already know about title sequences. From your analysis of the title sequence to *Friends* in Chapter 1, from the activities and discussions above and from your own experience of analysing title sequences more generally, you should have realized that a title sequence is a very highly constructed, concentrated text which very quickly and effectively has to convey certain information to the audience. To bring all of this together, we can state that there are a number of important facts about the extremely hard-working nature of title sequences:

- They generally indicate the genre of the programme to the audience (for example, soap opera) while, at the same time, differentiating the individual programme from others within the genre (for example, shots of

Manchester make it clear that the programme is *Coronation Street* and not *Eastenders*).

- Linked to this is the fact that they provide the audience with the back-story (useful information) about the specific programme to follow: where it takes place, the characters in the programme, etc. For existing viewers this provides a sense of anticipation which heightens the pleasure to come, while for new viewers it provides them with the information that they need to understand and derive pleasure from the programme.

- They are also used to 'grab' and hold a potential audience. Music for title sequences can function as a grab and let you know that it is time to make yourself comfortable for a programme that you like. Of course, if you do not like the programme, the signature tune can tell you that it is time to go and put the kettle on. The aim of the makers of the programme is to make the tune as familiar and as widely known as possible. Think, for example, of *The Simpsons* which is shown across the world with the same opening signature tune.

- They allow the programme-makers within the institution a level of creativity which often cannot be expressed within the confines of the generic production that they introduce. In the example given earlier of *House Invaders*, for example, the title sequence is much more imaginative than the generic programme that it introduces. This creative use of the elements of the title sequence can also function to give information about the institution to the audience. For example, as we have already seen, the style of MTV title sequences gives the audience important clues about the ethos of MTV as an institution: it is contemporary, it is 'wacky', it is for the young, etc.

- they allow new (and therefore expensive) technologies to be tried out in the production of a short (and therefore relatively inexpensive) piece of video before they are used on the finished programmes.

Producing a script and storyboard

Given that the normal rule when producing a drama script is that one page of script generally translates into one minute of screen time, your script is likely to be half to three-quarters of a page long. It is not likely to be a key document for this brief. In the production of your title sequence, it is the storyboard which is the key document that you will produce.

As we saw at the beginning of the chapter, attention to detail is everything for this type of production. Thumbnails are the starting point for getting your shots on paper. Use the thumbnail stage as an opportunity to explore ideas for shots: draw out every shot as it might appear in the final video but for each one think of alternatives and draw those too. Think hard about the pace that you want for your title sequence. This is related to the length of time that each shot is on screen: ten shots will produce a slow pace; twenty five and upwards is fast and edgy; any more than that and you are moving towards the subliminal! It is a good idea to remember that you only have about thirty seconds to work with, so, as a basic starting point, thumbnailing a shot which will last one or two seconds will provide reasonable pace to the sequence and will mean that you should finish off with between about fifteen and twenty shots. *Friends*, if you remember, had over thirty shots in a forty-second sequence. Now that you are starting to pin down the duration of each shot, start to consider how you will move between shots. Will you use a straight cut, a dissolve or something more sophisticated? Once everyone in the group is satisfied with the thumbnails, it is time to produce the storyboard. The final consideration should be the types of camera movement that you think you might want to use.

In many productions, especially longer ones such as dramas, you can get away with working from thumbnails or from relatively rough-and-ready storyboards, although we would *never* recommend it. Given the duration of the title sequence, the limited number of shots that it may contain and the importance of the music and the graphics, it is essential to spend time producing a detailed and comprehensive storyboard. This means representing each shot exactly as it will appear and with as much detail as possible with regard to framing and composition, movement and the other essential elements: sound and graphics.

Visuals

As this is likely to be a one-camera shoot, you need to think really carefully about the shots that you would like to get from that one camera.

The first consideration when producing your storyboard is to remember that you should always aim to cover your scene with the full range of simple shots: that is, those static shots such as LS, MCU, CU, etc.

It is essential that you also consider and work upon two other key elements at this point: the generic conventions of the genre of your title sequence and the *mise-en-scène* of each of the shots. In terms of the former, try to make sure that you have a variety of interesting and relevant shots within the storyboard. Given that the title sequence is one of the most creative parts of many programmes, really push the boat out and think of using different compositions and camera movements, but only if they are appropriate to your chosen genre. In terms of the latter, think really carefully about how each shot could be improved by including something more, such as people or props. The only way that this will happen is by looking at as many title sequences as possible, identlfying those elements that you like and thinking about how to do them with the resources at your disposal.

Sound

From your research, you are likely to have found that sound within title sequences is, more often than not, limited to music. The music within title sequences is the second of the key signifiers of meaning and is, therefore, one of the important elements that will make or break your title sequence. As such, it should definitely be sorted out at the pre-production stage. By sorted out, we mean that it should have been researched and sourced, it should be appropriate to the genre of the title sequence and of the right length and it should have been cleared for use.

With regard to sourcing, spend as much time as possible listening to music of all types and listen out, especially, for short snippets of music which may be suitable for your title sequence. Go on to general music websites such as Napster and i-Tunes or more specialist film and video music websites, such as www.royalty-free.tv, which will often have music of exactly the right length.

What kind of music should you chose for your title sequence? From the research, both content analysis and semiotic, that you carried out when assessing your ideas, you should have a relatively clear sense of the types of music which might be appropriate and, more importantly, the types of music which are totally inappropriate for different genres. Gangsta rap is suitable for a gritty urban drama but less so for a rural comedy; classical music is suitable for the rural comedy but less so for the urban drama.

The benefit of choosing the music at the pre-production stage is that it gives you time to obtain copyright clearance. Clearance can be obtained in the UK from the Mechanical Copyright Protection Society (www.mcps.co.uk). Be aware, though, that it can be very expensive (hundreds or thousands of pounds for a thirty-second clip) to obtain clearance, especially if it is for a very well-known artist or group. So, key tips for alternatives are:

- Try to use the work of a lesser-known artist or group, as their music is normally cheaper than more well-established artists. This can also be a good opportunity for up-and-coming groups to promote their music more widely, so they may be more likely to agree.
- Approach the management of any artist or group directly. They may own the rights to the song that you want to use and may be able to grant you limited rights to use the song. This often happens if there is a 'social' purpose to your video: one very well-known singer–songwriter allowed one of his tracks to be used for free on a video we recently made about disability. Make sure that you have this agreement clearly in writing

before you choose the music. However well-known the artists, make sure that they are clearly credited at the end of the video.

- Have your own music composed by a local group or by music students at your local college/university. You can normally make contact by placing an advertisement in the local press or by putting up a poster at the institution. Very often, you can give the composer some key words (urban, gritty) and they will be able to produce it. If you want to be more prescriptive, you can give them an artist or track that you want your music to sound like, although, in our experience, this often annoys them as it devalues their creativity. Make sure that you sign an agreement with the composer clearly outlining who owns the copyright of the piece and, if it is the composer, the conditions under which you are allowed to use the music.

- Choose some royalty-free music from the internet. There are numerous websites offering royalty-free music and there is a huge amount of choice. If you want music which sounds *exactly* like an established artist or specific song without actually being that artist or song, then this is often the best option. Note, though, that the music from these sites is not normally copyright-free. You do have to pay to *use* the music, rather than buying it outright, but the agreement you sign generally allows you to use it in your videos and means that you can show your work anywhere without paying any extra.

  If you make a final decision at this stage and decide to buy music, be aware that most sites give you the option of downloading the music in different formats. Wherever possible, avoid MP3 files as they are heavily compressed and opt for WAV or AIFF files: they are less compressed and better quality.

All of the options above require work on your part but it is important because without it you cannot legally play your video anywhere and it almost certainly will not be broadcast or chosen for inclusion at festivals.

Try to bear in mind the following tips when choosing your music:

- Be careful to avoid choosing music at the last minute, such as when editing the final cut.
- Using your own music collection can be quite limiting so look further afield.
- Your music has to work with the visuals to create the right feel for your title sequence so choose carefully to ensure that there is not a mismatch between the two, in terms of either the aesthetics or the pace.
- If you have not obtained copyright clearance to use your chosen music, you will not be able to show your video anywhere publicly.

Graphics

In terms of graphics, you need to think very carefully about how and why they will be used. Are they a major part of the title sequence or more secondary? Will they be static or moving? What font(s) will you use? How long will they stay on the screen for? Do you want to use digital titles bundled with your editing software or some other form? All these decisions need to be made now.

When storyboarding, you need to make sure that titles are clearly shown and that consideration has been given to the overall screen design. You can change it later but you must think about it now, purely because it impinges directly on your shot composition. When storyboarding, and later when shooting, remember to leave space for the graphics in the necessary shot. So, if you remember the rule of thirds from Chapter 3, have your subject on one of the horizontal or vertical lines, leaving the rest of the frame for the graphics.

You are not limited to digital titles created in your editing software package. It is possible to create your own which can be planned now and incorporated into the production stage. In the past year, we have had the following examples:

- A group shooting a title sequence for a cookery programme in a kitchen used magnetic letters on the fridge and made a nice stop-frame animation whereby a shot was held for a couple of frames and then the letters were moved into the next position, and so on, until the whole sequence was built up.
- A group shooting a dark drama, originally called *Pain*, noticed some graffiti on a dirty wall: 'Nothing but heartaches'. A tracking shot of this brightly coloured graffiti made a superb title sequence.
- A group planted some cress in the name of the title of their video for a gardening programme and, over the course of a week or two, filmed time-lapse footage of it growing – another creative title sequence.
- A group producing a title sequence for a programme on surfing used letters in the sand which were obliterated by the tide. More creatively, they ran this backwards in the final edit so that it looked as though the sea was writing the letters.

Once you have produced a relatively final draft of the storyboard, usually after many other drafts, you then need to go through each shot on the storyboard with a final critical eye for detail. This involves looking, for the last time, at every single shot and asking how it could be improved and how it fits in with the shots before and after it on the storyboard. Always think in terms of what will be seen on the screen in the finished edit. Remember, though, that it is the process of constant drafting and redrafting of the storyboard at this stage which will bring your idea to the best possible stage of development and, as a result, save you a lot of time and effort (and possibly punch-ups) at the production and post-production stage. Make sure, however, that you do get to a point where everyone in the group agrees that no more changes can, or should, be made: in the industry this is called 'locking' the storyboard

Finally, whatever happens, do not think that you can ignore storyboarding and just make your title sequence up at the production or post-production stage. We sometimes have students who, to 'save time', do this but then quickly realize that it actually takes them much longer at both the production and post-production stages as they have not fully thought through what shots they want and how they want them.

Producing a shot list and shooting order

This will consist of as many shot descriptions as there are pictures on your storyboard but should offer more detail than your storyboard. Given that this production requires high production values and a reliance on attention to detail around issues of *mise-en-scène*, use the shot-list descriptors as a means of describing in detail the shot content and what you are trying to achieve with each shot. This will be very good practice and discipline for future, much larger projects.

Given that you may be shooting in a number of locations at different times of the day and night, the shooting order needs to be carefully planned. You need to make sure that you schedule all the shots in one location for the same shoot.

Producing a shooting schedule

Once you are happy with the final drafts of the production documentation listed above, they can be locked. You are now ready to produce the final document of the pre-production stage: the shooting schedule. This document details the key information needed for the shoot(s).

Do not be misled by the fact that this may only be a one- or two-day shoot. It is easy to fall into the trap of thinking, 'We don't need to schedule this; we will just go and do it.' This is a big mistake. Even though the video will be very short, your shooting schedule needs to be as detailed and as accurate as it would be for a much longer video.

The reason for this is that, although it may well only be a one- or two-day shoot, you may have selected a number of different locations with a number of different actors requiring a number of different shots. In addition, the concentration needed to ensure high production values may mean that you will need a significant amount of time for set dressing, setting up equipment and rehearsals. You may be working on perhaps fewer than twenty-five storyboarded shots, but each one will need to have significant time spent on both the technical and creative aspects. Scheduling allows you to plan out the order and timings of each shot. It is unlikely that you will shoot in the order shown on the storyboard or that each shot will take exactly the same time to shoot, so the shooting schedule allows you to make sure that you do this properly. Realistic and accurate scheduling is good professional practice and will stand you in good stead for future, larger projects.

When scheduling, allow travel time for the crew and actors to reach the different locations and think carefully about when you want everyone to be on set. Do not call everyone at the same time: the director and set dresser need to be there first, then camera and sound and then the actors. Do not keep people waiting around unnecessarily: they will get too cold/too hot/fed-up and they will need feeding and watering!

Production

The production stage is when you actually record your video, either in a studio or out on location. Given the extensive process of pre-production that you have carried out, you should be well prepared and in a position to complete it relatively quickly. You will have considered each shot carefully when producing your storyboard and so it is now perfectly possible to go out and produce those shots using just the shooting kit that we introduced you to in Chapter 4 to achieve a good finished product. This is much more likely if, as we suggested, you have been familiarizing yourself with the equipment by taking it out and practising with it. In this section of the chapter, we shall look at the practices and considerations which are specifically associated with the three main areas that you need to consider in the production of title sequences: visuals, sound and graphics.

Visuals

We will reiterate, because it is so important, that title sequences are very hard-working pieces of video. As they are very short and contain very few shots, each shot and each sign within that shot must be perfect. The visuals, therefore, need to do the job that you want them to with the highest-possible production values. By visuals we are referring to the footage, either live or animated, which will probably form the bulk of your title sequence.

However comfortable you feel with the kit, you *will* have to go through exactly the same process at the production stage: set up for your shoot, shoot and pack away.

When you get to your chosen location, you need to make sure that everything is in place in order that you get all the shots you need and that they are of the highest quality possible. This requires you to dress your set and set up the kit you have brought safely and appropriately for the shots you want to get. This can be difficult, especially if the location is one that you have only seen once before at the recce. If possible, therefore, you should always try and carry out a test shoot at the location, using the kit and crew that you intend to use on the actual shoot but without your actors or any other hangers-on, such as friends.

Dressing the set properly is vital. In the industry, this would be planned and carried out by an art director. Make sure that you have all the props that you need *before* you leave for the shoot. Make sure that the people dressing the set have enough time to do their job properly, even though it might feel as though you are eating into the 'real' job of shooting. Do not set up the equipment until the set is properly dressed, making sure that when you do you are extremely careful not to disturb all the hard work. You have already seen that if the dressing is not right, the finished title sequence is likely to be poorer as a result. Of course, you may have limited time at a location and may need to work more quickly than you would like. On these occasions, do not panic: be flexible but do the job to the best of your ability in the time you have available.

It is likely that this project may be undertaken early on in your course and, therefore, your expertise at producing detailed and usable storyboards may be limited. This means that you will need to think on your feet while filming in order to shoot material which will work in the edit. Ensure that you have plenty of time at each shoot so that you can make the best of each shot on the storyboard. Some of the shots you had planned may be impossible to shoot or may not work. Although we shall keep stressing the importance of scripts and storyboards throughout the book, it is also important that you see scripts and storyboards as guidelines and not as overly prescriptive. You should shoot every shot on them, you should also have the confidence to get a good or excellent shot when you see it. This skill will come to you as you develop more experience and become more confident. Be flexible. If a shot on your story-board does not work or looks ordinary, do not panic. Ask yourself whether there is anything that you can do to get the shot or improve the quality of the shot. Discuss the possibility of moving the camera, the lamps, the props or the actors. If nothing you do seems to work, make sure that you shoot a shot that you know will work in the final edit. Keep working at shots until they look great: adequate, ordinary or OK won't do in a title sequence!

If you feel confident about using the basic shooting kit, you might want to consider how you can improve the production values of your piece. One of the key ways in which you can do this is by carefully considering the lighting for each of your interior shots.

If you are not, for whatever reason, using a lighting kit but need more light for your interior shots, there are a number of things you can do to increase available light and improve the overall look of each shot:

- Use the metallic side of a reflector for a harder reflection or the white side for a more diffuse reflection. You can also use other material which reflects light, such as polystyrene sheets. Position them so that the available light is 'bounced' to where you need it to be. It will, of course, not be as intense as the available light.
- Put higher-wattage bulbs in the location lighting, Make sure, for Health and Safety purposes, that you do not exceed the fitting's maximum wattage.
- Bring in more table lights from elsewhere.
- Adjust the iris control to made good use of the light which is available to you, but if it is too wide the footage will be very grainy.
- Select a room which has a lot of natural light (big windows and skylights).

The more confident among you may feel ready to use the lighting kit we introduced in Chapter 4. If you do, remember that if you decide to light your interior shots, you will need to light *all* interior shots to maintain lighting continuity.

Sound

In your research you may have found examples of title sequences which contain sync sound: that is, sound recorded at the same time as the visuals on set. However, the vast majority of title sequences do not use it at all. Even though it is probably not going to make it to the final video, you should develop the habit of always recording sync sound. The reason is quite simple: it is very easy to get rid of in post-production if you do not need it but almost impossible to add at a later stage if you did not record it at the time. So, even with a brief like this, you will aim to record sync sound.

What this means is that you will need a dedicated sound person on the shoot. There are no special skills which are peculiar to this brief so he/she will perform the usual functions of a sound recordist: that is, recording any dialogue, location sound effects and wildtrack or *atmos* (atmosphere).

Graphics

Graphics are the third key feature of most contemporary title sequences. You will already have decided what titles you are going to include in your title sequence by the time you get to the production stage. The key thing that you need to think about at this stage, therefore, is making sure that you frame your shots with graphics in mind: that is, leaving the space within the shot for titles. Use a monitor to check that you have enough space and that the background is suitable for the titles you have chosen. We had one group who decided that they wanted to use crisp, white graphics in their video but then proceeded to shoot all their characters against a white wall!

Although we have stressed the need for every shot to have been rigorously considered and storyboarded at the pre-production stage and although it is possible to produce a huge array of graphics at the post-production stage, it is also possible to produce effective ones as a separate shot at the production stage. Often, as we saw earlier, the idea for such graphics comes to students when they are actually on a shoot. What this should suggest to you is that you need to think creatively not just at the pre-production stage but at the production stage as well.

Roles and responsibilities

In Chapter 4 we mentioned that it is important to allocate specific production roles, preferably on the basis of the strengths of individuals. For this project we would recommend the usual student production team: director, camera operator, sound recordist, PA and, if the size of your group allows it, lighting operator and editor. If you have a small team, lighting and camera could double up. For a full description of the responsibilities of all of the above we would refer you back to Chapter 4.

Post-production

Once shooting is over, you will move on to the final stage of the production process: post-production. This is the stage where all the rough footage that you took in the previous stage is logged, transferred on to your computer ('captured' or 'digitized') and edited on an edit suite to create the finished production using video editing software. It is also where any sound, visual effects or titles are added. Given the work you have already done – 70 per cent at pre-production and 10 per cent at production – this stage should be relatively short (although, in this case, it could still represent days of work).

The reason for this is that the post-production for this brief is extremely important. If we think about our earlier discussion of production values, what the audience want to see and hear in your title sequence is thirty seconds of *good-quality* video. This means that every shot counts, every edit decision counts and everything which is added counts. Although your title sequence may be 'only' thirty seconds, it will take you hours, and possibly days, of work in the edit suite to make sure that the piece is of the highest possible quality. This means that before you even sit down at an edit suite, your group needs to do the following:

- Discuss and finalize roles for post-production. Are you going to edit democratically or is one person going to take responsibility for the bulk of the editing?
- Allocate sufficient time for the edit. In your pre-production discussions, you should have gained a clear awareness of how sophisticated your final video would be and, as a result, how much edit time you need. If you have to book edit time, do this as early as possible.
- Do some practice editing before starting the final edit, to make sure that you are competent at Dancyger's *technical* level: that is, you feel comfortable using the different features of your editing software. The technical level is, for the moment, the key level that you can do something about so do an assembly as a dry run. Given that title sequences are probably that part of television output which requires you to use *all* the elements of the edit and, moreover, to use them in as skilful and creative a manner as possible, this brief will develop the other two levels at the final-cut stage.
- Maintain good group dynamics. It is a mistake to think that, because the production stage is over, the project has almost finished. For the title sequence this is an equally important stage. All members of the group should try to remain engaged with the edit, even if not working on it collectively. The editor should be working to the storyboard and disputes should be kept to a minimum and resolved with the minimum of fuss to avoid the possibility of the group falling apart at this late stage.

The process of editing

Before you begin the editing process, you will have logged your rough footage. If you have not done this, then now is the time to do it. It involves looking and listening carefully for the right example of each of our three building blocks of a title sequence: visuals, sound and graphics.

Examine carefully the material you shot as a group and decide which shots will be used. You have a number of main options: use it as it is, use it but play around with it in the edit, go out and reshoot, or panic and give up. The option you choose will determine the success (or failure) of the finished title sequence. Always refer back to the genre you are working within, the brief, the outline and your storyboard. Because you are using a limited number of shots, you need to be brutal in your quality control of each shot. You will constantly need to:

- establish whether or not the shot succeeds in doing what it was meant to do;
- assess its technical quality, primarily with regard to colour and focus;
- decide whether it matches the other shots which will be in the final edit.

If the shot is very poor, do you have the option of shooting it again? Remember the key rule: garbage in, garbage out! At this stage in your production career, you may not have noticed bad shots at the production stage but you will all have had enough experience of watching film and television to know a bad shot when you see it on a monitor. If there are any disputes about which shots to include in the edit, this is where they should be resolved. If you have a limited amount of editing time, you should not waste hours arguing over one shot, only to run out of time and have to 'bang' everything else together too quickly.

The assembly

Now that your shots have been carefully logged, you need to digitize those you have selected and move on to the editing stage. As you may recall from Chapter 5, this involves the digitized clips being dragged from a clip box or bin on to a timeline into what is called the assembly.

You have two main options in constructing your assembly for a title sequence:

1. *Put the soundtrack on to the timeline first and edit to it.* If your music was chosen at the pre-production stage when storyboarding, it should already have been sourced, purchased and cleared for you to use. This means that, when it comes to the edit, you can put your music on to the timeline first and then edit *to* the music. Although most other types of production will add music towards the end of the editing process, title sequences often achieve their rhythm and pace from editing to the music.

2. *Edit the visuals and then add the soundtrack.* You *can* edit a visual sequence together and then test it by adding a number of tracks to your final edit

and hoping for the best: we have seen videos which are so tight that the music could almost have been written for them. However, this is *always* by accident and *never* by design. While you should make the most of such happy accidents, we would not advise you to do this as a working practice as it is haphazard and it suggests that you did not think clearly enough about the music at pre-production. Most importantly of all, it doesn't usually work!

Whichever method you choose, do not agonize over the assembly. You will have an idea of the shot order from the storyboard and so should be able to produce the assembly quickly. At this stage the clips are likely to be the wrong length and, as a result, the title sequence will be either too long or the pace will be incorrect. Ignore that for now and concentrate on shot order and the general continuity of shots. Play the assembly again and again to confirm that all the shots are in the right order and that they work together. It is often at this point that you realize either that your sequence needs something that you did not shoot or that something you did shoot needs to be reshot because the quality is poor. Now is the time to tell the director and crew and send them back out to film while you carry on editing.

A key tip is to complete a number of different versions of the assembly. It is amazing how, by slightly altering the order of clips on a timeline, a completely different video can be constructed. If you produce only one assembly, you may miss a much better one and, as a result, a much better video. Keep going until all your options are exhausted.

Now is also the time to bring theory back into your practice. Remember, from your contextual research, that title sequences do not necessarily use the rules of continuity editing, so now is the time to look at alternative techniques. One of the key techniques for the production of title sequences is what has been termed 'montage'. Montage, in general terms, means editing and is derived from the French word, but there is a more specific use of the term which comes from a style of film production pioneered in the Soviet Union from the 1920s. More specifically, it is associated with the writings and work of Sergei Eisenstein. Space does not permit a full examination of the concept of montage but suffice to say that it is almost the opposite of continuity editing. Whereas the techniques of continuity editing are designed to invisibilize the process of editing, theories of montage state that it is the job of the director and editor to foreground it to highlight the constructed nature of the text (see Nelmes 1996: 394–416 for a fuller discussion of montage). What this means, in practice, is that you can afford to neglect the rules of continuity editing and, instead, concentrate on the meanings conveyed by each individual shot and its relationship to the shots around it.

The rough cut

With the shots placed in the correct order, you can now commence the rough cut. The primary aim at this stage is to trim the clips to the agreed duration without negatively affecting the overall coherence of the sequence. Be brutal about the length of your clips: they should be long enough to give the required information but not so long as to affect adversely the pace of the sequence. Given the length of the title sequence, this may be as little as half a second.

As title sequences do not have to follow the rules of normal continuity editing, it is likely that you will need to concentrate on pace at this stage. This will have been considered at the storyboard stage but what often worked on paper at the storyboard stage does not always work on screen. Don't forget that your storyboard is a guide, so if a sequence is not working, now is the time to find out why and to change it. Very often, these changes are concerned with the pace.

The pace of editing

This refers to the length of time that each shot is on screen and the subsequent pace generated for the whole sequence. Within a thirty-second title sequence the pace may not vary very much, simply because there is very little time for it to do so, but in drama, as we see later, the pace frequently varies according to the action: for example, a love scene may be very slow with lots of slow cross-fades; a chase sequence is fast-paced with a lot of clips. The key considerations with regard to the pace in title sequences are:

- *Timing*: the length of each of the shots and where they are placed in relation to each other. You need to justify what are you attempting to achieve with each edit and why.
- *Rhythm*: the length of the shots in relation to the length of the other shots around them. Because they need to allow the audience to absorb a lot of information, establishing LSs are held for longer than CUs. The use of a number of LSs together, therefore, leads to a slower rhythm in a piece than using the same number of CUs, which need to be held for a shorter time.
- *Transitions, such as cross-dissolves:* these need to be carefully timed in terms of how long it takes to cross-fade from one clip to another. If your title sequence needs to be fast-paced, you would normally use cuts or dissolves of about seven frames (one-third of a second), while a slower sequence can afford to have dissolves of up to one second in duration.

Getting the pace of the edit right is much easier if, as mentioned above, the music was carefully selected at the pre-production stage and was put on to the timeline first during the assembly. This should allow your pacing to be perfect as you will edit to 'hit points' within the music: that is, points where the music changes or where there is a definite beat. In the title sequence of *Friends*, for example, one of the key hit points is the hand-clapping. A word of warning though: for such a short sequence you only need to use four or five hit points.

The final cut

The final cut allows you the opportunity to construct a more sophisticated sound edit and to add graphics to the piece. This is also the opportunity to grade your piece by matching the 'tone' of the different shots: that is, ensuring that the colour and lighting in each shot is broadly equivalent.

The sound edit

You will have discussed the sound design for your title sequence during pre-production but, as sound is equally as important as the visual and graphics within your sequence, a significant amount of time should be spent on sound at this point.

The simplest use of sound in title sequences is the music soundtrack. Indeed, for many it is the *only* sound. However, a more sophisticated use of sound might involve the inclusion of different sound elements. If, as we suggested above, you recorded sync sound at the production stage, you need to decide at this point if any of it will now be used. Non-sync sound at this stage is likely to include two more main elements: voice-over and sound effects.

Voice-over

Certain types of title sequence may benefit from the inclusion of a voice-over. This can be planned as an integral part of the meaning of your title sequence or, in an emergency, as a means of getting you out of trouble if the visual edit needs support in conveying its meaning.

If you are going to use a voice-over, you need to make sure that:

- you craft the script carefully (each word will carry significance and needs to be chosen with care, so you need to draft and redraft the script, even though it is only thirty seconds long and may contain only a couple of lines of dialogue);
- the voice you use is totally appropriate for the genre of title sequence that you are producing: think of it in terms of the right class, age, gender, ethnicity;

- it is recorded properly (if possible, this should be in a studio but, if this is not possible, with a professional microphone into camera in a space with the right acoustic environment);
- it is balanced correctly (it is neither too loud nor too soft in relation to the other sounds within the sequence).

Sound effects

Sound effects can add another layer or dimension to your title sequence: they can be the difference between a good title sequence and a great one!

There are three main ways of obtaining the kind of sound effects that you need: recording them at the production stage, creating them in post-production using the Foley process or accessing existing effects libraries, either on CD or via the internet.

Wherever possible, it is best to record your sound effects in the location as they will contain the right atmos for that location. However, there may be reasons why this is not possible. If you read the bonus chapter on the website, you will remember how Foley artists created most of the sound effects for *Friends* at the post-production stage, as the sound of the studio audience made it impossible for all the effects to be recorded at the time the programme was being recorded. If, as we suggested, you looked at the behind-the-scenes documentary about the production process, you will have seen how this involved the Foley artists working in a recording studio to create exactly the right sound for the visuals. In the case of the episode of *Friends*, this involved throwing rice in the air and allowing it to land on to a board, to simulate rice being thrown at a wedding chapel, and running across different floor surfaces to simulate Phoebe running from the outside to the inside of the chapel. You have this option available to you too. Once you have a rough cut, you can see what sound effects you already have and what are missing. Once you have this list, you can book a studio (or other soundproof room) and the appropriate kit and record them yourself.

Traditionally, sound-effects CDs were produced specifically for film and television production work. However, it is now possible to find almost any sound effect imaginable on the internet. A simple search will bring up hundreds. Be aware, though, that you will normally have to pay to use these effects and, more importantly, as copyrighted artefacts, they may well have conditions of use attached to them. Make sure that you know what these conditions are and that you adhere to them. If you break copyright law, you could end up in court and, even if you don't, it means that your finished video cannot be screened publicly. If the conditions of the contract allow, you can enhance them by, for example, adding effects such as reverb.

Graphics

Whereas, in many other types of video, graphics are secondary, in title sequences, as we have already mentioned, they are the third key building block. If you have not yet produced your graphics, post-production is the place to do so.

If you choose to use digital titles, one of the key decisions that you need to make is about the type of font to use. Even on the most basic of edit suites there are dozens to choose from. If your editing package does not give you enough choice, there are numerous websites where you can buy fonts (or typefaces). Give yourself time to familiarize yourself with them all: only then will you choose the right one. As a basic rule, use simple fonts because elaborate or very small fonts are difficult to read and need to remain on screen for longer.

Never choose a font just because you like it: it has to be appropriate for the type of video you are producing. You won't be surprised to learn that every font has a semiotic significance and therefore needs to match the type of video you are producing and the overall intended meaning of your sequence: period dramas will tend to use an older, seriffed font such as Times New Roman whereas contemporary dramas will use a more contemporary, sans-seriffed font such as Arial. We recently had one memorable romantic comedy which used a gothic, death-metal font throughout, simply because the editor liked it. It was memorable primarily because the font was totally inappropriate and looked terrible!

If you are producing text on the edit suite (as opposed to having produced it earlier in the production stage), make sure that the title safe-area template is turned on. This is the series of lines which overlay your video image and show you where you can place your text so that all of it is visible, whatever size and type of television or monitor it is viewed on. Make sure that your text is placed within these lines.

Most editing packages will offer the possibility of adding movement to your titles: from the simple scrolling (moving from the bottom of the screen to the top) and crawling (moving from right to left or vice versa) movement common to most television programmes to much more sophisticated three-dimensional movement. Again, choose only what is appropriate for your title sequence.

Colour-correction

Clips which cannot be matched in terms of colour will need to undergo grading. Your editing package should offer you a number of tools for this purpose. Because you are working with a limited number of clips, it is worth your time and effort to do this, colour-grading the entire piece if necessary. Dedicated software packages such as Magic Bullet offer a huge range of filters and effects. Don't forget that grading can also be used to creative a specific aesthetic effect.

Compositing

One final point to make. Students are increasingly aware of compositing packages such as After Effects or Shake which allow for really sophisticated layering and manipulation of the video image. If you are already familiar with such packages, their use can dramatically increase the sophistication and effect of your sequence. The reason we have mentioned them here and not in pre-production is that, when thinking of ideas for your sequence, you should never start with an understanding of what such software can do and form your idea around that; you should always start with the idea.

What you should have started to see from this brief is how the process of editing is fundamental in constructing meaning. The analogy that we like to use for all the aspects of the post-production process mentioned above is that of sculpting. You start with the rough footage and, via the process of producing an assembly, a rough cut and then increasingly finer cuts, 'sculpt' the finished piece: removing a few frames of a shot here, adding a transition effect here, altering the sound levels elsewhere. Unlike sculpting, however, and especially when using digital equipment, it is impossible accidentally to chip off a whole arm, which makes it a much more pleasurable process!

Exporting

The final aspect of post-production is exporting your finished title sequence to DVD and tape, or other storage medium, as a master copy. If you are handing these in for assessment, make sure that you keep a copy for each member of the group. As mentioned in Chapter 5, you should also save the entire project to your own hard drive, which will allow you to re-edit it at a later date, should you wish to do so.

Conclusion

The ability to convey a message in 30 seconds is an increasingly important skill. Although this chapter has talked specifically about title sequences, there are other types of production which could be seen to be quite similar, such as movie trailers, channel idents, advertisements and viral ads. Although they may increasingly be viewed using different types of technology such as the internet and mobile phones, they each require you to go through the same creative processes and to use the same kinds of technical and creative group skills.

Our top ten tips for the production of title sequences:

1. Watch more title sequences! By this we mean watch as many different title sequences for as many different types of programmes as possible. Keep notes of your research as this will help you later on.

2. Explore four or five genres in which you think you might be interested. From that will come your first ideas.

3. Don't give up thinking about ideas and don't stop until you come up with a great idea. You will know it when it happens!

4. Try to stretch yourself both technically and creatively but do not over-reach yourself. Be realistic with your ideas, especially if this is your first video.

5. You *must* produce thorough thumbnails and then a detailed storyboard. Play your 30 seconds through your head until you are completely happy with it.

6. Think really hard about the sound and graphics: they are not secondary but are key signifiers of meaning.

7. Plan and schedule everything thoroughly, even though you might be tempted not to do so because the production is so short.

8. As you may be using only fifteen to thirty shots, ensure that the production values of each and every one are as high as possible.

9. Always have Plan B (and Plan C!) ready for when things go wrong.

10. Sit down and watch your final cut as a group. Are you happy with every part of it? Does it meet the brief *and* work as an entertaining title sequence? If not, go and shoot more material or go back to the edit suite and sort it out! Don't be content with 'all right': you should be aiming for great!

7 The Magazine Programme

Introduction

Magazine programmes are a staple genre of contemporary television. In the UK, the genre is very broad and includes news and current affairs programmes such as *The One Show* (UK), *60 Minutes* (US) and *Today Tonight* (Australia), sports magazines such as *Sportsworld* (Al Jazeera), motoring magazines such as *Top Gear* (UK) and, increasingly, what we term 'lifestyle' magazine programmes such as *This Morning* (UK) and *Oprah* (US). So, wherever you live, it is almost certain that if you look at the television schedules for any one day, there will be at least one magazine programme.

We would initially define the genre as follows: *a magazine programme is a predominantly studio-based programme which is generally recorded live, or as-live, with regular presenters who guide the structure and content of the programme which, depending on the subgenre of the programme, contains a mixture of chat or discussion, interviews with guests (the public, specialists or experts and celebrities), phone-in or write-in quizzes and competitions, reviews and separate short articles, which are either live or pre-recorded.*

As part of the production process, you will need to research the specific characteristics of different subgenres of magazine programme. In the discussion within this chapter, though, we will refer primarily to lifestyle magazine programmes.

Despite their popularity with both broadcasters and audiences, current examples of the genre tend to have a relatively low cultural status. This is especially true of lifestyle magazine programmes. There are a number of possible reasons for this, all related to their main characteristics:

1. The programmes are informally presented by 'personality presenters' rather than serious journalists, often one male and one female, and with help from experts within discrete articles.
2. They have a number of separate short 'articles' about disparate subjects which are not explored in any great detail.
3. These articles tend to relate primarily to lifestyle issues (health and beauty, interior décor), personal stories (overcoming adversity) or the

current projects of celebrities, all of which are discussed by the presenters relatively uncritically, rather than explored as 'serious' issues

4. The programmes tend to be broadcast outside of prime time.

Despite what might look like a long list of negative points, magazine programmes are very popular indeed, possibly for exactly the reasons we have cited as negative points. *This Morning*, one of the UK's most popular daytime lifestyle magazine programmes, for example, regularly commands approximately a third of the available audience for that time slot. As a student brief, they are also popular and productive because they allow students to gain experience of studio-based production, they enable smaller production groups to produce high-quality single articles for a larger programme and they offer students the opportunity to experience live (or as-live) production. It is for all of these reasons that we are including them in the book. The points that we make about them, however, especially in relation to their production, can be applied to almost any studio-based programme that you might be asked to produce as part of your course.

Tasks to do

Before we go any further, we want you to look at a week's television schedules and make a note of how many magazine programmes are broadcast, at what time of the day they are broadcast and which channels they are on. Once you have done this, choose two examples of different types of magazine programme and conduct a more systematic analysis of each: a semiotic analysis of the title sequences, the sets, the presenters and a content analysis of the content and style of the programmes and of the types of advertisement in the advertising breaks.

You will remember that it is at this stage that you should be carrying out contextual research around your production, using our key concepts: I CARLING. It is worth stating at this point that, as with television title sequences, there is virtually no serious academic study of magazine programmes. So, although we have confined ourselves to talking mainly about lifestyle magazine programmes, more research on your part may well provide other ways of theorizing the genre.

Institutions

Institutionally, magazine programmes tend to be the preserve of major broadcasters because they require a relatively large infrastructure: they are studio-based and so require the expense of a studio; they are regular (weekly and, in some cases, daily) and so require an established crew; and, as research is vitally important to their success, they require committed and effective researchers. From the introduction to this chapter, you may have developed a sense of the importance of magazine programmes for broadcasters. Historically, the different types of magazine programme – science and technology, news and current affairs, consumer affairs, etc. – were an integral part of the schedules for terrestrial broadcasters and formed part of their public service broadcast remit: to inform, educate and entertain. The BBC1 magazine programme, *Nationwide*, for example, was one of the channel's flagship programmes of the period (1969–83). It was broadcast after the tea-time news, which was seen as a family-viewing slot. The content ranged from the mundane to the highly political: one famous article being about a skateboarding duck and another showing the Prime Minister, Margaret Thatcher, being challenged about the sinking of the General Belgrano in the Falklands/Malvinas War of the early 1980s. Not only did it attract an audience of a respectable size, it also performed the function of keeping that audience for later prime-time offerings. However, more recently there appears to have been a move away from news and current affairs magazine programmes which educate and inform towards lifestyle magazine programmes which appear to be purely entertainment. This is especially true of those channels which rely on advertising revenue: in the UK, ITV, Channel 4 and Five. We alluded in the opening paragraph to the fact that magazine programmes are popular with broadcasters and the selling of advertising space is one of the main reasons for this. The size, stability and regularity of the audiences for these programmes means that the broadcasters can sell appropriate advertising to a clearly identified and predictable audience. Institutionally they are appealing, too, as they are cheap to produce in relation to, for example, prime-time drama.

Contexts of production

One of the key contexts of production is the economic context. Despite our comment above about magazine programmes tending to be the preserve of larger media institutions, they are, in television terms, relatively inexpensive to produce, especially in relation to drama programmes. The recent popularity of lifestyle magazines with their relatively large and loyal audience can, as we shall see in a moment, be very appealing for advertisers, thus allowing the institution to recoup the money spent on production costs. The fact that they are usually produced by larger media organizations also has an important impact on the type of content: big media organizations have access to equipment, people and places which may be unavailable to students.

Another key context of production to consider when looking at the decline of 'serious' magazine programmes and the rise and continuing popularity of the genre of lifestyle magazine programmes is the socio-political context. The 1980s and 1990s saw a decline in collectivity as a result of the right-wing politics of Thatcherism/Reaganism and the corresponding rise of a more individualistic consumer culture. This led to a huge increase in the popularity of 'lifestyle', self-help and self-improvement and, most importantly of all, the birth and stratospheric rise of what has become known as celebrity culture. This in turn led to the rise of a range of media devoted to examining such issues, for example printed magazines such as *Hello* and lifestyle television programmes, and a move within existing media away from serious content to lifestyle issues. Such a move is also apparent in the types of advertisement aired during the advertising breaks within the programmes. From our very unsystematic and unscientific content analysis research, these advertisements tend to be for health and beauty products, cleaning products, life and health insurance, finance and loans, and home-based products. All of them are 'worry-based' in that they identify a sense of anxiety with regard to lifestyle in the minds of the audience.

It is also important to note at this stage that one of the key aspects here is the symbiotic relationship between magazine programmes and printed lifestyle magazines: the articles of each mimic those of the other in that they share exactly the same concerns, but the programmes themselves form part of the content of the magazines, and vice versa.

Audiences

On the surface, then, magazine programmes may appear to be simply a way for media organizations to produce relatively cheap TV to fill the schedules, sell advertising space and/or retain audiences for prime-time viewing. However, if we think about the audience for magazine programmes, the picture becomes much more complicated. You will remember from Chapter 1 that we suggested that, when thinking about the audience for a media text, you should not just think about *who* the audience is but rather ask a list of questions: *who, what, when, where, how* and *why?* If you do this, you can see that magazine programmes and the uses that the audience make of them are much more sophisticated.

With regard to the 'who?' and 'when?' questions, we have already mentioned that magazine programmes have tended to be on day-time or early-evening television, so it might be tempting to state that the audience for them is primarily female and figures have, in the past, tended to support such a statement. Certainly, the assumption of the producers in deciding the content of their programmes is often that the audience is primarily female (see Gauntlett and Hill, 1996, Bonner 2003). However, the fact that such programmes are, at least in the UK, starting to feature in the late-afternoon and early-evening schedules which were, in the past, the preserve of children's television, and the fact that the content of these programmes is starting to become more gender-neutral, seems to suggest that this may not be the case in the future.

The 'where?' and 'how?' questions are also deceptively simple: magazine programmes are examples of television which is watched in the home, normally alone or with close family members. This may be true but that is not to say that this is the only way in which these programmes are viewed. One of the key moves in thinking about audiences is the move away from seeing an audience as a monolithic mass all watching in the same way. So, like the readers in Janice Radway's seminal study of romantic fiction *Reading the Romance* (1987), the female audiences of daytime magazines may watch them as a 'declaration of independence', as a means of carving out a pleasurable, relatively solitary space away from their everyday family duties. The increasing number of televisions in many homes raises the possibility of a more solitary and atomized audience. Alternatively, they may, as did the audiences of soap operas in Dorothy Hobson's (1980) study, watch them at the same time as being engaged in daily housework. So, rather than paying full attention to the programme, audience members can dip into items which interest them while ignoring others or simply using them as background noise. But there is a third alternative, especially for magazine programmes: that of the social viewer. Much media theory about the audiences with regard to magazine programmes has posited the family as the locus of television viewing (for example Lull 1990 and Morley 1980), but many viewers of daytime lifestyle magazine programmes watch as a much more social experience: with friends over a cup of coffee or, even more of a social experience, away from the home in a public space, such as a student union.

Representation

If we think about *what* is being represented first of all, we would suggest that many magazine programmes, especially those which educate or inform, clearly represent the programme as coming from a television studio with all the key signifiers such as studio lights, an obvious set, and production technology such as microphones on show. There may be many reasons for this but we would suggest that what this does is to reassure the audience that the institutional might of the organization is behind the programme: if the BBC is giving up a studio and airtime for this, it must be important! However, other programmes within the genre, especially lifestyle magazines, tend to hide the industrial nature of their production and represent the programme as coming from an essentially domestic space. The key signifiers of furniture, carpeting and lighting are used to connote a space that is similar to your living room.

The content of the programmes and the issues raised by the content are the second area of representation that you might want to consider. We have already seen that the content tends to fall into certain recognizable and discrete categories:

- Celebrity interviews are relatively unchallenging and are often used to plug a new book, film or play.
- Health stories tend to focus on one person's fight against disease/the system/themselves.
- Lifestyle articles tend to focus on the fact that increased personal consumption is good and leads to a happier life.
- Fashion and beauty suggests that you must be fashionable and need to continue to work at it.

For the producers of such programmes, the idea appears to be to offer a mix of competitions, fashion, social issues, health issues, celebrity culture, house/garden features and an agony aunt.

If we think about *who* is being represented in magazine programmes and *how* they are being represented, there tend to be three main categories: the presenters, the support presenters and the guests. Each group is represented as being different from the others and as having different attributes and functions:

- The presenters on the majority of magazine programmes in the UK, especially lifestyle magazines, tend to be white and middle-aged. There is usually one male and one female presenter who, in representational terms at least, are likeable and have a good personal relationship. In programmes where there are more than two presenters, each presenter tends to have a different personality. More importantly, they are represented as being accessible to the audience both in their direct address to camera and in their chatty and informal tone: the phrases 'Do you ...' and 'Have you ...' are frequently used. They are also represented, even in the domestic space of the lifestyle set, as being in control of the proceedings owing to their experience of both broadcasting and life in general: keeping to schedule, linking between articles and managing the guests. As such, they have much of the screen time within the programme and enjoy a relatively high status.

- Support presenters tend to be younger and less recognizable than the main presenters. They generally take responsibility for only one of the articles in the programme, often outside the studio or in a separate part of the studio away from the main set, and their articles are introduced by the main presenters. These introductions and the banter between the presenters at the head and the tail of the article generally confirm the difference in status between the main presenters and the support presenters.
- Guests tend to fall into four main categories:
  1. *Celebrities:* they normally use the interview to plug their new book, film, CD, etc. However, 'troubled' celebrities are often interviewed to explain and validate their recovery from illness, alcoholism or drug dependency (or, in the best cases, all three at the same time!). Celebrities may also be interviewed about a career change.
  2. *Members of the public:* those who have a story to tell, from the superficial and trivial to the serious human-interest story.
  3. *'Experts':* those who are brought in to explain something specific to the audience. This can range from the faux expert such as a journalist commenting upon and predicting the result of an event such as a one-off news story to a real expert, a guest with a serious academic reputation explaining, for example, a medical procedure
  4. *Regular guests:* those who come in each week to talk about a specific area. Their expertise is normally related to relatively superficial areas: television programmes, the love lives of celebrities, the latest fashions, etc.

Whichever category they fall into, guests are invited on to the programme for a limited time to perform: that is, to be interesting, witty, challenging and exciting. In most magazine programmes, the interactions between the presenters and the guest are represented as a chat to which we are allowed access, possibly in a domestic space, but they are very highly constructed in that the questions (and sometimes the answers) are predetermined; the presenters lead the chat and guide it in certain 'safe' directions (away from legal challenge, for example).

The relative informality of the genre means that occasionally, and normally when things go wrong, a member of the studio crew may be represented. In the research for this chapter we saw one example where a fly was bothering the main presenter and a runner came on to set and into shot to deal with it, and a second example where the presenter was jokingly referring to the floor manager and the camera panned round to show him smiling at the joke. These occasions are relatively rare as they undercut the representation of the production space as a domestic rather than an industrial space and they highlight the fact that the programme is an industrial construction and not just a 'natural' occurrence. However, there are occasions when this is completely subverted. In the UK, for example, the Channel 4 morning magazine programme, *The Big Breakfast* (1992–2002), constantly had members of the crew both in shot and as an integral part of what was happening on screen.

Language

Key to the way in which such programmes produce their meaning is the type of visual and aural language that they employ. If we look at their title sequences, for example, most lifestyle magazine programmes tend to start with shots of presenters laughing, past guests, bright graphics and a light, upbeat piece of music. Other types of magazine will use different techniques to alert the audience to the style of the programme: for example, the title sequence for motoring magazines tend to have shots of cars as opposed to presenters, a faster pace of editing (to connote speed) and 'rockier' music.

The main body of the programme, too, will be constructed in ways which leave no doubt in the minds of the audience about what they are watching. You will remember that *mise-en-scène* is composed of setting, clothing, props and the non-verbal communication of the subjects and, once on air, the *mise-en-scène* of the lifestyle magazine programme creates an overall air of casualness, even though it is highly constructed: the sets are light, bright and casual, the clothing of the presenters tends to be 'smart-casual' and the bright backdrops, sofas and carpets all combine to give the impression that we are entering the living space of the presenters, not an industrial studio. This is confirmed by the relaxed manner of the presenters who joke among themselves and shift around in their seats as if they were at home (unlike, say, newsreaders, who remain static throughout), and the mugs of tea and bowls of fruit on the table in front of them.

Returning to our key questions in Chapter 1, lighting (as we shall see in more detail in a moment) tends to be flat and often includes domestic lights, transitions tend to be cuts between shots, especially in the studio-based segments, and the camera movement is related to the type of programme: for example, the UK motoring magazine *Top Gear* uses edgy and fast-moving camerawork while the lifestyle programme *This Morning* uses predominantly slow, gentle tracks and pans.

Ideology

Not surprisingly, given all that we have said above, most magazine programmes tend to have certain ideological assumptions built into them.

As we have seen, the main content of lifestyle magazine programmes can be broadly broken down into certain recognizable and often-replicated categories: fashion, health and beauty issues, social issues, celebrity/star culture, cookery, house and garden and agony aunt, to name a few. A key ideological construction in most of these categories is that they are what we described earlier as 'worry-based': they identify a sense of anxiety in relation to lifestyle and suggest that all the worrying aspects of your life can be overcome by consumption: buy this fashion item or make-up and you will look great, cook this quick and nutritious meal and your family will stay healthy, go and see this film and the meaning of life will be explained to you! As such, we would argue that most function as what Andy Medhurst terms a 'domesticated utopia': that is, a space where our dreams can seem achievable (quoted in Bonner 2003: 129). That is not to say that they do not tackle more serious issues but when they do, they tend to be approached in a 'commonsense', everyday, chatty manner or in a manner which relates strictly to the personal. Health issues, for example, focus on one person's fight to obtain outline rather than providing an examination of the underlying structural problems against which the person is fighting.

So, it is possible to argue that magazine programmes function as an example of what Frances Bonner (2003: 2) characterizes as 'ordinary television': television programmes which are noticeable by 'their lack of anything special, their very triviality, their ordinariness'. For her, the main characteristics of any ordinary television programme are the 'direct address of the audience, the incorporation of ordinary people into the programme and the mundanity of its concerns' and these characteristics are the characteristics of the magazine programme *par excellence.*

At 'best' then, it is possible to assert that magazine programmes function as an apolitical space where, with a little *personal* transformation – of home surroundings, of diet, of self – everything will be all right. This diet of content about self-improvement has the negative effect of encouraging what Bonner has termed 'cocooning' on the part of the audience: that is, 'retreating to one's personal space and investing time and money to produce it as a bulwark against the unpleasantness of the surrounding world' (Bonner 2003: 130). We consider that magazine programmes are, at worst, an inherently conservative space which focus purely on 'piffle', palatable little dollops of unchallenging content which ignore key political issues, articulate the dominant ideology and maintain the political status quo: just because something is on television doesn't make it good or right!

Narrative

The key feature of the structure of magazine programmes is that the programmes *as a whole* do not normally have a narrative, except in the sense that they have a recognizable beginning and end: they are ordered by what John Ellis (1992) has termed 'segmentation': that is, each programme is broken down into small, recognizably different segments. These segments tend to be between three and five minutes long but may, on occasions, be longer and include studio-based, location-based and pre-recorded material. We will look at the importance of the order of these segments in our later discussion about creating a running order.

Each individual segment is organized and structured differently according to where it is shot, how it is shot and the content of the segment; For example, a studio-based interview will have a clear beginning, middle and end: the beginning functions as an introduction to the item under discussion, the middle is a list of questions (either structured or in the heads of the presenters) and the end is the link into the next article. The scripted narrative can be altered by the presenters, depending on what actually happens within the article and on the level of interest it generates. This is a real skill: in the research for this book we saw, on a visit to the studio, how the presenters on *This Morning* used their skills to create a moving and well-structured interview which went over time but was superbly handled. It was the presenters who made the important decision to continue with the interview because of the level of interest that they felt it would generate.

Pre-recorded VT will tend to be more structured and potentially has a more coherent narrative structure.

Genre

From the comments above and from the activity carried out at the beginning of the chapter, it is relatively easy to isolate some of the generic conventions of the genre, however tentatively. We would argue that a magazine programme:

- is a regular programme which is broadcast daily or weekly in the same time slot;
- contains a light, bright title sequence with upbeat music;
- is shot in a light, bright set;
- generally has two anchor presenters, one female and one male;
- rigidly adheres to certain types of content appropriate to the subgenre of the programme;
- is segmented: the larger programme is broken down into narrative segments.

It is these conventions which will form the basis of your own ideas but, once again, we would remind you that the best student work is that which, while acknowledging the conventions of a genre, is able to step outside them and do something different. We will return to this in the section on the practice of producing magazine programmes.

Tasks to do

Now that you have read this section, watch the interview with Pete Ogden, the day producer of *This Morning*, on the website. Under the different I CARLING headings, make notes on the basis of his comments.

Pre-production

As with all your video productions, you must work through the production process systematically if you want to produce a video of the highest possible quality.

Thinking of ideas

Thinking of a range of ideas and narrowing it down

Once again, we would urge you to start with the brief provided by your tutor and see whether it is a closed brief or an open one. If the brief is relatively closed, it may be that you have little choice about what you produce; if it is relatively open, it will allow you to make key decisions about the content and style of the programme that you wish to produce and the target audience for the programme. Remember at this stage that you are thinking of ideas for a whole programme. As for any of the other briefs in this book, it is a mistake to think of only one idea so, once you have examined the brief more closely to make sure that you are very clear about what it is asking you to do, carry out a brainstorming session with your group until you have at least ten ideas.

From the introduction to this chapter and the 'Tasks to do' activity, you already have a sense of the different types of magazine programmes which exist, so use these as an initial trigger but do not stop there. As we saw with the title sequence in the previous chapter, it is tempting to ape the conventions of a genre because it is easy, but you should be trying to think of something a little more imaginative. For magazine programmes this is important because although you can follow the structure of existing programmes, you simply cannot compete with them in terms of content and quality: you are unlikely to have the necessary budget, be able to access a professional studio and crew or have the opportunity to interview celebrities.

Bearing this in mind, think of magazine programmes which are realistic to produce, are interesting *and* have a definite audience. So, as always, you should start with what you know. This may be something quite general, such as student life or your local community, or could be more specific and based on something in which, either individually or as a group, you are interested: extreme sports, gymnastics, music, student life, your local community. It really is down to your imagination. Remember, though, that when thinking up your ideas, you must have a clear idea of the target audience: the more general the idea, the broader the audience; the more specific the idea, the more 'niche' the audience.

Assessing the feasibility of your ten best ideas

One of the main differences between this brief and the others in this book is that the magazine programme is, by definition, more segmented and less coherent than other types of video. As it contains both the main studio segments and different pre-recorded articles, in assessing the feasibility of the programme you also need to think carefully about the practicalities of producing enough high-quality, three-minute articles for your programme. At this stage you will need to think of potential articles for each of the programme ideas and then apply the limiters detailed in Chapter 3 *both* to the programme as a whole *and* to each potential article.

Carrying out research on each of your remaining ideas

You now need to carry out the initial research for *both* the three programme ideas that you have selected *and* for their respective individual articles.

Given the complexity of a magazine programme, what you might want to do at this stage is to produce a written outline programme proposal for each idea. Remember in Chapter 3 that we introduced the idea of a pitch (description of your programme) of no more than twenty-five words? Well, this is the starting point. Your twenty-five words should summarize the intention of the programme and the proposed audience and provide a very brief outline of the content of the programme. If you can do this, it suggests that you have a relatively clear idea of what you want your programme to include, but it will also focus your mind on the types of research that you need to carry out and where you might find the information.

Think, too, about your likely audience for each idea: Who are they? How homogeneous are they? What do you think they want to watch? How do you know? Might you be wrong? It goes without saying that your systematic initial research about the types of content for each of your suggested programmes and the articles within them *and* how they will be received by your proposed audience is paramount. Without articles which appeal to your audience, you do not have a magazine and so you now need to function as a professional researcher. Looking at each of the limiters in more detail will help:

- *Finance:* the main costs are likely to be for constructing and dressing your set, paying for presenters, paying expenses for guests and the costs of producing each of the separate articles. Consider each idea and think about how much it is likely to cost and whether there are viable and less expensive alternatives.

- *Logistics:* if you are constructing a physical set, you will need to source materials, transport them to the place where you are able to construct and store the set and then move it into the studio for filming. Similar considerations apply to props and dressings. One of the joys of shooting a magazine programme is that it should all take place at one location. However, this may mean that you need to consider how you are going to transport everyone from where they live or work to the same place at the same time.

- *Health and Safety:* now that you have a clearer idea about the types of programme and the likely articles within them, you can start to think about the specific Health and Safety issues for each idea.

- *Technical resources:* television studios are typically made up of two distinct areas: the studio itself and the control room or gallery. A studio is usually a large, soundproof room with a smooth, clear floor area and a relatively high ceiling, as it also includes overhead studio lighting, air-conditioning and often a *cyclorama* a coloured, flat material background. A gallery is a smaller soundproof room, usually close to the studio, which contains both the equipment necessary to control images, sound and lighting and a bank of monitors displaying images from each of the different sources or *feeds*: usually cameras, videotape or hard disc and graphics. The crew within the two rooms are in contact with each other via what is known as *talkback*: a system of microphones and headphones which is a one-way means of communication from the gallery to the studio floor.

  You will have to think carefully about the resources to which you have access and the technical limitations of the kit in the gallery and studio in relation to the ideas that you have generated. For example, if you have an idea for a show which requires you to have two presenters and three guests on at the same time when you have only three radio microphones, then clearly you will have problems. If any of your ideas are too ambitious for the resources available to you, you will need to select another, more achievable idea.

- *Human resources:* the key human resources upon which you are likely to draw for this brief are presenters, guests and your institution's technicians. We shall look in much more detail at the first and second of these below but, for the moment, we would just say that you need to be able to source guests. There is no point in having ideas for content for which you cannot find an expert, or anyone else, willing to talk on the subject. With regard to the third human resource – your institution's technicians – without them, you have no programme, so never take them for granted and always be professional: provide them with clear and accurate instructions about what you want them to do, giving them as much notice as possible, and never expect them to do your job for you.

- *The experience and ability of your crew:* a crew with little experience of set design and construction or of lighting design should not agree to an idea which requires the construction of a hugely elaborate set. Similarly, an idea which relies on live links to outside locations is likely to be over-complicated.
- *Time:* magazine programmes take a lot of time to research and produce. At this stage it is worth making the obvious point that programmes with a number of articles require more research, especially if those articles are complicated. Similarly, complicated articles usually take more time to shoot and edit.
- *Output:* consider how your ideas might be distributed. A different medium may be suitable for each. Technology now allows studio-based productions to be screened with relative ease either live or as-live on the internet, or you may wish to enquire about whether your institution will permit you to screen your programme via its own intranet or the monitors frequently located in public areas such as foyers and reception areas. Alternatively, you may decide to screen it on a community, cable or satellite television station. Whichever route you choose, you need to consider the implications of your decision.

Deciding upon your final idea

In deciding upon the final idea that you want to take into production you need to be clear as a group that the idea is the strongest one. We cannot give you hard-and-fast rules about which decision you should go with: it should be the one which fully meets the brief while at the same time being challenging, feasible, creative and fun to do!

Writing an outline

Having agreed on a programme, you will now need to write a detailed outline so that everyone is clear about the intentions for the programme (see Figure 7.1). This will need to establish the target audience and the content of the programme: the types of articles and features and the topics for discussion. You will also need to discuss briefly the overall theme and purpose of the programme, as well as its suggested structure and style. This might include information about lighting, the set design and the presenters and their

---

Outline

Title of programme: *Gothic*

Duration: 27 minutes

Time slot: 11.30 pm

Audience: Male/female, 18–25 years, Goth and non-Goth

Format: MiniDV

Résumé: A magazine programme aimed at exploring the world of the UK Goth. Studio-based male and female Goth presenters who examine all that is Gothic. Studio design, lighting and presenters reflect the overall theme of Goth; black and deep red being the predominant colours. Articles are fairly lightweight and short in duration (2–3 minutes maximum). Articles and features include fashion, music, design, art, film and Goths at home. An informal, relaxed and at-ease meander through the life and world of Goths, through the eyes of Goths.

Suggestions on style: Dark, sinister, lots of statues, gargoyles, black and red velvet drapes and assorted artefacts associated with Gothicism. Camera work to be quite informal, using handheld as well as mounted. Intro and outro music to be composed by local Goth band and played in and out by them. Lighting to be subdued and only pockets or certain areas of the set to be lit, some dramatically, from single lamps above and below certain props and dressings.

Suggested elements:
1 Music and gig reviews
2 Film and DVD reviews
3 Live music/performance
4 Interview with band
5 Interviews with Gothic hair and clothes stylists, Snitch and Snatch
6 Gothic tale of the week (3-minute drama, location)
7 Interview with UK Gothic 3-D artist and designer Sophie Dunroon (studio and location)
8 All that's Gothic – Gothic architecture and design (location)
9 The Gothic home – this week's must-have item

Film days: 2 days studio, 2 days location filming, 2 days editing

Estimated budget:

Transport	£60
Stock	£40
Studio dressing, inc. props and costumes	£110
Location props and costumes	£90
Presenters	£120
Original music for titles sequence/credits	£65
Total	**£495**

Figure 7.1   A sample outline for a magazine programme

approach to interviewing and presenting. Finally, your outline should also compare and contrast the proposed programme with existing and past television magazine programmes in order to offer a more concrete description of how it will look.

Carrying out research

In the real world of magazine-programme production, the research stage forms the bulk of the pre-production work and this is likely to be the case for your programme too.

Using your outline as a basis for discussion, you should hold an initial meeting which explores the idea for the programme as it currently stands. At this meeting, you should discuss the two remaining areas of research: technical and logistical research and content research.

This is where the project-management and time-management skills that we outlined in Chapter 2 will really be needed. This is because this brief is potentially vast and, as a result, requires you to work in a different way from that in which you worked when you produced the title sequence. The main difference is likely to be that, following your initial meeting, you will almost certainly be forming subgroups and working within those as well as within the single larger group. So, as part of this meeting, it is vital that the team should agree and draw up the formal, written group-project planner which highlights the tasks for each of the production areas, is distributed to all team members and must be adhered to without fail!

From this point onwards, having *regular* group and subgroup meetings and producing written action plans at each meeting is vital, as it offers the opportunity to plan and review, move ideas forward and set workloads and targets. The pattern for this stage is likely to be: meet as a large group, divide up into smaller teams, conduct further work in those teams, meet with the large group, divide up into smaller teams, conduct further work in those teams, etc. At the larger group meetings, each subgroup will need to update the rest of the group on the progress that they are making within their area of responsibility. It also gives them the chance to take on board the progress of other members of the team. This cross-communication is vital to the overall success of the programme. Remember that you are part of a larger team working to a shared timescale and budget, so be supportive of other team members and, most of all, be professional.

Technical and logistical research

A significant part of the research for this brief involves looking at production roles, and the skills and responsibilities needed to carry them out properly, and familiarizing yourself with the equipment you will be using.

At this point, therefore, you need to finalize roles and responsibilities, if you have not already done so. The main difference between the brief for the title sequence and this brief is that this one will almost certainly be produced in a studio. For many of you, this may be the first time that you have been involved in a studio-based production. At the same time as starting to think about the content of your magazine programme, therefore, you need basic information about studios, which will inform the way you work in them.

Roles and responsibilities

You need to think carefully about what the main roles are within studio production and who in the group has the necessary skills to carry them out.

Professional television-studio production teams are made up of a large number of specialists, each with a specific role, who should knit together seamlessly in order to make the production work effectively. Studio production is not democratic; it involves a hierarchy with a strict chain of command: producer and director at the top, runner at the bottom.

For downloadable outlines of all the roles and responsibilities for magazine programme production, the key skills required for each role and the key tasks for each of the stages of production, visit www.palgrave.com/culturalmedia/ dawkins (the book's website).

There are two main things to consider when setting up your production team:

1. The number of different people required is much greater than for a basic location shoot, such as that for your title sequence or, as we shall see in following chapters, for documentary or drama production. It is essential, therefore, that all crew members understand the protocol of working in a studio. As with the location work that you carried out for your title sequence, each person has specific functions to carry out and *thoroughly* understanding your role and how it fits into what is going on overall, is paramount. It is also important to have a good technical and creative understanding of the kit you are using: people are relying on you and your ability to carry out your job professionally. That is why we are providing so much detail about the roles at this stage.
2. The different jobs require very different skills, so the allocation of roles is one of the key tasks that you need to undertake as early as possible if you are not to encounter major problems at the production stage. Given the smaller scale of your production, you may not be able to fill all the key positions with different people and so each member of the group may well have to carry out more than one role. This is multitasking: one of the key skills that you need to develop if you wish to succeed in the media industries.

Think about how you chose who did what when you were producing your title sequence. Did you select the person who was most suitable for that job, the person who made the best pitch, the person who shouted the loudest or the only person who was willing to take on the responsibility? For this brief especially, you should make sure that you choose the most appropriate person for each of the production roles. When you are thinking about the role that *you* would like, consider two things: what skills are needed for the job and whether you have those skills. Don't aim for a plum job simply because it is a plum job but be very honest with yourself: if you think that you don't have the skills to do the job, then either don't go for it or, more positively, do go for it but pledge to gain the necessary skills to do it properly.

The equipment

We saw earlier that television studios are typically made up of two distinct areas: the studio and the gallery. Although initially they look very different and quite complicated, it does not take long to understand how each of the areas functions and what each piece of equipment does. As we say to our students, it takes a couple of days to learn how to use the studio and gallery but the rest of your professional life to learn how to use them really well. The good news is that this will be fun to do so there is no need to panic. If you research the kit fully and practise in the studio as much as possible before starting production, you will find the whole process enjoyable rather than frightening.

Let us go first go through the types of equipment that you will be using in the studio:

- *Cameras:* the cameras used in studios are similar to any other video cameras in the way that they work but are likely to have certain important differences when compared with those that you used in the production of your title sequence, and this will affect the way in which you operate them.
    - They are very large and will probably be mounted on some form of studio support: normally, a pedestal mount (*ped*), a mount with wheels which allow for smooth movement over the studio floor and with a control for moving the camera up and down easily (*pedding*, in industry parlance)
    - The main set-up of the camera (iris, white balance, etc.) are controlled from the gallery via a camera control unit (*CCU*).
    - They normally have a monitor mounted on top of the camera to allow the camera operator to stand comfortably while recording.
    - They have a large, red tally light on top of the camera to show the presenter and guests which camera is being used (or 'live') at any given time.
    - They may have a teleprompter on the front.
    Most studios will be 'multi-camera' studios: that is, they will have more than one camera. As we saw in the *Friends* bonus chapter on the website, the 'three-headed monster' set-up used within sitcoms allows the director to choose one camera to be live while the other two cameras set up the next shot.
    Some of the articles in magazine programmes will cut live to another location, often an exterior location, to cover that article. A studio camera would obviously not be suitable to cover such a feature, so one or two

portable cameras of the type you used to produce your title sequence, frequently shoulder-mounted, are used as they are quick and easy to set up and allow for free and easy movement within the feature. Like the studio cameras, they become one of the feeds into the gallery.

- *Teleprompter (autocue):* a teleprompter, or autocue, is a device which allows presenters to speak without appearing to be reading from a text. It can be slowed down or speeded up, depending on the presenter using it.

- *Lighting equipment:* within the television studio there is an array of different lamps which hang from a metal grid fixed to the studio ceiling. This is called the lighting rig. The individual lamps can be moved to anywhere on the rig and are controlled in the gallery by the lighting desk operator. Traditionally, studios have been closed rooms where all aspects of the environment – sound, lighting, sets – can be carefully controlled. While some contemporary magazine studio sets incorporate both natural exterior light falling on to the set through windows behind the presenters and also studio lighting, the majority of magazine programmes are produced in a traditional studio with the full range of professional studio lamps. Often some domestic lighting is incorporated, such as a desk or table lamp, to reinforce the sense of domesticity mentioned above.

- *Sound:* the sound equipment in the studio is essentially the same as that to be found on location: a range of microphones and supports. Sound is one of the feeds into the gallery. For the magazine programme, radio tie-clip microphones are the most often used, as they allow for the movement of presenters and guests and for the types of LS which are favoured, ensuring that a boom operator need never be in shot. Each person who will speak on the programme will need to be set up with a microphone, and levels should be tested on the set prior to recording. All microphone signals go from a transmitter carried by the person wearing the microphone to a receiver and then through to the sound mixing desk in the gallery. Each microphone is allocated a separate channel on the desk which is clearly labelled and the sound mixer operates the desk according to the script and running order. Apart from the studio sound, other inputs to the desk would include sound from pre-recorded material run from videotape, such as the title sequence, articles, and interviews and live sound from an exterior location.

- *Monitors:* many studios will have monitors on the studio floor so that the floor manager, and, in larger professional productions, the studio audience can see what is being broadcast at any given time. Use monitors sparingly as they encourage people within the studio to look at the monitors when they are on screen and can distract the presenters. If you decide to use them, position them so that only the floor manager can see them.

For those who have never been in a studio gallery before, they can be intimidating places because there is a wide range of equipment with which they are probably unfamiliar. However, all galleries from the smallest college or university studio to the largest broadcast studio will contain essentially the same equipment and once you have mastered the basics, you should feel comfortable working in any studio setting:

- *Monitors:* all galleries have a bank of monitors. Individual monitors show what is coming from each feed – normally cameras, VT and graphics – as well as having one which shows the final programme which is being transmitted and/or recorded.
- *Vision mixer:* this desk receives all visual feeds such as images from the studio and exterior location cameras, pre-recorded material and graphics. Each separate feed is viewed on its own clearly labelled monitor in front of the crew in the gallery. The most important feed or signal is the 'feed-out', which is the output for broadcast and/or recording.
- *Sound mixer:* this allows the sound from the studio microphones and the VT from the gallery along with other sound such as that from computers and hard drive recorders to be mixed together for output in the final programme.
- *Camera control unit (CCU):* this allows the settings of the studio cameras to be altered from the gallery. From the CCU, it is possible manually to control the iris and white balance. It allows for all cameras to be set up and balanced in relation to each other with regard to their visual uniformity: mainly their colour and contrast levels.
- *Talkback:* there needs to be constant communication between the gallery and the studio while a programme is being recorded and all studios have some means of doing this. This is called talkback. Microphones and headsets are worn by crew in the gallery, allowing individuals to talk to anyone connected to the system, in either the studio or the green room. The floor manager has a microphone which allows him to talk back to the gallery during the studio set-up and during breaks but, during recording, all crew on the studio floor will use hand signals, to keep unwanted noise to a minimum.
- *Titling:* most studios have the capacity to lay down graphics on to the pictures from the studio or VT. This can be as simple as the title of a presenter or guest (in the industry, a 'name super') or more sophisticated graphics.

Presenters
Presenters have one of the most important jobs, as they are the public face of a production. Remember our main rule of video production: garbage in,

garbage out? Presenting to camera may seem simple, but you only have to try it to realize that it is an extremely difficult job which requires a great deal of skill. If you choose a poor presenter, then the final output is also likely to be poor, so *never* choose a presenter from within the group. We would always suggest that you look outside your group for a presenter who can do it properly – try local theatre companies, performing arts courses, advertisements on casting websites and industry bulletin boards and in actors' magazines such as PCR – and that you carry out auditions.

Make sure that your chosen presenters are given their scripts well in advance of shooting so that, even if using an autocue, they can gain a good sense of what they will be presenting. Magazine-programme presenters talk both to the camera and to each other and their guests. In order to ensure that your presenters talk *to* guests and not *at* them, produce a script which is made up simply of topic headings and links. It is important that they should able to work without using the autocue for dialogue but simply for prompts to assist with the running order, initiating conversation with guests, timings and links. A good presenter will be able to work from a very basic script made up of simple and short sentences which act as prompts, thus ensuring natural speech, eye contact and body language.

Locations

It is likely, but not inevitable, that your programme will be studio-based. As such, it will be relatively easy to recce. Your institution will carry out regular risk assessments to ensure that the studio is safe to use. However, this does not mean that you can abdicate responsibility for safety. You need to maintain high standards of Health and Safety at all times and to report immediately any faults or problems which occur. We shall return to this in the production section below. Articles within the programme may be shot outside the studio and for these it goes without saying that you need to carry out recces and risk assessments for all locations used.

Most magazine programmes have some form of set which needs to be constructed. A set can be as simple as hung drapes or fabric or as complex as a full-scale mock-up of the interior of a large room. Whichever you decide to use, you must remember that your set provides the audience with key information about the programme. In designing and constructing a set you are creating an illusory world; you are responsible for creating every aspect of what the viewer will see and what they will believe. Your brief may provide you with no option about the set that you use but, if it does, you have a key decision to make: whether to design and build a physical set or whether to create a virtual one.

Unless you have someone in your crew who already has the necessary expertise to be able to build a set (or knows someone who does!), we would recommend that you do one of two things:

1. Construct a simple physical set.
2. Construct a virtual set using chromakey. This is where action is shot in a television studio which is either completely blue or, more normally for video, green, which allows for video (in this case a set) to be overlaid electronically.

Whichever way you chose to construct your set, you will need to work on set design plans which will in turn determine your lighting plans. It is also a very good idea to construct a detailed model of your proposed set, based on your research, sketches and plan drawings which need to illustrate both elevated and plan views. Your set model could be built using simple materials such as card or foam board and must be constructed to scale. For a physical set, mark out the true dimensions of your design in the studio itself, using chalk or masking tape to define edges. Does it allow sufficient space for cameras and crew? Does it take into account your lighting rig? If the set is too tall, will it create unwanted shadows? Will all the props and talent fit comfortably into the set?

Your set design should incorporate all props, particularly furniture and dressing. Consider style first: what type of look do you want to achieve? Then go through furniture catalogues and build up mood boards which reflect your chosen look. Cut out examples of sofas, fabrics and colours from magazines and catalogues to build up a picture of what you wish to have within your set. Are you going for a very modern, high-tech look – clean lines, metal and glass – or do you want your set to be softer and more homely? It really is up to you! As with all media, preparation and research are imperative as they will inform your decisions later.

Creating a physical set
Whatever the scale of the set, all studio sets must be designed with the camera in mind. Everything about the set – size, colour and props – must be adapted specifically to what the camera sees. It is essential that your set design and construction meet the artistic aim of transporting the viewers to a specific place or time or creating a particular theme or mood. This is clearly seen in a variety of magazine programmes where viewers are led to believe that the presenters and guests are sitting in someone's home, chatting on the sofa and drinking cups of tea, rather than in a television studio with an entire production team working around them and, in some cases, a live audience in front of them.

Just how elaborate your set will be is determined by factors such as the space, budget, time and materials available, and the labour, experience and skills you have at your disposal to design and construct the set. The most achievable option is to design and construct a simple set using the cyclorama as the backdrop. Adding a few basic props such as a coffee table, a sofa, a lamp and some flowers may be sufficient for the effect that you are seeking. It is surprisingly easy to acquire good quality props, such as sofas, rugs, lamps and other furniture, to fill the basic space if you know where to look. A useful skill for video production is *blagging* (obtaining goods and services without paying for them), so approach local businesses to see if they will lend you props and dressings.

Creating a virtual set

Alternatively, you may decide to be adventurous and construct a more sophisticated set. If you do, you must work with someone who has the tools and the know-how to construct the set properly, for example someone from the theatre or performing arts department of your college or university. Vitally, as they do it all the time, they will have the necessary knowledge of construction techniques and current health and safety requirements, which means that you will have both a professional and a safe set.

A chromakeyed background can look extremely professional and effective, as the background can be anything you choose, from any still or moving image. Most modern studios and editing software allow you to chromakey very quickly and easily but, whichever studio or software you decide to use, the key thing that you need to ensure is that the lighting on the background is entirely even, mainly with backlights at floor and ceiling level. If there are any shadows or bright spots on the background, the image that you wish to superimpose will be uneven. The other thing to remember is to make sure that neither the props nor the clothes of anyone appearing in shot are in the same colour range as the background colour: if they are, the image will appear on them.

Moving people and equipment

Arrangements for transporting guests and presenters will need to be made and you may have to accommodate them overnight. If they are travelling to the studio, ensure that they are provided with accurate details about the venue and the time of arrival. As with other productions which rely upon guests, look after them: meet and greet them and make them feel welcome.

So far, we have spent a long time discussing the logistics of production but very little on the content. Content research is the second thing that you need to do, simultaneously with your technical and logistical research.

Content research

For this brief, content research will be the key research. There is a saying in film production, 'the script is king': that is, having a good script is the key to a good drama. For the magazine programme, the three-minute story is king. Good-quality content research will result in good articles and a good final programme: poor content research will result in uninteresting and unengaging articles and a poor final programme. It is as simple as that.

So, once you have the idea that you are going to put into production, you need to carry out some detailed research into the proposed content:

- *Fully research the type of programme that you intend to produce.* You must have a clear understanding of the conventions and likely content of programmes which are similar to yours. This will almost certainly come from your detailed content-analysis study of similar programmes.
- *Come up with interesting content.* Very often, what seems interesting at the beginning can turn out to be very boring. You only know this by carrying out research. What is more exciting, however, is that often something which initially seems quite boring can prove to be very interesting, especially if you are able to unearth new information about it or present it in an unusual manner. You must remember, too, that the running order of your overall programme has to be both coherent and exciting *and* have enough differentiation in the content of the different articles to make it interesting to everyone in the audience.
- *Isolate possible guests.* Persuading guests to come on to your programme to talk about something is relatively easy; finding *good* guests is much harder. If you have an article that you need a guest to explain, do some research on that guest but, more importantly, see if there are alternatives. What you need are guests who have something relevant to say about a subject and who will say it in an interesting, exciting and challenging manner. For example, we recently had some students who were producing a magazine programme about the local music scene. They had identified a possible guest – a 'man from the council' – to talk about the problems of a club with a late licence. However, as a result of talking to him, the group realized that he would not be a very interesting guest and, after some hard work and detailed research, they found a local woman who had started a campaign group against the club. Not only did she know as much as the man from the council about the law and the specific circumstances surrounding the club, but she was a much better speaker. Without the research, they would not have found the more interesting guest. Don't be afraid to aim high in your search for guests; very often, people whom you consider to be out of your league may well (for whatever reason) agree to your request.

- *Find out how to contact them.* Most people do not normally publicize their contact details widely, so it will take some digging on your part to find out how to contact them. Use your library, and more importantly, your librarian if you want to save yourself a considerable amount of time here: there are accepted directories for different professions and organizations and these include contact details. Contact is often made through an agent. Students are sometimes able to contact personalities via websites or by e-mail. As with any research, try all means at your disposal.
- *Find out more about them.* Do not accept at face value everything that your guests (or their agents or PR companies) tell you about themselves. As we saw in the introduction to the chapter, one of the criticisms of many magazine programmes is that they are unchallenging, simply providing an opportunity for guests to plug their new book/play/lingerie/CD. Don't let your programme do this. Carry out in-depth research into your guests and find out as much as possible about them or the group or organization that they represent. Only by doing this will your presenters be able to ask questions which prompt interesting answers and respond to those answers knowledgeably, taking the interview to unexpected places.

Producing scripts

The scripts for magazine programmes are, by their very nature, quite sparse. Given that interviews are interactive and develop organically, articles are presented live and, as a result, are often equally organic: the script may often contain only scripted links between articles, using stock phrases such as 'Coming up in the next half hour ...' and 'And now, it's time for ...'. Whatever they contain, make sure that they are not too wordy and they are 'sayable'. You can ensure both of these by letting your presenter have a copy of the script as soon as it is produced. They will soon let you know if there are any problems with it.

Producing a storyboard

In the title sequence brief, the storyboard was the key document for the production; for this one it is almost inconceivable that you will produce one for the whole programme. Of course, you should storyboard the individual articles that you intend to shoot outside the studio for VT feeds and your title sequence.

For the studio sequences, the storyboard is replaced by a floor plan which clearly shows camera positions at each stage of the production. You will remember, from the *Friends* bonus chapter on the website, that studio productions go through the process of camera-blocking in rehearsals and run-throughs. During this process you will isolate where your cameras will go and the type of shot they will be required to provide. It is a good idea to mark the camera positions on the floor with tape, as it allows the camera ops quickly and easily to move into position during the recording. Once these positions are agreed, produce the final floor plan. Especially for the studio shots, it is likely that the shots you choose to use and the movement of the cameras will be relatively conventional. If not, you might want to storyboard the relevant sequences.

Producing a shooting script and shooting schedule

It has been suggested that your programme might be recorded as-live and as such will follow the running order. Producing a shooting schedule for the magazine programme provides all those involved with a breakdown of the times when they are required and of what tasks will be undertaken. As studio time may well be limited, the schedule needs to be realistic and strictly adhered to. It should show when to clear the studio, to construct the sets, to rig and focus the lamps, to dress the set, to conduct rehearsals, run-throughs and the final run-through, to carry out the live recording of the programme, to dismantle the set and to clear up the studio prior to departure. Any material which needs to be filmed prior to the recording of the magazine programme also needs to be scheduled so that it is ready for inclusion in the programme. This could include interviews with members of the public or a location report.

The key document in magazine programmes is the running order. It enables all members of the crew quickly and easily to see what is happening, in what order, with whom, when, how and for how long. Figure 7.2 shows part of a running order for a student magazine programme on the subculture of goths: *Gothicism*.

Once all the research has been carried out and all the production documentation is complete, you will need to turn your attention to three things specific to studio production:

1. set erection;
2. dressing the set;
3. run-throughs.

All of these will be carried out in the studio so, before looking at them in any detail, we need to alert you to the specific issues relating to Health and Safety

Group B: Gothicism Magazine Programme Running Order				
Item #	Item Name	Source	Item Duration	Overall Time
1	Titles	VT	0' 25"	00' 25"
2	Show intro – Hello and welcome. Presenters Meg and Tim	Live	0' 20"	00' 45"
3	Intro to item: Goths on Campus Pres M	Live	0' 15"	01' 00"
4	Spotting Goths/Vox Pop Presenter Josh	VT	1' 25"	02' 25"
5	Interview with guest – why be a Goth? Pres Meg and Tim	Live	1' 30"	03' 55"
6	Uni Goth Music Scene Review – guest Silas Macan	Live in studio Lounge area	1' 30"	05' 25"
7	Interview with guest band – 'Marquees' Meg and Tim	Live	2' 30"	07' 55"
8	Link Pres Tim	Live	0' 10"	08' 05"
9	Fashion in the High Street	VT	2' 15"	10' 20"
10	Food of the Gods/Goths – guest chef	Live	3' 20"	13' 40"

Figure 7.2 A sample of a magazine programme running order

in the television studio. The studio, even in an educational establishment, has the capacity to be either a very dangerous place or a place where you could do a lot of costly damage to equipment so issues relating to Health and Safety should always be at the forefront of your mind.

There is basic studio etiquette, or as Bermingham *et al.* (1994: 172) call it, 'studio discipline', which is accepted professional practice that you need to abide by at all times. Such discipline includes the following:

- *Make sure that all fire exits are kept clear and unobstructed.* In larger studios, this means that no equipment should be placed and no action should be carried out at a a distance of less than one metre from any wall.
- *Do not eat or drink on set.* Not only is it possible to damage expensive and sophisticated equipment (or yourself) if there is a spillage, but it causes the studio to be untidy.
- *Keep the studio as tidy as possible and free from obstructions.* The most common accidents in studios involve people tripping over things. Make sure that cables either have a cable ramp over them or that the cables are gaffer-taped down. Props, sets and additional lighting should all be secure. Never rest things against potentially unstable items.

- *Always do exactly as you are told by the floor manager and/or director and without question.*
- *Make sure that you do not touch or move equipment unless you have been asked to do so by the floor manager and have all the necessary equipment and assistance to do so safely.* If you are likely to be moving or lifting equipment, make sure that you know how to lift properly and safely: knees bent, chin in, back straight and elbows in! If in doubt, get someone to help you!
- *Make sure that, if possible, you have a registered first aider in the studio.* If that is not possible, make sure that you know who the nearest first aider is and where he/she is located.

Most educational establishments will, of course, run workshops on the correct and safe use of the studio. Do not attempt to use the studio unless you have attended such workshops. Also make sure that you know what the rules and regulations are for the studio in which you will be working. Both educational establishments and professional studios eject those who break the rules!

Set erection

Your allocated studio time may be very limited. Ideally, therefore, you need to design and construct your set beforehand so that it can be erected quickly and easily when you gain access to the studio. Remember that these are temporary constructions which need to be built, moved around and taken down without too much difficulty. When erecting the set, allow sufficient time to make last-minute alterations. Even if you are erecting the set as a team, make sure that one member of the group has overall responsibility as set designer for erecting it properly. It is this person who should take the appropriate tools needed to erect the set.

Once your set is erected, switch on the studio lighting that you intend to use in your programme. Using only the gallery monitors to view the set, decide how it looks: are there any areas which are overlit, underlit or in shadow? What, if any, changes do you need to make? Have you allowed time to make these changes? If your set doesn't work under lighting, it is probably too late to do very much, other than make minor changes. However don't despair as you are now able to move to Plan B (media students always have a Plan B): dressing your set.

Dressing the set

Now that you have created a physical space within the studio, it is time for the person who has been allocated the role of art director to dress it to create the mood that you want your finished programme to have. So, it is time to transport your props and dressing from wherever they have been stored. Once the main seating and presenting areas have been set up, it is a good idea to place people (anyone will do) to check that the lighting still works. If it does, you can continue the process of dressing the set. You might want to turn off the majority of the studio lighting at this point as it will get very hot if you don't.

Attention to detail is the key skill in set-dressing. Make sure that props are placed correctly according to the model of the set that you made at pre-production. Now is not the time to have arguments about the set but if the group, or more correctly at this point the director, is unhappy with something, dress it again, replace it or lose it! As we keep saying with regard to *mise-en-scène*, there are no half measures! Now re-examine the set under the lighting you intend to use, again using only the gallery monitors and adjust where necessary. At this point you might want to step back from the production and ask someone who is not involved in the production to look at your handiwork with a critical eye.

Run-throughs

A run-through is a rehearsal where you can stop if problems arise or repeat a section which doesn't quite work for some creative or technical reason. Carrying out run-throughs allows all members of the team to practise both running the studio and working their way through the actual programme, albeit without the actual guests. If this is the first experience of a studio, it helps the crew to feel much more comfortable about what they are doing and can make the difference between an ordinary and a very good or excellent programme. It is at this stage that you will consider carefully both the technical and creative aspects of your programme and carry out any necessary final fault-finding and problem-solving. This could be creative (for example, if an item doesn't work, you can drop it or, if it is too long, it can be trimmed), technical (for example, the lighting isn't right so lamps need moving) or a mixture of both (for example, the camera composition doesn't look good so alternatives have to be found). Guests should not be present for run-throughs as this will adversely affect the final interview. You will therefore need to ask a stand-in to come on to set and do the interview as fully and professionally as possible. This can be a member of the crew, a friend or a tutor, but the key point is that he/she must complete the whole interview. For presenters, doing a run-through allows them to feel comfortable with the set that they will inhabit for the duration of the programme. At the run-through, minor changes can be made: if major changes are needed here, you are in trouble and have a very long night ahead of you.

If you have time, you should attempt a final run-through, which should be a complete run-through *without stopping*.

Only now are you ready to enter the production stage.

Production

The production stage for the magazine programme is extremely important as it is recorded live and, as a result, you only have one real shot at your takes: any mistakes that you make are there for all to see and cannot be covered up in post-production. That is why spending so long on the pre-production stage really does pay dividends. If you took the time fully to research and develop your ideas and to prepare for the production date, the shoot itself should be relatively straightforward.

Although this puts a lot of pressure on to you as a group, it should also focus your minds on the importance of making sure that you know exactly what you are doing long before the production date. There is relatively little to say at this point other than that you need to understand the correct working procedures and potential problems.

Studio procedures and roles and responsibilities

At the pre-production stage you should either have chosen or been allocated a specific production role or, if you are working in a relatively small group, multiple roles. Each one has specific functions and these knit together seamlessly in order to make the production work effectively. Even though you are now splitting into the two distinct production areas of studio and gallery, it is vital that you continue to function as one team. What is equally important is that everyone in the team should know both his/her responsibilities and the procedures which should be followed in the studio.

Potential problems (and how to overcome them)

The problems which are faced over and over again by students working in a studio for the first time fall into three main areas: lack of confidence about the equipment, the pressure of a live shoot and members of the group not doing what they should. All of these problems can be avoided:

1. *Lack of confidence about the equipment* results when students have not spent sufficient time learning how to use it. Make sure that you have all had enough time to research your jobs properly and that you have allocated enough pre-production time to learn how to use the equipment properly. If you do that ...
2. *the pressure of a live shoot* will disappear. People normally feel under pressure when they are unsure or lacking in confidence. If you know what

you are supposed to be doing, then you will do it without even thinking about it. If you are in that lucky position, then the problem of …

3. *members of the group not doing what they should* will disappear: nobody within the group will be treading on anyone else's toes and the shoot will go swimmingly!

The problems are all related: sort one aspect out and the others will resolve themselves!

Finishing off

In the elation of getting through the recording, make sure that you finish off properly. This is good professional practice and includes the following:

- Tidy up the studio, making sure that you leave the equipment in the order that your institution requires it.
- Remove every trace of your production from the studio. Not only is this good professional practice but it also means that the group which follows you does not have to spend a large part of their precious studio time clearing up after you. Put yourself in the situation of having to do this and think about how you would feel and you should never forget to tidy up.
- Make sure that all props and costumes rented or borrowed are returned in the condition in which you received them. Make sure that you write a formal letter of thanks and ensure that you use the name of the person or organization who lent them in the final credits. It really does mean a lot to people outside the production to see their name on the video. Make sure that you send them a copy of the video.

Post-production

It is possible to produce studio productions which are recorded and then edited in exactly the same way as other videos. The great thing about producing a live, or as-live, production is that once the programme is over, so is the production process. This means no logging, digitizing, editing, etc. However, you should make sure that the master copies of your programme, along with all the production paperwork, are suitably stored.

Distribution

As with all the briefs in this book, we think that you should always see the final stage of your project as an opportunity to promote your work to the largest possible audience so that everyone else can see how wonderful it is. We mentioned above that magazine programmes tend to be produced by large media organizations but increasingly there are some very good examples on the internet that you should investigate. It is here that you might want to think about screening your work: if your product is good and innovative, there is nothing to stop you either setting up a website and producing regular programmes (that your audience can videocast) or pitching your idea to a community channel or internet broadcaster.

Our top ten tips for the production of magazine programmes:

1. Plan, plan, plan! As this a complex project which effectively ends at the production stage, you need a very clear timeline to take you there.
2. Know your audience and what they want, not what you think they want.
3. Keep your articles short and sweet. Three minutes is good, five minutes is flabby!
4. Remember to have a good mixture of articles to keep your audience happy and entertained.
5. Get the running order right. It helps the crew, set and programme to work effectively.
6. Designing, constructing and dressing your set is time very well spent. It creates the appropriate backdrop within which your presenters will work.
7. The presenter is the public face of your production so make sure that you find a good one!
8. Find guests and interviewees who have something interesting to say and give them the space to say it.
9. Work as a team! Studio production is all about individuals uniting and working like a well-oiled machine.
10. Presenters' scripts should be very basic, allowing them the space to perform their magic.

8 The Documentary

Introduction

Despite the huge number of different types of documentary, it is often the brief that students find 'boring'. One of the main reasons for this may be the relatively narrow range of documentaries to which many of us are normally exposed. As Sheila Curran Bernard (2004: 5) notes:

> It seems [...] that general awareness of the documentary form has been confused by a crowded schedule of 'reality' programming that is often anything but and by programming that is rightly called 'documentary' but is often mediocre, if not stale – stories of predators and prey, autopsies, deadly weather and celebrities. Like junk food, it may be temporarily satisfying but offers little in the way of actual nourishment.

Following the success over the last few years of a range of cinema documentaries such as *Fahrenheit 9/11*, *Supersize Me*, *The Story of the Weeping Camel*, *Touching the Void* and *An Inconvenient Truth* and as a consequence of the number and importance of documentary festivals worldwide and the proliferation of imaginative and stimulating websites which both analyse and screen documentary work, that situation has changed and documentary is now more likely to be perceived as being an interesting and valid brief. It is the kind of brief which allows for truly exciting and innovative work to be produced and it is precisely this type of documentary, rather than the mediocre or stale, that we want you to produce.

Before you can begin the process of pre-production for your own documentary, though, you need to know exactly what is meant when talking about documentary. If we look at two definitions of documentary, one from a 'practitioner' and one from a 'theorist', we can see that they define it as follows:

> *[Documentary is] the presentation of factual information about real people, places and events, generally portrayed through the use of actual images and artifacts.* (Bernard 2004: 2)

Documentary is the loose and often highly contested label given, internationally, to certain kinds of film and television (and sometimes radio programmes) which reflect and report on 'the real' through the use of recorded images and sounds of actuality. (Corner 1996: 2)

Although Corner's definition provides a sense that defining documentary is not without its problems, both definitions consider documentaries to be factual in that they show real events which are recorded, or portrayed, by documentary makers. This is a good starting point.

Tasks to do

So that you may explore the broad range of documentary practice before beginning production, we would suggest that you carry out a content analysis study and do the following:

1. Construct a grid which allows you systematically to record the following information: the title of the documentary, its subject, its main elements (interviews, presenter, reconstructions, etc.), the likely audience, where it was screened, the time of screening and the duration.
2. Watch as many different documentaries as possible – on television, in the cinema and on the internet – and fill in the grid. We would suggest that a minimum of six documentaries of different types should be studied. We would also suggest that you look at documentaries produced from the beginning of the twentieth century onwards, not just those from the last five years.
3. Once you have completed the grid, look at the examples you have chosen and compare and contrast them to see what the differences and similarities are. If you can, characterize them into subgenres of documentary in terms of form (for example, docu-soap or fly-on-the-wall) or content (for example, medical or wildlife).

Contextual research

You will remember that we strongly urge you to contextualize your work by considering theory at all stages of the production process, but especially at the initial stage, before you begin the pre-production of your own ideas. So, at this stage you must either let your ideas be informed by theory or at least be aware of how theories of documentary relate to your own ideas and have a clear understanding of the full range of documentary styles which exist. The reason that contextual research is so important at this stage is that it allows you to establish:

- the kinds of ideas which would or would not be produced in the real world and the form that they would be likely to take;
- how similar subjects have been treated in the past;
- the different styles of documentary which exist and upon which you can draw in the production of your own documentary.

Luckily for you, documentary is a popular area of academic study and, as a result, there is much academic writing about documentary. Unfortunately for you, it is in reading these resources that you will start to realize why it is, as is made explicit in Corner's definition of documentary above, such a contested term and what difficulties this may pose for your production.

An integral part of your research for documentary should involve you actively researching this documentary theory and supplementing it by using the key concepts of I CARLING to contextualize and inform your own practice. Let us go through the key concepts and see how they can do this. Remember, though, that the following discussions only point you in the direction of the key issues and writings and are only the beginning of your research, not the end.

Institutions

Space does not allow us to provide a detailed history of documentary. For that, you should consult the resources listed in the bibliography. What should be apparent from even the most cursory of research is that there have been, and remain, many different institutional sources for documentary. What should also be evident is that the institutional source of a documentary almost inevitably affects both the form and content of the resulting documentary.

So, if one thinks about the institutional status of contemporary documentary, the majority of documentaries are commissioned by major broadcasters – Richard Kilborn and John Izod (1997: 166) give a figure of 90 per cent for 1995 – and this will almost certainly affect their form and content. The fact that they are produced within the confines of major media institutions means that they will often share both the values and attitudes of the institution and the relatively conventional form of the institution's products. Much of the documentary work within the UK, for example, has been the output of such media organizations. It is a crass generalization but, on the whole, the desire to attract audiences and the public service ethos of UK broadcasters have led to certain types of broadly educational and informative documentaries being produced by the people working within those institutions. The converse is that, with certain notable exceptions through the years, overtly political and stylistically radical productions have tended not to be produced within the institutional confines of the major broadcasters.

That is not to say that major institutions *always* produce relatively conservative documentary. For example, a key moment for British documentary production came with the founding of Channel 4 as a result of the 1981 Broadcasting Act. Uniquely in British broadcasting, the channel did not produce any of its own programming but was required by the terms of the act to source it from independent production companies. It gave a whole new institutional ethos to the channel and what subsequently became known as the Workshop Agreement was one of the key results. This agreement meant that novice and community documentary-makers were able to produce work that to this day looks and feels fresh and vibrant owing to its political and stylistic innovation. This was certainly not characteristic of the output of the other major broadcasters in the 1980s.

However, the stranglehold of the major institutions on documentary production may now be ending or has, according to certain commentators, already ended. The increasing number of cable and satellite television stations in all parts of the world has meant that a much wider range of documentary practice is now screened on television. More significantly in the last ten years, the growth of dedicated user-generated documentary websites such as *Four Docs* in the UK and *Trigger Street* in the US, which rely on people submitting their own documentaries produced outside the usual institutions, has meant that fresh and vibrant documentary has a space for distribution which was previously denied to it. Even more importantly, more general user-generated sites such as *YouTube* and *My Space* have enabled those with access to a camcorder and a computer to produce 'documentary' work which has no institutional constraints, although clearly there are still residual legal and ethical guidelines to which such work has to adhere. The vibrancy of the work on user-generated sites may be one of the reasons why most young people today define mainstream documentary as 'boring', although, like Bernard, we would argue that much of this type of documentary work is superficial, lacking in rigour, has only a superficial relationship to the real and is ultimately unsatisfying.

Remember that although, for this brief, you will working outside the institutional constraints of mainstream broadcasters and this should allow you a degree of freedom that people working within major media institutions would envy, you will be working within those constraints imposed by your educational institution, by the specific brief and by the distribution channel(s) on which you exhibit your work, all of which need to be at the forefront of your mind throughout the process of production.

Context

Andrew Britton (quoted in Nelmes 1996) makes the point that:

truly great documentaries are analytical in the sense that they present the corner of reality with which they deal not as truth there to be observed, but as a social and historical reality which can only be understood in the context of the forces and actions that produced it.

While many good documentaries do contextualize the reality that they are representing, few (even great ones) explicitly address the 'forces and actions' which give rise to them *as a documentary*. As a student of media you must be able to analyse critically and to contextualize both the reality being shown within documentaries and the production of the documentary by reflecting upon what those forces and actions might be.

John Corner (quoted in Nelmes 1996: 190) has suggested that there are three main contexts which need to be explored when examining documentary:

1. technological factors;
2. the sociological dimensions;
3. aesthetic concerns.

We would add one more: the economic context of production.

If we look at the first of Corner's contexts, the technological context, we can see how changing technologies of production and distribution have had, and continue to have, a direct influence on the form and content of documentaries. At the birth of film at the end of the nineteenth century, *all* films were documentaries in the sense that they documented real life and real events as they happened. One of the main reasons for this was that the cameras used could only hold a certain amount of film, which meant that the films produced were limited to one or two minutes and, as a result, there was little time to develop a narrative. In addition, the cameras were relatively large and cumbersome and therefore not easy to transport. The result was that this early documentary cinema was formally characterized by static shots in one location recorded with no sound. The early films of, for example, the Lumière brothers in France documented such a reality: *La Sortie des ouvriers de l'Usine Lumière* (*Workers Leaving the Lumière Factory*), widely acknowledged as the world's first moving picture, and *L'|Arrivée d'un train en gare à La Ciotat* (*Arrival of a Train at La Ciotat*) tended to show real events or, in the French term which is still widely accepted, *actualités* (Cook 2004: 9–11). Clearly, more recent technological developments such as the introduction of 16mm film, and later Super 8, in the 1960s, portable video technology in the 1970s and 1980s, DV and HDV technology in the 1990s and sophisticated mobile phones with high-resolution cameras in the 2000s has significantly affected, and continues to affect, the subject and form of documentary.

There is also a social and political context to documentary production.

Documentary makers live and work in a particular time and place and in particular political circumstances and their work is inevitably informed by these conditions. So, for example, the documentaries of two of the earliest documentary makers, John Grierson in the UK and Dziga Vertov in the Soviet Union, were inextricably linked with the social and political conditions of the time. For Grierson, an institutional base within the state-run GPO Film Unit meant that his documentaries and writings on documentary had a liberal notion of the social responsibility of documentary to educate and inform its viewers. For Vertov, a similar position in the Soviet Union's revolutionary film unit meant that his output was able to be more formally revolutionary.

Corner's third context is the aesthetic context. The term 'aesthetics' refers to the 'look' of the finished video. For Corner, there are certain tools that the documentary maker can use to help construct the aesthetics of a documentary. He usefully highlights and tries to categorize the main rules of documentary language in terms of the 'visual modes' and 'modes of speech' used within the range of documentary. He characterizes these 'modalities of documentary language' (1996: 27–30) as shown in Table 8.1.

Table 8.1   Modalities of documentary language (taken from Corner, 1996)

Visual modes	**Evidential mode 1: reactive observationalism** Minimal directorial influence … fly-on-the-wall.
	Evidential mode 2: proactive observationalism Here, a scene or sequence adopts the basic mode of observationalism, but with the management of the pro-filmic allowing increased scopic mobility … a more discursive use of *mise-en-scène* and smoother time compressions.
	Evidential mode 3: illustrative The visualization is subordinate to verbal discourses, acting in support of their propositions or arguments, which they can frequently only partially 'confirm'.
	Associative mode Here, the visualization is primarily engaged in the making of second order meanings, producing a kind of visual exposition or visual evaluation.
Modes of speech	**Evidential mode 1: overheard exchange** This is the speech of overheard subjects, whose ostensible reason for speaking is to be located in the pro-filmic action.
	Evidential mode 2: testimony This is interview speech, variously obtained and used.
	Expositional mode The 'classic' mode of documentary speech, including full and partial commentary, occasional out of frame bridging, presenter direct address, etc.

Increasingly, and especially since the 1980s and 1990s, there has also been an overriding economic context to much documentary production, even for public service broadcasters. The need for existing channels to maximize their audiences and for the increasing number of terrestrial, cable and satellite television channels to fill up their schedules meant that new types of 'documentary' programmes began to emerge. Rather than having any sort of social responsibility, the main aim of such programming was often entertainment in order to maximize audiences. As a result the 1990s saw the emergence of, for example, the docu-soap: a hybrid of documentary (in that it dealt with real people and real situations) and soap opera (in that it narrativized for entertainment purposes the situations and interactions between the people involved). This commodification meant that an increasingly prevalent strain of what might be termed 'branded documentary' programmes began to appear: in the UK, for example, there was a range of sensational medical documentaries on Channel 5. It is frequently this type of commodified documentary that Bernard isolates as being mediocre and stale in the initial quote in this chapter.

Audience

We have seen in previous chapters that there has been a move away from simply analysing texts for embedded meaning and then assuming the audience's response (as in a semiotic methodology) towards a more nuanced notion of the audience as being active in making meaning. So, it is in the relationship between the text and the audience that the meaning of the text resides (Barthes 1977; Hall 1980).

For Richard Kilborn and John Izod (1997: 215), there are two main issues to consider when thinking about documentary audiences:

1. 'Broadcaster–audience relations': that is, the strategies that 'broadcasters have devised to attract an audience'.
2. 'Audience–viewer relations': that is, the 'ways in which viewers make sense of documentaries: what enlightenment or pleasure they derive from them and what impact, if any, individual documentaries might have on influencing their views on a range of contemporary or historical issues'.

Clearly, both issues need to be considered not only when analysing existing documentaries but also when considering the audience for your own documentary.

Representation

While there is a general perception that documentaries are *objective*, showing things 'as they really are', as a student of communication, media or culture, you should be extremely critical of such an idea. From earlier chapters and your wider reading, you should already be aware of some of the debates around the problematic relationship between reality and its representation within any media text. You should also be aware that at each stage of the process of production – thinking of an idea, thinking about how to present it, choosing what to shoot and what to leave out, and making decisions about editing – the personal, *subjective* ideas of the film-maker and the institution for which he/she is working will pervade the documentary. One of the key theoretical ideas that you need to consider in terms of documentary, therefore, is that of the truth status of the video: what has been termed its *verisimilitude*.

We saw above that the earliest films produced at the end of the nineteenth century were termed *actualités* because they appeared simply to record actuality: that is, what was there. However, as technology and film-making techniques changed following the birth of film, fiction and *actualités* diverged. Narrative cinema started to develop the rules of continuity editing discussed in Chapters 5 and 6 in order to heighten the pace and excitement of the narrative.

By the 1930s, the term 'documentary' had been coined by one of the UK's leading film-makers and theorists of documentary, John Grierson. For him, documentary was superior to 'fictional cinema' in that it engaged with the real rather than fantasy. In what was one of the earliest and now one of the most famous declarations of the purpose of documentary, Grierson noted that documentary was not simply the reporting of the real world: for him, this was the job of journalists and newsreels. Rather, it was about the *creative outline of actuality*: that is, the revealing or enhancing of reality through the 'arrangement, rearrangement and shaping of it' (in Corner 1996: 12). So, in a famous sequence in one of Britain's most well-known documentaries, *Night Mail*, the creative outline of actuality is achieved by matching the reality of postal workers on a post train to a W. B. Yeats poem, the rhythm of which echoes the rhythm of the train's wheels.

As Brian Winston (1995) notes, however, the extent of the creativity used by many documentary makers throughout the history of the genre actually problematizes the idea of 'reality'. The most famous example of this creative outline of actuality for entertainment purposes was Robert Flaherty's film, *Nanook of the North*. The first feature-length documentary in the world, this documentary about the Inuit people of Northern Canada staged certain sequences using clothing that the Inuit no longer wore and activities that they no longer undertook so that it looked more 'real' and reflected the outdated expectations of people in America.

It is this tension between actuality – the real world and events within it –

and the range of possible representations – the ability of the documentary maker creatively to enhance it – which has exercised documentary makers and theorists of documentary, often one and the same, since the inception of the genre. It is something that you will inevitably have to consider, whatever subject you choose for your documentary. The waters are now even muddier. Brian Winston (1995) makes the point that, in his opinion, we have entered a period of 'post-Griersonian' documentary: that is, that the truth status of documentary can no longer be relied upon. The reason for this is that the scale and pace of digital technological developments have meant that 'the challenge of digitalization cannot be resisted. Digitalization destroys the photographic image as evidence of anything other than the process of digitalization' (1995: 259) and he calls for a rewriting of the relationship between actuality and its representation within such documentary. Of course, technological developments have since advanced at an even greater pace and an awareness of the truth status of documentary has to be central to any documentary maker. What is interesting for us, especially on the user-generated content sites we mentioned above, is the apparent move towards a 'pre-Griersonian' style, a style that the Lumière brothers would have instantly recognized: static single shots, long takes and a lack of any visual or sound effects.

This idea of representation is one that you have to consider fully with regard to your own idea, as it is *your* choices which will influence the content of the video and, as a result, your viewers' opinions. It is a position that you, as a documentary film-maker, cannot ignore or indeed underestimate. What you decide to film or not to film and what you decide to include or omit in the edit will influence the preferred reading of your documentary.

Language

We saw above that documentaries, like every other media text, are constructed artefacts and use rules to make meaning in specific ways. We saw, for example, John Corner's useful categorization of the main rules of documentary language in terms of the 'visual modes' and 'modes of speech' used within documentary. If we think about the building blocks of documentary of whatever type, they tend to use similar elements – for example, interviews with experts, vox pops with members of the public, illustrative footage, graphics, footage from archive sources – all of which can be put together in any number of ways.

In *Introduction to Documentary*, Bill Nichols begins to categorize the different types of language used within documentary by defining six 'modes' of documentary related both to their institutional manner of production and their content and style:

- *Poetic mode:* these are documentaries which rely upon a more abstract, lyrical form and are usually associated with 1920s documentary and modernist ideals: for example, the work of Dziga Vertov's *Man With a Movie Camera* (1929) and Walter Ruttman's *Berlin: Symphony of a Great City* (1931). However, this is still a popular mode for documentary makers.
- *Expository mode:* these documentaries contain a direct address to their audience. The elements which make up the subject of the documentary are assembled into a coherent form by what is known as a *voice-of-God* narration. As Richard Kilborn and John Izod (1997: 58) note: 'The script is no less than the primary organizer of meaning, and lays out the argument or story which the images themselves sometimes do no more than confirm.'
- *Observational mode:* as technology had advanced by the 1960s and cameras had become smaller and lighter and able to document reality in a less intrusive manner, so less control over lighting etc. was required, leaving the social actors free to act and the documentarists able to record without interacting with them. This is often divided into two distinct subcategories: direct cinema, which relates to those observational documentaries produced by North American documentary makers working within this style, and the *cinéma vérité* of French documentarists It is what has become known in general parlance as fly-on-the-wall documentary. Kilborn and Izod note that the rise of this mode of documentary was directly related to the demands of, and viewing situation for, television.
- *Participatory mode:* in this type of documentary, the encounter between film-maker and subject is recorded and the film-maker actively engages with the situation he/she is documenting, asking questions of the subjects and sharing experiences with them. It is heavily reliant on the honesty of the witnesses. This type of documentary is associated with documentary makers such as Nick Broomfield, Molly Dineen and Michael Moore.
- *Reflexive mode:* as the name suggests, this type of documentary actively and consciously engages with the process of producing and reading documentary. By that we mean that such documentaries do not claim to be transparent 'windows on the world' but encourage the viewer to question both the subject of the documentary and the form of the documentary itself. It is largely seen to have arisen in the 1970s and 1980s.
- *Performative mode:* such documentary acknowledges the emotional and subjective aspects of documentary and presents ideas as part of a context, having different meanings for different people. They are often autoboiographical in nature.

However, these categories are not without their critics. Stella Bruzzi, for example, takes issue with Nichols's apparent premise that 'documentary has evolved along

Darwinian lines' (2000:1). For her, the periodising nature of Nichols's categories is problematic as, in seeing the modes as being representative of a certain era, there is a suggestion that each mode improves upon the ones which preceded it. For her, this is untenable. More fundamentally, though, she argues that such a periodising is misguided by providing examples of documentaries of different modes which were produced before they were supposed to have evolved.

Ideology

If we accept that all documentaries express some sort of representational position, then all documentaries, however hard they strive not to, will exhibit an ideological position. As with any media text, this may support the dominant ideology or, which is less likely, may go against it. A key part of your research when analysing existing documentaries is to isolate their ideological position through, for example, semiotic analysis.

Clearly, the institutional position that we discussed earlier will affect such a position in that documentary makers, either consciously or subconsciously, will be affected by and will internalize the institutional ethos within which they are working. As a result, individual documentaries will exhibit an ideological position with regard to the subject that they are supposed to be examining objectively. However, that may substantially overestimate the institutional power of most media institutions and significantly underestimate the relative autonomy of documentary makers and the extent to which documentary has, historically, been a space for the examination and criticism of established ways of seeing the world and existing structures of power.

More fundamentally, though, the notion of objectivity which underpins both documentary as a genre and individual documentaries is one of the key ideological aspects of the genre. The idea, from the birth of film onwards, that documentary merely records 'the real' conceals the fact that all media texts are constructed and that, in their construction, the views, biases and predilections of the documentary maker will inform each of the stages of production. The fact that the production process and the lack of true objectivity is effaced or hidden in most documentaries, especially in observational documentaries, is, for most theorists of documentary, their key ideological position. See Bruzzi (2000) for an informed discussion of such criticisms about documentary makers and their documentaries.

Of course, some documentaries make absolutely no claim to be objective but, on the contrary, glory in their constructed nature and subjectivity. Modernist documentary makers of the 1920s and 1930s, for example, especially those in what was then the Soviet Union, highlighted the production process within the film, precisely to make points about the constructed and ideological nature of film. A key example of this is the documentary mentioned above, Dziga Vertov's classic documentary *Man With the Movie Camera* (1929), where the man with the camera is deliberately shown throughout the film, as is the editing process (see Petric 1987 for a full discussion of Vertov's theoretical deliberations about documentary and his practice). This foregrounding of the process of production was a key feature of the first avant-garde of the 1930s, the second avant-garde of the 1960s and 1970s and more contemporary documentary production in, for example, a subgenre of reflexive documentaries called essay-films (Lopate 1997).

Narrative

If one starts with an idea of documentary as a 'factual' genre which simply shows what is there, then the idea of narrative seems to be an odd concept. However, an examination of narrative is central to the analysis and production of documentary. We saw above that all documentaries treat reality creatively in order to convey a message and, in so doing, tell stories about people, places or events.

What this means in practice is that most of the techniques of storytelling that you have already explored and will explore in more detail in the next chapter are utilized by documentary makers to construct and structure their documentary. Documentary makers give thought to characters and how they are represented, narrative structure, point of view and style. You must research this area more fully as it has direct relevance to the content of your own documentary.

Genre

If we accept that the defining characteristics of documentary are those that we isolated at the beginning of the chapter – they are factual, showing real events which are recorded or portrayed by documentary makers – then it might be possible to talk about documentary as a discrete genre. However, theorists of documentary would argue that these features are so general and are common to such a wide range of media output that it makes such a claim almost impossible to bear out. As Kilborn and Izod note, 'the label "documentary" is now attached to a much wider range of audio-visual material than when it began to be used in the pre-war era [...] "Documentary" has in short become a *portmanteau* word with multiple points of reference' (1997: 13). For them, the idea that it is possible to talk about *one* genre of documentary which shares a coherent set of codes and conventions is problematic and, as for other theorists of documentary, for them it makes much more sense to talk of subgenres of documentary.

From the activity at the beginning of the chapter and from the discussions above, you should have begun to see that different types of documentary have discrete and distinct codes and conventions. So, it is possible to talk about the widely accepted subgenres of documentary that Nichols categorizes above.

Finally, it is worth making the point that there is an increasing hybridity of output both within the documentary genre as a whole and within the different subgenres, with the codes and conventions from different subgenres being combined. As Corner (1996: 1–2) notes, these 'inter-generic mixings and explorations [open up] new imaginative possibilities for documentary'. It is for this reason that many students now find documentary exciting to work on and it is these possibilities that we hope you will take up in the production of your own documentary.

Pre-production

Anyone working professionally within documentary production is likely to agree wholeheartedly with Cartwright's 70–30–10 rule. Central to the success of any documentary, whatever its form or content, is the 70 per cent of time that should be spent on pre-production. All of you will, by now, possess the necessary technical skills to go out and shoot a documentary but it is only with a lot of thought and effort that you will be able to produce a *good,* or even great, documentary. In this section of the chapter, then, we will focus primarily on those aspects of the pre-production stage which are the most important in order to complete this brief successfully: most notably, coming up with good ideas for your documentary and researching for production.

Thinking of ideas

Thinking of a range of ideas and narrowing it down

As we have already discussed, there are a large number of subgenres within documentary: from the relatively unsophisticated video diary to fly-on-the-wall documentary to highly constructed, artistic, impressionistic documentary. Each works to different codes and conventions with regard to style, structure and content, but to be successful they all need to be interesting in terms of style, structure or content. That is to say that either the chosen subject needs to be unusual, novel, entertaining, emotive or stimulating *or*, if the subject is ordinary, it needs to be explored in an innovative way. That is why a range of good initial ideas is fundamental to the success of the finished video.

In addition to the usual places where you might look for ideas, as outlined in Chapter 3, it is worth remembering the widespread adage: start with what you know. Many students faced with producing their first documentary think that a good idea involves addressing a vast subject such as global warming or world famine, but you don't have to tackle such a huge subject. Local events can be just as rewarding to make and interesting to watch and are more readily accessible because they are on your doorstep. So, think about *your* world and the things within it as a starting point. Although you may think that your life is boring and of interest to nobody, it might be a rich source of ideas: have you recently learned a new skill? Are you in any clubs or societies? Have you done anything that nobody else you know has done?

An equally fascinating subject matter for documentary is other people. The interaction and behaviour of a well-chosen group of people will provide you with instant content for your documentary. One of the most interesting student documentaries we have seen recently was concerned with the coverage of a My Little Pony convention. The documentary dealt with the obvious fascination shared by the people at the convention for a simple plastic toy animal: who are the people who collect them and why do they do it? Why would anyone go to a convention such as this? What do they talk about? What do they have in common? Do they collect anything else and, if so, what and why?

You will remember from previous chapters that we recommend that you come up with ten ideas at this stage. To show you how easy this should be when producing a documentary, we conducted an experiment. Returning on the train from a meeting in London, we arrived at our station at about 8.30 p.m., took the ten-minute walk from the station to our car and tried to think of as many ideas as possible during that walk. Below are some of the ideas generated, all of which could, with time and effort, make for a great documentary:

- *Train-spotters*: at the far end of Platform 4 stood a gaggle of train-spotters. What we noticed was that modern train-spotters don't use just notebooks; they use high-end digital still and video cameras, presumably to share their findings with other train-spotters over the internet: 199 websites when we looked! So, any documentary about modern train-spotters could include the following: discussion about why they do it and what they get out of it; how they share their passion with other train-spotters; what they do when they are not out train-spotting; what jobs they have. A second potential documentary could focus on capturing the excitement and genuine interest of the activity itself: you could record the train-spotters as they exchange stories about trains; you could create wonderful sequences with careful shooting of visuals and recording of the sounds which can only be found at stations; you could record the ebb and flow of travellers and what they think of train-spotters. This is the real joy of your documentary: you have captured the essence of what makes a railway station and indeed what continues to attract individuals who are prepared to spend hours standing on the platform in all weathers. Also interesting to note was the fact that one of them was a woman: a third potential documentary.

- *A messy subject*: narrowly avoiding treading in some excrement as we walked away from the station led us to consider dogs and their owners. We've probably all done this and have an opinion about owners who let their dogs foul the pavement and so interviews with members of the public, dog owners, doctors, environmental health officers and local dog wardens could all be used to explore the idea of responsible dog ownership. Personal opinions from members of the public and discussion about health implications and the process of prosecuting dog owners could all go to make a great documentary.

- *Novas and Fiestas*: just around the corner from the railway station was a large car park. To our surprise, it was full of cars all parked randomly, not in the usual straight lines. Furthermore, all the cars were small hatchbacks which had been customized and adapted. Most of the occupants were young people. What were they doing there? Do they meet every week? Their cars must be what bring them together, but what else do they talk about? How much have they spent on customizing their vehicles? What have they done to them? What do the authorities and the general public think of them gathering like this? How much is their insurance? Do women become involved and, if so, how? This was yet another potential documentary waiting to be filmed.

- *Heel boy, heel!*: further on, we passed a dog-training session in progress. A documentary about this could include interviews with owners and trainers, footage of the animals in training and the owners and their dogs working as one. What types of training do they go through? Is it the dog who is being trained or the owner? What happens when dogs don't do as they are told? Is there a social aspect to the club? Are there any love-interest stories or scandals among either the owners or the dogs? Are there any funny dog stories?

- *Local organic farmers:* on the wall at the side of the local supermarket was a small poster promoting the local organic food market. Again, this could be an interesting documentary which could include any or all of the following: interviews with organic farmers, especially if they were interesting characters and prepared to talk about what their jobs entailed; interviews with the customers; shots of the farm and the produce; a discussion with farming experts about the benefits of growing and eating organic food; discussion about lifestyle choices, costs, health; interviews with people who eat only organic foods and/or interviews with people who eat only fast food or pre-prepared meals.

- *A day in the life of ...*: just as we were getting into our car, we noticed the torn front cover of a copy of *The Big Issue* lying in the gutter. Our thoughts turned to the many individuals we had seen selling copies of the magazine, which prompted us to consider other individuals or characters who might be worth looking at:
  - the local eccentric;
  - a local radio station, DJ or band;
  - any interesting or colourful well-known local characters: the gymnastic champion, the war hero, the man who has built a full-size replica of the bridge from the Starship Enterprise in his lounge;
  - people within local clubs and societies who are fanatical about their interests;
  - the people doing the jobs that nobody sees or wants to know about: the person who sifts through the waste at the local sewerage plant, refuse collectors, those who work at the local crematorium.

The points we are making here are that:

- all these ideas were really easy to come up: we were just looking around while doing what we normally do;
- there are endless opportunities for creating good content with only a little bit of thought, even from the most basic of ideas;
- although the ideas you come up with may initially seem 'boring', they all offer the opportunity for you to make something really interesting out of them, especially if you work hard on creating an innovative structure or style.

At this stage, it is up to you to go out and find ideas that you think are interesting. If each person in your group does what we did, within ten minutes you could have thirty or forty ideas on the table to choose from!

Assessing the feasibility of your ten best ideas

This brief is likely to be different from those for your previous productions because it is a noticeable step up. Your title sequence was probably restricted in its scope and duration and the magazine programme was recorded as-live in a controlled environment in a short space of time. The documentary is likely to be more complex in that it potentially involves multiple locations, numerous members of the public and the production takes place over a longer period of time.

You need to test each of your initial ideas with regard to its feasibility by talking through the same limiters as in the previous two briefs. However, we would add one more limiter which is specific to assessing the feasibility of ideas for documentary production: ethics. By ethics, we mean the codes of moral behaviour which govern the production of truthful and objective documentary. Whereas in your previous videos you did not really have to consider the ethics of the content of your video, for documentary production it should be central to your considerations. The reason for this is that you will be representing real people and real events and, as a documentary maker, you have a responsibility to represent them fairly and truthfully. This is not solely a legal requirement when broadcasting your documentary, it is the minimum that people agreeing to appear in your video should expect from you.

Carrying out research on each of your remaining ideas

The documentary brief really does require more work at the stage of having three ideas than the previous briefs, owing to its depth and its 'unknowability'. As you are dealing with actuality, you need to know as much as possible about each of the ideas to prevent problems later on in the process. You should, therefore, use the limiters to help understand your three ideas. Key points of your research might include:

- *Finance:* each of your ideas will cost something to produce, no matter how local you decide to keep it. The actual cost will depend on the idea but is related to the main items of expenditure:
  - *Transport:* this is fundamental to the success of your production, as you will need to move crew, kit and contributors around, possibly to multiple locations on a number of different days. So, at this stage, you really need to think about convenience, time and costs. Convenience and timing are important considerations. You must fully investigate all of your options at this stage and compare and contrast each potential travel option for each your three ideas. If you have access to a car, this is often the most convenient and cost-effective option, as you are free to travel where and whenever you wish. Buses or trains may appear to be cheaper but are likely to be much more limited. Don't forget that your transport costs may rise significantly if your documentary is not based locally. Do not, however, dismiss the possibility of filming outside your immediate locality. Flights to a faraway destination, for example, can be cheaper than taking a train within your own country, especially if you use your student discount!

- *Stock:* although it depends on the type of documentary you are shooting, a typical shooting ratio for documentary is 20:1: that is, twenty hours of footage are recorded for every hour of screen time. It can be much more: we recently shot 25 one-hour tapes for a 28-minute documentary. You will therefore need to think about how many tapes or how much storage media you will need for each of your ideas and how much it will cost.
- *Kit:* most documentary crews use only one camera and so you will probably not have a long list of kit, but make sure you think about what you might need to realize each idea fully. If you cannot obtain all of it from your educational institution, you may need to hire some of it, so you need to think carefully about what you might need to hire, where to get it from and how much it will cost. Don't forget that the more specialist the kit, the more difficult to source and expensive to hire it is likely to be.
- *Accommodation:* some of your ideas might require you to book accommodation for the crew and contributors. If so, how much will it cost? This will depend on where and when you are filming, for how long and the type of accommodation you choose.
- *Catering:* the cost of feeding the crew and contributors should be taken into account. If you are acting as host for a number of contributors, you should cater for them in return for their contributions. Feeding your crew and contributors could be expensive so think about the different options: from making your own meals to feeding everyone in a restaurant.
- *Presenters:* if you intend your documentary to be introduced by a presenter, you should aim, wherever possible, to use a professional and to pay him/her. Although you may not be able to afford to pay the full union rate, you may be able to afford the student Equity rate or, at the very least, cover expenses. Be as accurate as possible about the number of days you will need to pay the presenter for. If the presenter is central to an idea you should factor in the cost of auditions.
- *Contributors:* although interviews are generally given free of charge, some individuals may need to have their expenses met, especially if they are travelling to you to be interviewed.
- *Logistics:* whatever your documentary, you and your crew need to get to places to set up and shoot. Each idea will have different requirements logistically. Ideas which involve a considerable number of locations or long distances will pose more of a logistical challenge than, say, an idea which uses one or two local locations. When thinking about each idea, consider your crew size and the equipment that you will be using, how you intend to move it and the time that you have available for filming.

- *Health and Safety:* now that you have definite ideas, it should be possible to start the process of carrying out a risk assessment for each production. This process is likely to be more complicated than previously as you will probably be working in public places, over a longer period, in different situations and with a larger number of people.
- *Technical resources:* you should already have made a mental list of the kit that you need for each of your ideas. You should now find out whether it is available on the days that you are likely to require it. It is pointless to pursue an idea which requires equipment that you cannot access when you need it or, in the case of specialist equipment, that you cannot afford.
- *Human resources:* your remaining ideas are likely to include people from outside the crew and your immediate circle of family and friends, so the key consideration at this stage is whether you are able to find these individuals and, if so, whether these individuals will agree to appear in the documentary.
- *Expertise and ability of the crew:* does your crew have the necessary skills and expertise to realize each of the ideas well? What sort of training will they require, not just in terms of using the equipment but also with regard to interview techniques and working professionally while under the scrutiny of the general public?
- *Time:* you will need to consider how much time will be required to conduct thorough research for each idea, especially if numerous locations need to be recced, many individuals need to be contacted or permission sought. You will also need to assess the number of days required for filming and the ease of access to the various locations. This is important because it can occupy much more time than you may at first imagine and may need more time than you actually have available.
- *Output:* you should consider where each of the ideas may end up. It seems a very obvious point but certain ideas may find a place on mainstream broadcast channels while others may, owing to their content or style, be much more suited to specific websites. There are also numerous documentary festivals around the world, some specifically catering for student productions, which actively seek out more innovative and imaginative documentary.

Deciding upon your final idea

You should never decide upon your final idea on the basis that it will be the easiest to produce. Students who do this show a lack of real commitment. Rather, you should choose the idea that offers you the best chance of producing an exciting and worthwhile documentary. At this stage, it may come down to which of your ideas you are, personally and as a group, most interested in.

If you are not fired up about the idea, it will be much more difficult to produce an exciting and worthwhile documentary which is of interest to other people.

Don't forget, too, that the two ideas which you have eliminated will now become Plan B and Plan C if your chosen idea, for whatever reason, fails.

Producing an outline

Producing a detailed outline for your proposed documentary is essential, as it will allow you to focus clearly on how you, as a group, intend to 'creatively treat the actuality' of your chosen subject. As with all moving-image production, this will need to be a succinct and focused document, so ensure that your material at this stage is detailed, not vague!

It needs to be produced in such a way that the reader, without further guidance from you, can comprehend exactly what your *intention* is in making the documentary and what the audience is likely to see. It should, therefore, outline both the content and the style. You can compare your idea with existing documentaries in order to make the description more succinct. However, your outline must not only offer a résumé of the structure and content of the documentary, but must also highlight its most attractive and exciting elements in terms of style, content and characters. Include anything which makes your proposed documentary different or special in any way. It is a good idea to mention those who have agreed to contribute to the documentary, especially if you have managed to attract some big names who are happy to be interviewed. Provide detail about those involved, where the docuementary is likely to be shot and how many days it will take to shoot it. Don't be afraid to enthuse in your outline but be realistic and don't include anything that you cannot possibly achieve.

Carrying out research

One of the main failings of many student documentaries is that they simply describe something out there in the real world, often superficially. Your aim should be, through what Richard Kilborn and John Izod call the 'transformative work' (1997: 4) of the documentary maker, to explore that reality for your audience and let them explore it with you.

As Sheila Curran Bernard (2004: 5) notes, 'Documentaries should do more than help viewers pass the time: they should demand their active engagement, challenging them to think about what they know, how they know it and what more they might want to find out.' The only way you can do this is to have better knowledge of your chosen subject than your audience: you need to become an expert in your chosen area. We have already seen how researching the area theoretically and contextually will enable you to expand your view both of what documentary is and of what it is capable of being. The main aim at this stage, therefore, is to carry out all the remaining research necessary to develop and produce your own documentary effectively. You will do this by building on the very basic research that you carried out previously but increasing its scope and depth. You now have only one idea, so you can really go to town on it!

Technical and logistical research

Your logistical research will be guided, to a large extent, by the categories that you have already used in assessing the feasibility of your ideas: indeed much of that work actually *was* research. So, this stage should really just involve you 'putting meat on the bones':

- *Finance:* now that you have your definite idea you can prepare a budget. Though your budget will not be large by industry standards, this is likely to be your most expensive production to date. As such, you need to produce a formal budget which details both income and expenditure. Most student documentaries are funded by the student production crews, but there are a number of alternative means of raising income, such as packing bags at a local supermarket, asking your institution for financial help and organizing sponsored events. You need to put a price tag on each of the funding headings discussed earlier in this chapter:
  - *Transport:* a detailed breakdown of costs is imperative and must take into account the costs of getting you, your kit and your contributors to each location. Make sure that you also include the cost of recces, especially if you are working far from your base.
  - *Stock:* now is the time to obtain accurate costings for the type of stock you intend to use. If your idea requires you to use HD or film stock, you also need to include potential additional costs, such as transferring your film to video or to a format that you can use to digitize from.
  - *Equipment:* produce a final list, with costings, of the kit that you cannot source from your institution and therefore need to hire. Investigate as many hire places as possible and as soon as possible: it is standard practice to obtain three quotes. It is good professional practice to familarize yourself with new equipment and so you should ensure that you also include the cost of any necessary test sessions.
  - *Accommodation:* obtain accurate costings for all accommodation needed. At this stage, research the cost of alternatives: we have found rooms in youth hostels to be much more cost-effective in the UK than

hotel rooms. Think also about who you are accommodating: a middle-aged contributor may not want to stay in a hostel with the student production crew. Try and reduce costs by negotiating on prices. Once you have the most appropriate deal, book it.

- *Catering:* obtain costings for each of the options that you considered previously with regard to feeding the crew and contributors.
- *Presenters:* obtain accurate costings for posting your casting call on websites, advertising in magazines or through acting agencies and auditioning. The cost of auditioning might include room hire, travel costs, accommodation and food on the day of the auditions.
- *Contributors:* it is difficult at this stage to know the true costs of contributors but you will need to consider the cost of you travelling to them compared with that of them travelling to you and your chosen location.
- *Logistics:* you will need to produce a logistical breakdown for your idea, detailing how to transport all the necessary people and equipment to each of your locations. This involves careful consideration of the following key factors:
  - the size of the crew;
  - the amount and type of equipment that you will be transporting;
  - the different options for moving the crew and equipment;
  - how much travel time will be required for each of the locations.

  You will also need to consider the logistics of obtaining the necessary permissions, passes and access:
- *Health and Safety:* conduct a thorough recce and risk assessment for each location.
- *Technical resources:* produce a comprehensive list of the technical equipment that you need, ensure that it is available when you want it and book it. Also book it for practice sessions, if needed.
- *Human resources:* now is the time to contact all those who will assist in the production. Approach key contributors, talk to them about what their possible involvement might be and assess their enthusiasm. In doing so, you will be ascertaining both whether you have sufficient numbers of people prepared to contribute and who the best of the potential contributors might be. If potentially vital contributors seem hesitant, for whatever reason, then this is a clear signal that you may need to approach others without delay. Meeting potential constributors will offer you the opportunity easily to identify what they are likely to contribute and how. An enthusiastic, articulate and intelligent contributor can make your documentary a success; a poor, inarticulate contributor can cause it to fail. If your documentary requires a narrator or presenter, now is the time to book him/her.

- *Expertise and ability of the crew:* allocate roles and responsibilities and encourage your team to start producing test pieces where they can assess their specific skills and, if necessary, do something about improving them. This ranges from the generic skills of setting up quickly and professionally to the more specific skills of lighting and filming location interviews, selecting and using a variety of suitable microphones and interviewing techniques. At this stage of production, all crew members should have the requisite skills.

- *Time:* it is at this point that you can draw up your final project plan. From the brief, you should already have a number of important dates to work to: critiques, screenings and the final deadline for the completed documentary. You can now begin to add those dates which are unique to your production: when you intend to complete all the elements of pre-production, when you intend to shoot and when you will complete the various stages of post-production. Remember that this planner is a live document and starts life as a basic plan which becomes much more sophisticated as the research and the project progresses.

- *Output:* now is the time to carry out full and detailed research around the proposed output for your finished documentary. This should involve researching the technical guidelines for submitting your final documentary and any other requirements. With regard to the former, it may be a specification about the final format of master tape for submission to a festival or the required type of compression and file size for uploading, if for a website. With regard to the latter, this may include the requirement to submit certain documentation along with your master tape or file: for example, copies of all release forms or music permissions. The point we would make here is that you must have all this information *before* shooting.

Content research

Michael Rabiger (2004: 92) makes the point that 'unless the film is of the highly controlled essay type, the documentary author is at the mercy of whatever materials he or she manages to acquire'. For documentary, therefore, content research is possibly the most important, as it allows you to have a much better sense of what it is possible to acquire. It enables you not only to become knowledgeable about your chosen subject but also, more importantly, to begin to make a judgment about whether there really is a documentary in your idea.

It involves the gathering, through primary and secondary research, of all the materials which may inform or impact on content. It requires you to seek out information from all the usual places: libraries, the internet, newspapers and magazines. However, as we have already stated, documentary generally involves people and places, so you should also aim to spend time with the people who may feature in your documentary in the places that they inhabit. Look not only for what is typical about their world but also for what is unusual. When contacting experts, learn from them and be guided by them.

Remember, it is only with detailed, systematic and wide-ranging research around content that you will discover interesting facts which make your idea attractive to your audience. This is a continual and exhaustive process which often does not seem to have an end point: indeed it can still be in process after production has started. It covers all aspects of the chosen subject, often revealing what initially appears to be innocuous information but may later become paramount.

A group of our students recently filmed a documentary in Spain. Their initial aim was to explore why retired British people went to live in Spain and often ended up living within communities of similar people. However, after some relatively basic initial research, it became clear that such a community did not really exist and so the documentary changed direction. After a chance conversation with a hotel manager, the students decided that it would explore what it was about Benidorm which attracted so many elderly British people to go there for long winter holidays. Content research started six months prior to filming and initially involved gathering information on the history of the resort, what it was like before people started to holiday there, how it had developed over the previous seventy years and the type of holidays which were now available to the elderly. But it did not stop there. Further research included unearthing information about building regulations and how land is used in the resort, the effect of building on the environment, the old town and how it contrasts with the new town, crime, entertainment, transport, how the resort meets the needs of its many and varied visitors, Spanish politics, facts and figures on the holiday season and how the type of holiday-maker varies according to the time of year, temperatures, geography, how much the city consumes in terms of food and water, its annual turnover, how the tourism industry has affected the local area and what the future holds for Benidorm, to name but a few!

It is vital to collect all this information because some of it will become content in the finished documentary – which is why it is called content research – and some of it will remain as background information, often useful for stimulating questions in interviews. It is also important to know as much about the documentary subject as possible for practical reasons.

The recce for the Spanish documentary was conducted about a month prior to the start of filming. This is also an integral element of content research as it allows on-site visits to specific locations and conversations with individuals there. It allows important contributors to meet the crew and talk over the intentions of the documentary and ensures co-operation from all parties. Meetings with such people are as important for them as they are for you, as gaining their trust in you and your intentions is integral to the success of your documentary. Over two hundred digital photographs were taken of buildings, specific locations and individuals. All the information gathered on the recce was fed back to the crew and formed an important part of the documentary research. As with all research, the materials were discussed at length by the production team and stored for reference. The questions which would be used in interviews with the elderly holiday-makers were substantially influenced by this research. The same could be said for the subject and style of the camera shots, which benefited greatly from the photographs and video footage taken during the recce. Information gathered about daily activities on offer at the resort where the crew were filming and staying became potential content. They continued to work with the benefit of the knowledge they had gained, rather than in ignorance.

While you are busy gathering all this data, you should also be considering more seriously the style of your proposed documentary. You will have had ideas about this earlier on in the process and recorded them in your outline. It is at this point that our students re-evaluate their earlier suggestions about style and sometimes arrive at ideas which are more sophisticated or more effective. This requires you to continue your contextual research by watching a wider range of documentaries on television, at the cinema and on the internet than you might normally watch. Systematically consider the complex nature of what makes a documentary, both visually and aurally, and what types of content are present (and, of course, absent). So, once again, you need to make sure that you carry out both significant content analysis of your chosen subgenre and detailed semiotic analysis of individual documentaries within that subgenre. You will notice from such research that the relationship between subject and camera varies dramatically. You will need to decide what is suitable for your chosen subject: tripods and carefully contrived shots tend not to work in documentaries about subjects such as weekend binge-drinkers or car thieves, while CCTV footage and shoulder-mounted camera work is probably inappropriate for a documentary on your local chess club.

Do not be afraid, at this stage, to reconsider how you intend representing your subjects. Think about and discuss the other documentaries that you have seen in order to extend your thoughts about the relationship that you, your crew, the camera and the audience will establish with your subjects. Consider what steps you will need to take in order to accomplish this. One of our own student documentary production teams recently reconsidered how they would approach their subject – obsessive compulsive disorder (OCD) – and agreed that they would need to spend much more time than they had initially planned just visiting and befriending their subjects in order to build up a real relationship with them before they could start filming. They agreed that it was only by doing this that they would be able truly to represent what it was like to suffer from this illness and to do justice to the individuals who had agreed to participate in the documentary. This decision naturally affected the overall style of the documentary because they planned to ensure that the presence of the camera was in no way intrusive and thereby hoped that the material they gathered would be more factual and honest.

Just as in industry, when producing a student documentary you need to adhere to the, by now familiar, stages of the production process. You have probably already realized, however, that the production process for documentary is somewhat different from that for the earlier briefs in this book. There are many variables which are outside your control and there are no real definites upon which you can rely. That is why good quality research into the logistics and content of your production must be your starting point and why it is imperative that you research your chosen idea fully.

The 'ping' moment

Obviously you started with a basic outline of your documentary but the information you have collected to date will have added 'meat to the bones'. Only when all your research material has been gathered and collated will you know what to do with it and what shape your finished documentary might take.

You should not take your documentary any further until you have experienced what we call the 'ping' moment. The 'ping' is the comedy sound that a cartoon character hears in its head when it understands the true meaning of something, and this is only experienced when students really understand all aspects of their topic. Students who have 'pinged' make much better documentaries than those who have not, as they have sufficient knowledge actively to partake in the debate, are familiar with every stance or standpoint and have acquired sufficient content. Make sure that you 'ping' and that you 'ping' early.

Producing a script and storyboard

There is a widespread perception, shared by many students, that documentary makers 'shoot from the hip': that is, they take their camera and kit to where they want to shoot and, with little or no preparation and planning, simply respond to what is happening. While there may be some documentary makers who do this, if you read accounts of how they work, you will soon discover that this applies to very few of them (see, for example, Goldsmith 2003). Most leading documentary makers will have a very clear idea of what they are going to shoot before they shoot it. That is not to say that they do not respond to unexpected events, merely that such events are seen as an added bonus. Given that this is possibly your first documentary, we would advise you not even to consider shooting from the hip; in planning your documentary, you need to produce the same kind of documentation as for other video work: the script and the storyboard.

Script

The format of the documentary script is slightly different from that of the scripts you have produced for the previous briefs. Although it contains broadly the same information, it is in the form of what is termed a two-column script. The first column contains the visual elements of the documentary, while the second column contains the sound elements (see Figure 8.1).

Producing a script will give initial shape and structure to your video and will enable you to work out whether certain elements will work with others.

For example, if we think about why you might decide to include interviews

| **Home from Home** | |
| **Greenhouse Productions** | |
Visual	*Sound*
Fade in from black	Music: William Orbit … strings
Title 'Home from Home'	
Exterior: hotels on front	Narrator: Benidorm. Loved by thousands of Brits since the early nineteen-sixties,
Exterior: roof shot of vista	frequented by the stars, but why?
Exterior: beach	Narrator: Is it the sun-kissed sands?
Exterior: bars and clubs at night	Narrator: Or the colourful nightlife?
Interior: club at night	
Exterior: distant hills and mountains	Narrator: Or the eternal beauty of the hills that surround the city and contribute to its perpetual moderate climate?
Interior: hotel lounge	Mr and Mrs Boscombe
Exterior: hotel poolside	The Planters family
Exterior: goods in shops	Narrator: Irrespective of why you might come here, you cannot deny that it does have a charm peculiar to itself.
Exterior: ice creams on beach	Welcome to Benidorm!
Montage:	

Figure 8.1   A sample of a documentary two-column script

in your documentary, we might conclude that it is for all of the following good reasons:

- to hear a person's point of view or reminiscences;
- to hear an expert opinion;
- to allow for some staged, and therefore high-quality, footage to be included as a counterpoint to what might be very raw footage of the events being shown;
- to interest or challenge the audience in terms of the contributor, content or style.

In scripting, however, you realize that the inclusion of too many interviews unbalances the final documentary and so you might make the decision to include, to use Corner's terminology, 'expositional dialogue', or narration.

Storyboard

It is clearly not possible to storyboard every sequence of every documentary. Indeed, some documentary makers would argue that it is not possible, or desirable, to storyboard *any*. However, some documentaries, or elements of them, are much more structured than others and it is these structured elements that it is possible to storyboard: title and credit sequences, interviews and reconstructions. Because this may be your first documentary, you should aim to storyboard as many sequences as possible.

Once again, the starting point of the storyboarding process is the production of thumbnails. Thumbnails are vital for generally exploring the overall style and structure of the documentary, along with the specific elements which can be planned in advance. Thumbnails enable you to think of different ways of constructing each of these elements. They obviously work for the more highly constructed elements such as title sequences but they can also allow you to think of different, more innovative ways of shooting the less obvious ones: they may, for example, offer you the chance to explore the type of composition you will use for an interview.

This is particularly useful with regard to documentary, where a director may want certain interviews or sequences to be filmed and edited in a particular way and the drawings help to show both shot style and content. Because they represent the director's vision for the final documentary, storyboards will guide not only the shooting but also the way in which these shots will be put together in the edit.

The main responsibility of the director is to come up with the overall vision for the documentary. This should largely be decided at the pre-production stage and requires the director to translate this vision into interesting or exciting sequences. While you cannot be absolutely certain of the content you will gather, you can make sure that part of the interest comes from the way in which your shots are composed. There is a widespread perception that the majority of documentaries rely on a hand-held camera and a jerky style, but even a cursory examination will show that this is a fallacy. Your camera should always be mounted on a tripod with a good fluid head unless your style of documentary calls for hand-held or shoulder-mounted shots. If you do choose such shots, it should be the result of careful consideration early on in pre-production, based on your research around a wide range of documentaries and should be appropriate to your idea. For example, if the majority of the camera shots are shoulder-mounted, loose and constantly on the move, you need to be able to justify why you chose to film that way, for what purpose and how this affects the viewer and the dynamic of the overall documentary.

In terms of the non-interview footage, in addition to the usual rules of composition, your key considerations are with regard to the effectiveness of each shot. You therefore need to consider the following:

- *The subject of the shot*. What might it contribute to the intended sequence and the documentary overall?
- *The background of the shot:* failing to think about this could mean that you have inadvertently failed to consider something which could either undermine the shot you require or, in extreme circumstances, land you in trouble. For example, if your documentary is about shops selling out-of-date food and you have a supermarket in the background, the audience could infer that this is one of the shops involved, in which case you could open yourself up to potentially costly legal action.
- *The mise-en-scène*: that is, what you could add to the shot to help support the shot or to create additional meaning. As with any production, you have the power to construct what the audience see. As we saw above, however, unlike other productions, you have to give consideration to how far you can 'creatively treat actuality' before it ceases to be reality.

For interviews, you need to think carefully about how you frame your interviewee. If using one camera, there are accepted ways of framing the subject:

- *A two-shot with both interviewee and interviewer in shot*: this is often the worst shot as, if it is poorly composed, both will be in profile and, as a result, the audience will not be able to see the eyes and mouth of either or both. It can be used as an establishing shot in a studio interview.
- *Interviewee only:* this is much better and can either be composed *on-axis* with the subject looking directly at the camera or *off-axis* looking past the camera to the interviewer out of the frame. The camera would normally be on the subject's eyeline.

- *An over-the-shoulder two-shot 'favouring' the interviewee:* this is a standard shot, especially in investigative documentary. It frames mainly the interviewee but also part of the interviewer's body, thus providing a sense of their physical relationship.

If using two cameras, it is possible to set up one on the interviewee and one on the interviewer and 'cross shoot'. This can look much better.

Producing a shooting schedule

The shooting schedule for documentary is probably more important than for any other production, with the exception of the drama short. Given that you may well be shooting in multiple locations, with multiple contributors and at all times of the day (and possibly night), it is clearly important that this document should be detailed, accurate and up to date.

Many documentaries use interviews and it is therefore important to organize and schedule these interviews in a practical and realistic manner. If your documentary has a number of contributors, the schedule is likely to be heavily influenced by their availability. Contributors are not generally paid for their work and so it is vital that they should not be kept waiting, as this may impact negatively on their contribution to your documentary. As with all schedules, you will need to consider locations, travel, set-up and preparation times and the participants themselves, who will need to be in the right place at the right time. Treat them as you would want to be treated and give them time to adjust to their situation and to feel comfortable with you and the crew. Be organized, professional, punctual, practical and polite.

Production

Once you have spent 70 per cent of your available time on pre-production, you need to move on to the production stage. You must not only draw upon and use the skills you have already developed in the previous briefs but also develop new ones specific to this brief. These are technical in terms of both individual roles and responsibilities and the idea of constructing a story within documentary.

Roles and responsibilities

If you haven't already done so, now is the time to start inhabiting your production roles. A typical student documentary crew is likely to consist of the same crew that you used when producing your title sequence.

At this point you should visit the website, where you will find download-able sheets which clearly outline all the roles and responsibilities for documentary production, the key skills required for each role and the key tasks for each of the stages of production.

Whatever the size and composition of your crew and whatever role they are taking, every member of that crew must be disciplined and professional at all times. Documentary filming often puts the crew among members of the public. You will, therefore, be subject to public scrutiny every time you shoot in a way that you will not have experienced before and so need to consider the following:

- Each member of the crew must understand *exactly* what his/her function is and how it fits in with those of the other members of the crew. Practising as a team prior to filming is essential.
- You *must* have a code of conduct which should cover the obvious, such as Health and Safety and your conduct when shooting but should also include considerations which students do not always take into account, such as dress code and use of language. Agreeing to and abiding by such a code is essential: a scruffy, poorly organized and unprofessional crew is unlikely to instil confidence in anyone participating in the documentary.

Telling a story

Whatever the subject of the documentary, a good director and crew should always be consciously planning for the edit *while* they film. Given that you are filming actuality, with all its potential problems, having even a rudimentary storyboard will help. An interview with a war veteran, for example, will be much enhanced by the use of planned cutaways and inserts which will help to tell the story: a CU of his medals, a photograph on the mantelpiece of him in uniform, a faded newspaper cutting or a CU of his hands as they turn his wedding ring. Cutting to such footage during an interview will afford you the opportunity to cut around a poor edit or jump cut.

However, as with other types of moving image, be creative and be smart about how you use your kit. Always remember that the art of the documentary film-maker is constantly to seek out the *interesting* story. Unlike drama, where there is a high level of control, documentary filming can and often does go off in unexpected directions. So, while you are filming, other stories and directions for the documentary which you have not considered may emerge. Do not be afraid to let this happen. It can be unpredictable and surprising. An important opportunity can be lost if the members of the crew are not alert to what is taking place around them: if something happens and it has a link to the documentary, shoot it! You may not use the footage, but you do at least have it. By watching and listening carefully you may also be able to enhance the story by including other material which your contributor mentions, which will, in turn, add value to the documentary.

A final word of warning, though. While we *are* advocating that you think about the edit while you are shooting, we *are not* suggesting that you can ever make up your documentary's structure in the edit. One of the key pieces of advice that we would give you is never to think that you can shoot large quantities of footage and then produce your documentary in the edit. Such practice is sloppy and unprofessional.

After each day's filming, it is good practice to check your footage for a number of reasons:

- to see if there is any material missing;
- to see if there is anything that is, for whatever reason, of poor quality and needs to be reshot;
- to address any problems before it is too late;
- if you are using more than one camera, to compare and contrast the material shot and to put your mind at rest regarding the camera set-up and shot style.

Having the whole crew look at the footage affords an opportunity for discussion about the quality of the material and about the direction in which the documentary is moving, but it can also generate a useful sense of solidarity and achievement. Build the meeting into your production schedule. Even if you have had a full day, it is a vital part of building a successful crew.

Recording sound

The first rule of sound recording is, as you already know, never to use the camera microphone: the sound is likely to be unusable. With this in mind, you will need to think carefully about what type of microphone you use for each part of your documentary. The important thing is to consider your recording circumstances and have the right microphones to hand for each situation. Depending on the type of documentary you are producing, you may need to use a combination of microphones: rifle and tie-clip microphones for interviews; omnidirectional microphones for wildtrack. Although certain decisions can be made as the result of your recce, taking a selection of microphones with you will provide a number of options, particularly if on location: for example, if your set-up time is limited, then a rifle microphone on a fishpole may serve as the quickest and most effective means of recording, whereas if you have ample time to set up, then a tie-clip microphone may prove to be your best option.

Recording sound for documentary can be very different to other types of recording as it represents one of the few situations where the crew may have to record events while on the move. They may have no real control over what is happening and must react to the circumstances around them. A busy subject may not necessarily wish to stop and afford the crew the opportunity to set up an interview and may need to be interviewed on the move. This involves the sound recordist and camera operators working together so that neither is in the other's way and so that the microphone remains constantly out of shot while being as close to the interviewee as possible in order to obtain the best quality sound. This type of choreography between sound, camera, director and interviewee is not easy and takes practice to be successful.

The role of the PA

The PA is one of the most important members of a documentary crew. His/her primary role is to support the director and to do anything which helps the director to move the production forwards.

One of the key roles of the PA is to make sure that all the necessary production documentation is kept: primarily, log sheets and release forms. It is vital to keep an accurate log when shooting, especially if there is more than one crew working. The log sheet must be detailed, showing all the necessary key data: crew, location, date, time, tape number, a description of what was recorded, the number of takes, the timecode for each shot and any comments. It is the PA's job to store these sheets carefully, as they will be needed later.

Other essential documentation includes release forms for those who participated in the documentary. This is a form which gives the group permission to use the participant's contribution in the finished documentary. Without such a form for each contributor, you may not be able to broadcast or screen your documentary. Copies of release forms are readily available on the internet. Make sure that they are completed properly, even when busy doing something which seems more important. At the end of the shoot in Spain we had a large number of release forms which we stored carefully. However, when it came to using the information to write letters of thanks to all the contributors, we found that although the participants had signed the forms and written their addresses, in some cases we were unable to read them.

Interviewing

Depending upon the type of documentary you make, one of the key elements that you may have decided to use is the interview or what, as we saw earlier,

Corner terms 'testimony'. For many of you, this may be the first time that you have carried out an interview. Whether or not you conduct a successful interview can make or break your documentary. Although interviewing may be seen as a case of just sitting people down and asking them a few questions, good interviewing is much more sophisticated than this. So, what makes for a successful interview?

You will already have made the first key decision at the pre-production stage: how you wish to frame your interviewee. If you remember, this could be:

- a two-shot with both interviewee and interviewer in shot;
- interviewee only;
- an over-the-shoulder two-shot 'favouring' the interviewee.

Once you have decided this, the first key skill that you need to develop is the ability to build up a good relationship between you and the interviewee. Take as much time as possible to get to know the person, preferably before the interview. The presence of a film crew often changes people's behaviour so you should not expect them to react normally when you point a camera at them. If your interviewee is not coming to you, plan shots by visiting him/her at the place where the interview will take place, observing what goes on during the time you wish to film and talking to people there. In this way the people involved will feel far more comfortable with you and the camera when you do actually shoot. It can take quite some time but pays dividends in the quality of the resulting footage. It is especially important if you are taking the interviewee to an unfamiliar place that you should spend time talking to him/her prior to filming, telling him/her about your film and introducing the crew to help him/her to relax and feel at ease. Cunning also has its part to play in documentary. Many of the best shots for our own documentary work have been produced by setting up the camera for the desired shot, say of a group of people, turning the tally light off and then turning our backs to the camera as if we were busy with something else.

The second key skill that you need is to be as prepared as possible: never just turn up and shoot, no matter how easy you think the interview may be. Look professional and people will treat you professionally and take the project seriously: look unprofessional and you will be treated as such. Professionalism extends to three main areas: before the interview, during the interview and after the interview.

Before the interview

Before the interview starts:

- Make sure that you choose the right setting for the interview. It is not just what is said in an interview which is important: the setting can provide extremely useful information for the audience. An obvious example of this is an interview with an expert which takes place in front of a bookcase full of academic books. If your recce has highlighted the fact that the location needs dressing to make it more suitable, make sure that you schedule enough time for dressing it.
- Set up your kit in good time. Allow double the amount of time that you think you will need, especially if setting up in an unfamiliar place. It is much better to be sitting around waiting for your interviewee to arrive than to be setting up when they do.
- Make your interviewee as relaxed as possible:
  - Always greet your interviewee with eye contact and a smile. It is amazing what a difference this makes to people who are nervous about facing a camera.
  - The director should introduce himself/herself and the crew.
  - The director should give the interviewee a basic idea of what to talk about and what not to talk about. The interviewee should be given some time to think about these areas and may suggest other good areas for discussion.
  - The director should encourage the interviewee to start his/her answers with part of the question.
  - The director should make the point that all or part of the interview can be rerecorded if necessary. For really nervous interviewees, tell them you will do a run-through as a practice but record it without telling them, making sure that the camera's tally light is off. This is often the best interview you will get as they visibly relax if they think it is not being recorded. There is nothing to stop you recording another interview as insurance. Never let nervous interviewees read off script: the results are always appalling.
  - The PA should ask the interviewee if he/she needs anything (for example, a glass of water) and make sure that all mobile, or cell, phones on the set are turned off.
- Make sure that you and the crew are also relaxed and comfortable:
  - You, as interviewer, should look at your notes to remind yourself of the questions you are going to ask, especially the first question.
  - The rest of the crew should make themselves physically comfortable as they may be in the same position for a long time.

During the interview

During the interview:

- Have a list of about eight questions on an index card. These are your safety net and a guide but should *never* be all that you ask. Rest the card on your knee so that you can see it quickly and easily if necessary.
- Make your questions relevant and understandable:
  - *Don't* ask *closed* questions: Do you like fish? What size shoes do you take? Who is going to win the World Cup? They allow the interviewee to answer in one word and, as a result, are unusable in the final edit.
  - *Do* ask *open* questions; Tell me what you like eating? Take me through the kinds of exercise that you take?
  - *Don't* ask very general questions: What do you think of Christianity? What happened during your first ten years at school?
  - *Don't* ask very complicated questions/multiquestions: How old were you when you first rode a bike and, if you were under the age of seven and a half, tell me where you rode it and how it felt to be on a bike for the first time?
  - *Don't* ask questions which leave no room for an answer: Your grandmother's accident was obviously a terrible shock and must have left you drained of emotion. How has this affected you?
- Avoid any sounds that you might normally make in conversation, such as 'hmm' and 'yeah', as it makes the interview *extremely* difficult to edit. Instead, use non-verbal communication: smiles, nods of the head and interested facial expressions. It may feel unnatural to start with but you will soon get used to it.
- Treat the interview as a conversation and listen to what your interviewee is saying:
  - You might not need eight prepared questions. First-time directors often ask questions without listening to the answers and it may be that the interviewee has already answered your next question. This is unprofessional and annoys the interviewee.
  - Don't be scared of asking unscripted supplementary questions: the interviewee might take you into a more interesting area.
  - The director/interviewer should not be nervous about redirecting the interviewee if he/she is digressing, but this should be done gently!
  - At the end of the interview, always ask the interviewee whether there is anything that he/she would like to add. This can often be the best part of the interview, especially if the interviewee thinks that the interview has finished. This is when interviewees often tell you everything they have rehearsed as well as anything that pops into their head, and in a much more relaxed manner.
- Take a minute or two at the end to check that you have everything you need. It can be very difficult to get someone back to rerecord the interview

and, even if it isn't, rerecording may cause problems with regard to continuity and the mood of your interviewee. The sound recordist should use this time to record wildtrack.

After the interview

When the interview has finished:

- The director should thank the interviewee and let him/her know what will happen to the interview and when he/she will see or receive a copy of the finished documentary.
- The PA should ask the interviewee to sign a documentary release form

Interview filming tips

When filming an interview:

- *Do* keep coherent composition.
- *Don't* keep reframing or zooming. Only change the shot composition if necessary: for example, when moving to tighter shots to heighten emotion and during questions (not answers). Michael Rabiger argues that you should only ever use three shots: a wide shot for questions, a medium shot used when an answer is under way, and a close shot for anything intense or revealing.
- *Do* remember to take reaction shots (or *noddies*) of both interviewee and interviewer. Do them before the interview, not after.
- *Do* record shots for cutaways: hands are the most obvious.
- *Do* record practice interviews: these may be the best (or the worst) take.
- *Don't* feel that just because you and your interviewee have taken the time to record an interview that you have to use it. A judgement needs to be made at the post-production stage as to whether it fits into the final video.

Avoiding problems

A number of problems may arise when filming documentary and these generally come under the headings of technical, human or natural problems. Rather than seeing them as problems, see them as challenges which require solutions.

Technical problems can be minimized if you make sure that you check all your kit before you leave for the shoot, especially cables and connectors, adapters and batteries. Always carry spares and always keep a basic repair kit in case problems do arise.

Human problems can be minimized too. You should always be dependable and should try to select production team members on whom you can rely. The worst kind of let-down for documentary is when an important interviewee or participant pulls out or, even more disastrously, when the actions of someone in the group result in an interviewee being left waiting. Plan for more participants than are needed and, if possible, have other people lined up for interview. If there are doubts about whether participants will remember to turn up at the right place at the right time, contact them a couple of times to remind them about their interview, send someone to meet them and take them to where you are filming. Schedule well and reiterate to your participants how important they are and how vital it is that they, along with the crew, work to the shooting schedule.

As Michael Rabiger (2004: 326) advises: 'prepare for the worst and you will seldom be disappointed'. When the worst *does* happen, take a deep breath and collect your thoughts. You won't be the only person to have faced the problem. Think practically, think logically and think laterally. Seldom is everything lost, so gather your team together, discuss the problems and share your solutions. Most of the problems that you are likely to face can be resolved with some thought and work on your part.

Post-production

We are assuming that the previous briefs in this book have allowed you both to understand the correct process for post-production and to develop the necessary technical skills to use the editing equipment at your disposal. In this section, therefore, we are going to focus on what, in previous chapters, we have called the craft and art of editing for documentary.

Sheila Curran Bernard (2004: 2) notes that documentary is 'what the documentary maker does with the factual elements, weaving them into an overall narrative that strives to be as compelling as it is truthful'. This idea of editing as 'weaving' is a really good analogy. The director has acted as the overall designer and, with the crew, has been responsible for collecting all the materials for weaving the documentary. What you, as the editor, have at your disposal is all the different strands which have already been produced – the visual material, interviews, reconstructions, sound – to which you will add those available to you at post-production, such as sound effects, colour-correction, graphics and titles. Using your skills as an editor, you now have to take these seemingly disparate items and weave them together into a finished documentary.

The editor and director should have discussed the director's intentions with regard to the structure and style of the documentary at the pre-production stage. They will now resume the discussion based on the direction that the documentary may since have taken. Unlike drama, which works to definitive storyboards and scripts, documentary can take on a new lease of life during production and may deviate significantly from the original story and ideas. As Rabiger (2004: 416) notes, 'Absolutely nothing beyond what can be seen and felt from the dailies is any longer relevant to the film you're making. Any documents such as the proposal or outline are historic relics ... Stow them in the attic for your biographer. The film must be discovered in the dailies.'

This can be a very testing period for the director and the editor and it is important that their relationship should remain positive and creative. Some directors will want to work in close proximity with the editor: discussing, arguing and debating which material should or should not be included. Others will retire to a distance and allow the editor to do his/her job without interference. It is up to you and your group which route you take.

Viewing the material

If, as we suggested, the production team have checked and reviewed the footage at the end of each day's shooting (what are termed 'the dailies' in Rabiger's quote above), then all the footage should already have been viewed. It is now the job of the editor and the director to view the material again, this time noting the timecode of any particularly interesting or sincere interviews, emotive visual or audio material, beautifully framed and executed shots and memorable dialogue. Given that the normal shooting ratio for documentary, especially fly-on-the-wall documentaries, may be as high as 20:1, you may have to spend some considerable time watching and taking detailed notes which will act as your guide in structuring your finished piece. However, it is an exciting and productive process because it is at this point that you realize, possibly for the first time, that you do actually have a documentary.

As a result of viewing the material, the director and the editor should have identified the strongest material, possibly unexpectedly so, which can be used to structure and drive the documentary. They will be developing a fairly clear idea of what is likely to structure the film at this stage: either the spoken word, such as interviews and voice-over, or the visuals. The process of weaving can now start.

Structuring the documentary

Michael Rabiger (2004: 421) notes that 'You will need a narrative and thematic structure, no matter what genre of document you're making.' If you were able to keep to your goals during the shoot, then structuring the assembly [edit] may now be straightforward. Usually it isn't. So, in planning the structure of your documentary, there are three broad positions:

1. As a result of good planning and production, you have all the material that you need to produce the planned documentary.
2. For whatever reason, you do not have the required material and so have to make a documentary from the material that you do have.
3. You had one documentary in mind but, in the edit, a new and better documentary has emerged.

Ideally, your pre-production discussions will have given you a clear sense of what the structure of your finished documentary will be. If you are in the lucky position of knowing what you wanted to shoot and having achieved that, then you don't need to worry: you can simply get down to work on your assembly using your scripts and storyboards to structure the documentary. Otherwise, you need to go back to your material and assess what you have in order to decide exactly what you want to do with it.

There are a number of ways of constructing a structure. Rabiger suggests two possible ways of structuring a finished documentary – the action-determined structure and the word-driven structure – to which we would add one other: the image-orientated structure:

*   *The action-determined structure*: some documentaries are structured around what is seen. If you feel that the visuals are your starting point in terms of structuring your documentary, you now need to group your shots according to the themes or stories that they explore.

    Very often, students think that the term 'narrative structure' refers only to fictional video but, as we saw earlier, it is also an essential element of any documentary. Having viewed all the footage, now is the time to ask: what is the story and how should it be developed? There may be a noticeable visual linear pattern to your footage, such as a journey, or the passage of time which could offer the narrative structure you need. This could be something as simple as the movement through from dawn to midday to afternoon to dusk and then to night. Looking for other developments or changes in the emotions, themes or characters is vital, simply because it is the change which *is* the story and it is the *developing* story which hooks the audience: that sense of what is going to happen next. A contemporary example of this is the police-action documentary. Officers on patrol in their car spot a suspected stolen vehicle, they call it in and chase the vehicle across the city and into the suburbs. The offenders decamp and head off on foot through the local housing estate, the heat-sensitive cameras in a police helicopter show the offenders being pursued by the police officers and eventually caught and arrested.

The next task is to digitize the footage that you think you are going to use and then collate it, according to the various themes or stories which are now apparent, by storing grouped material in bins. In the industry this process would be carried out as a paper edit.

At this point, Rabiger (2004: 424) suggests that you do the following:

1. Put together an assembly edit [...] view it without stopping [...] does it, for instance, tell a story, convey a mood, introduce a society, or set an epoch?
2. What time period do you know your material spans, and how well does the assembly convey that lapse in time?
3. What memorable interchanges or developments did you capture on-camera?
4. What would your film convey were it a silent film?
5. How many clear phases does the observational film fall into, and what characterizes each phase?
6. What verbal material do you have that adds new dimensions to the 'silent film' assembly?
7. What does it add and what new dimensions does the original action and behaviourally based film acquire?
8. How little speech material do you need to further shift the film toward something you want?

- *The word-driven structure:* these rely less on what is seen and more on what is said. Such documentaries still require a narrative structure and a sense of development but rely upon the spoken word to move the story forward.

As a result of looking at and listening to your footage carefully, you may have noticed certain things of great import. These might include something which has been said several times during interview and which can become a theme, a consistent viewpoint, a feeling or a mood. Particular interviewees may have developing stories to tell or, collectively, elements from the interviews can be grouped into sequences, each sequence providing a development from the previous one.

Now digitize the footage that you think you are going to use and collate it according to the various themes or stories now apparent, by storing grouped material in bins. Rabiger (2004: 425) recommends that you should, '[t]o prevent your film from turning into solid speech, first deal with your action sequences, that is, those that show human processes with a beginning, middle and end. Make a list of these sequences and design an overall structure that moves them logically through time.'

- *The image-orientated structure:* like the action-determined structure, this starts with what is seen. However, unlike the action-determined structure, this may not be action as such but rather visual imagery which expresses a theme or emotion or contributes to a narrative. As with the other two types of structure, you will need to collate the images prior to digitizing.

  It is important to recall at this stage that visuals need words, and vice versa. By this we mean that while your documentary may be word-driven it will still need appropriate visuals to support what is heard; if it is visually driven, it will still need appropriate words to support what is seen. Don't forget to identify and digitize this supporting material.

Transcripts of interviews and conversations can be given headings or names based, for example, on topics and can sometimes be grouped. If transcripts are not appropriate, they can be named and grouped as digitized material stored in bins on the edit suite. The visual material (that is, shots which rely not on dialogue but on their visual content) are also listed as descriptions of the action. Once you are familiar with all the transcripts and visual material, it is possible to edit the documentary on paper by deciding the order of the above. We have seen it done by students who have literally cut out key topics covered in the interviews, put them in a linear order and then decided which visuals would most appropriately accompany them. One problem with this is that it can result in the documentary being mechanical and too heavily reliant upon what is said, as opposed to what is seen.

The assembly

Whether your documentary is action-determined, word-driven or image-orientated, or a combination of all three, you will need to put it into a coherent and watchable format in preparation for the first screening and for review by a wider audience than the production team.

In some senses, in constructing your assembly you are pre-empting the kinds of comments and questions that this audience will ask. You should, therefore keep asking yourself a series of simple questions about the edit while you are working on it:

- Does the documentary hook the audience within the first minute or so? If not, why not?
- Are the clips in the correct order? Does it tell the story? Are there places where this falters?

- Is it too long? Which clips, scenes or parts add nothing to the documentary and can therefore be removed or trimmed? Are any parts guilty of repetition?
- Which parts of the documentary do you like and why? Which interviewees hold your interest the most and why? Is there more material like this that you can add?
- Which parts do you not like and why? Can they and should they be replaced by something else?
- Does it have the right pace and rhythm? Is there sufficient variety in the pace? Are there emotional high points and low points? Are there counter-points?
- Where is the drama? Is it balanced? Is it too didactic? Can it be more subtle in its approach, for example showing images with no dialogue or utter silence?
- Does it have a range of emotions? Where should the emotion or tension come from?
- Are any sequences tedious because they are too similar in terms of content or topic? Is any material noticeably weak? Why?
- Is the conclusion clear?

These questions are in no particular order: they should all be in your head while you are editing.

Interviews are edited at this stage but this should be a basic edit without refinement or the addition of cutaways. It is important to remember that you, as editor, are responsible for quality control. The content of a clip may be what you want but if it is technically or creatively flawed, then it should not be included. You may have to be quite brutal, especially when it is a shot that you are particularly fond of or feel should be included. Do not be afraid to alter the order of sequences or the video overall if doing so improves the telling of the story.

Do not agonize over the length of clips or possible repetition: just put each clip on to the timeline in the order you have agreed and move on. Your production will take on a new lease of life. It is almost certainly going to be much longer than required but it should now start to have a wholeness in relation to the narrative, with a clear beginning, middle and end. Only now are you ready to conduct the screening of your assembly edit to other groups for feedback.

You will already have held a number of informal screenings within the production group prior to this and will have your own ideas about important considerations and changes which might need to made during the rough cut. During the viewing, the members of the audience are your barometer. Watch them carefully and note their reactions to each part of the documentary: for example, do they seem interested? Do they react appropriately to each sequence? Are there any sequences where they seem to lose interest? Conducting a wider screening to people who are seeing your video for the first time has the benefit of offering new perspectives on the process. Their reactions to your assembly may confirm what you already know or reveal areas which you need to address. After the viewing you may want to use a pre-written list of questions to acquire more detailed information from your audience.

Having asked the above questions, received answers to them and listed suggestions for improvement, it is often a good idea to take a day or two away from the edit before you dive back in, re-energized and ready to improve the assembly edit.

The rough cut

The rough cut concentrates on refining the visuals and the dialogue. Interviews will need to be refined, especially if the documentary is word-driven. Cutaways and inserts will need to be added, the dialogue trimmed and any extraneous sound removed. Concentrate on the duration of each edit within the documentary and its relationship with the previous edit and the one to follow. When you feel that the basic structure is good, apply visual effects, such as dissolves and fades in or out. The relationship between what is heard and what is seen can be more thoroughly polished at this stage.

It is appropriate at this point to outline some of the editing techniques which are useful specifically for documentary:

- *Counterpoint*: this is the combination of the sound from one shot and the visuals from another. This can be as simple as an interviewee sitting on her hotel balcony talking about the beautiful hills and endless nature walks surrounding her resort while the editor cuts to a shot of the hills as seen from the balcony, as if we (the viewers) were standing there listening to her while looking out across the lush, green, rolling hills.
- *Sound-against-image counterpoint:* this is more complicated. An example of this might be a head-and-shoulders shot of an interviewee describing her holiday resort in glowing terms which is then interrupted by footage of the half-built hotel and piles of rotting rubbish before cutting back to the interviewee. This sound-against-image counterpoint is a very powerful tool for the editor. When using this technique, however, you must have a clear idea of the truthfulness of such representations. By that, we mean that you cannot, and should not, creatively treat the actuality to such an extent that it becomes untruthful.

- *Image-against-image counterpoint:* an example of this might be an interview with a driving instructor who, talking about the skills required to do her job professionally, describes the absolute necessity of always remaining calm and in control while with a client. This contrasts starkly with footage of her screaming impatiently at a terrified client while clutching the steering wheel of the car. Viewers are left to make their own decision about the truth with regard to the instructor's professionalism.

- *The overlap cut:* this is another useful tool for the editor within the rough cut which brings the sound in earlier than the picture, or the picture earlier than the sound. This adds smoothness to transitions, particularly sound gaps between speakers, and avoids the obvious jarring of a straight cut. When editing interviews which show more than one person, the overlap cut can be used in conjunction with reaction, or noddy, shots which can offer a far more natural feel to the conversation and give the piece a sense of pace and continuity.

- *Sequence transitions:* this is another type of overlap cut. It is a tidy way of moving the viewer from one scene to another. This could be achieved through a fade or cross-fade, but a sequence transition is far more subtle. An example of this might be shots of a young woman preparing to go out for the evening. As she gets ready to leave the house we already hear the distant but increasing sound of night club music, the clink of glasses and the distant conversation of friends. The scene cuts to her at the club and the sequence transition is complete.

The best advice we can offer you in order to help you fully to understand how you can structure your documentary is to think back to the contextual research which you carried out in pre-production. Rereading some of the resources on documentary in the bibliography at the end of this book and watching more documentaries will allow you to gain a much better understanding of when these techniques are used, for what purpose and with what effects.

As an editor working on the rough cut, you will need to work on both the overall structure of the documentary and its individual parts, noticing the pace and rhythm or flow of its parts and its entirety. This is difficult and tiring so walk away from the edit as often as you need to, take a rest and return with renewed vigour.

Once you are reasonably happy with what you have achieved (as an editor you will never be totally happy), organize another screening. You might want to ask the following questions:

- Do any scenes or interviews require more attention with regard to inserts, cutaways, CUs or basic visual and sound effects such as transitions or overlaps?
- Do you need to shoot any new footage or dialogue?
- Do you need to reshoot anything?
- Do you need to restructure any part of the overall documentary?
- Do you need to add anything, such as voice-over or commentary, which may help to give meaning or provide an explanation?
- Do you need to lose any material?

As before, you will need to consider carefully and act upon the feedback acquired at the screening.

You are now ready to move on to the next stage: graphics, credits and titles, narration, sound and music, and colour-correction and compositing.

The final cut

This is done when the editor and director feel that the structure and content are largely correct and only require more subtle attention. Graphics, titles and credits are created and edited, additional effects may be needed such as colour-correction and compositing, dialogue can be further edited and balanced, and wildtrack is added, as well as sound effects. The music is edited and then all sound is carefully and painstakingly treated so that it is in balance: that is, the music does not drown out the dialogue, or vice versa.

Graphics, titles and credits

There are some very basic rules for documentary graphics (such as names and job titles of interviewees), titles and credits. These include:

- Keep text, titles and credits short and simple.
- Credit all those people who helped to make the documentary possible, ensuring that their roles or job descriptions are accurate.
- Decide upon an appropriate style. White on a black background is a good starting point!
- Keep text within the safe area. Consider carefully the font and size, remembering that small or elaborate fonts will disappear. Think about how the text will appear on the screen and for how long it will remain there.
- Check the spelling of all text, including the names of the contributors.
- Watch the credits and titles for existing documentaries as a guide.

If you are clever, you will have had other members of the production team working on the credits while you were editing. If this is the case, you simply have to check them for style and content before dropping them in on the timeline.

Narration or commentary

You may well be using narration by design in that it was predetermined and an integral element of your documentary from the pre-production stage. However, you may realize at this stage that it is needed as a means of giving explanation or additional meaning to your footage. More importantly, especially in your first documentary, narration can be useful in resolving certain common problems. Rabiger (2004: 444) highlights the circumstances where narration may be required and the problems that it can resolve:

- Difficulty getting the film started.
- Failure to establish background or historical context so that the audience can enter the movie.
- Failure to identify the origin and therefore authenticity of material (it might be a reconstruction, for instance).
- Film lacks momentum.
- Audience wants to know more about participants' thoughts, feelings and choices.
- Complicated storyline is incomprehensible.
- Getting from one good sequence to the next takes too much explaining by the participants.
- Lack of resolution to the film because the evidence never achieves a satisfying focus.

There are two quite distinct ways of producing narration: the first is to have it thoroughly scripted; the second is to produce an improvised version by conducting an interview or conversation, normally best recorded on location or in a place which is familiar to the interviewee.

The first method requires you to use simple, direct, natural language which should not sound contrived or scripted. Being economical with words is advisable as this also reflects normal speech patterns. The second method has the advantage of sounding much more natural, simply because the narrator is not working from a script. You should, however, create a basic outline script or, at the very least, produce a list of questions which can guide the interview or conversation. Whichever you choose, make sure that you record a presence track. This is the background noise of the studio or location where the recording takes place which you will need in the sound edit in order to fill in the gaps between narration and to extend a pause.

Don't forget that the voice you choose will become the voice of the film and so you need to spend considerable time and effort auditioning potential narrators in order to select the person with the right voice. The sound of the voice you choose, in terms of gender, class, accent and timbre, plays as important a role in making meaning as what is actually said. This is a job that the rest of the production crew can be carrying out while the editor continues crafting the final cut.

Sound

It is time to watch the whole documentary again, but this time you need to make detailed notes on the documentary's audio, highlighting where sound needs adding, blending or mixing to eradicate an abrupt sound edit, a change in sound levels or a gap in the sound. In each sequence, think about which sounds should dominate and which should be subsidiary. Look for areas where location ambience or presence tracks are absent and add the required sound. These may have been recorded in production but can also be acquired in post-production. An example of this would be an interview with an elderly lady in her home; through the lounge window, behind her, children can be seen playing. It might be appropriate to include that exterior sound of the children playing as background. Cross-fade sound edits by using short fade-ins and fade-outs so that there are no abrupt changes in levels as one sound ends and another starts. This is particularly useful with certain types of documentary which move abruptly from one scene or location to another.

Music

Now that your documentary is almost complete, you need to decide whether music is needed, where, why and what music is appropriate for the documentary *that you have now*. This may be completely different to the music that you had considered using at the pre-production stage.

You should sit down and go through the documentary again, but this time listening to it rather than watching it. Make notes on where music could be used to enhance the visuals. This process is called music sound-spotting. If you are very fortunate you will have had music composed for the video; otherwise, you will need to use pre-recorded music. It is worth remembering that if this music is not copyright-free or has not been cleared for use, this will prevent you from showing your documentary publicly. Adding the wrong type of music or including music where it is inappropriate can seriously damage your documentary, so you should take this process seriously. Your choice of music should always be guided by what is appropriate for the emotive or inner workings of a scene, character or subject. The music itself will evoke emotion from the audience, either by supporting the visuals on screen or through the juxtaposition of music and visuals which are intentionally at odds with each other.

Once all the music has been selected and added, the final audio mix can take place. You will need to go through the video once again, but this time close your eyes and concentrate on the balance of the sounds: for instance, is there a little too much ambient traffic noise which is starting to encroach on the detail of what the presenter is saying? Are there any areas where the viewers' attention is being shifted unnecessarily and therefore leading to confusion about where their attention should be focused?

Colour-correction

Now that the documentary is visually tight, it will require the editor to go through the final aspect of post-production: that is, to look at each section or scene and ensure that there is a continuity of colour between shots. You will remember that, in the video industry, this process is known as grading. This can take some time as it requires the editor to go through the whole documentary shot by shot, scene by scene in order to achieve an overall balance. If only one camera was used, it may be that colour-correction within a scene is not required. However, footage which was shot in the same place at different times or from different camera positions or footage from each camera of a two-camera shoot may require colour-correction. Grading for creative and stylistic purposes, if done correctly, can add another layer of sophistication to the finished documentary.

Distribution

We started this chapter by saying that there are an increasing number of opportunities for documentary makers, especially those working outside major media institutions, to have their work screened to a wider audience than previously. These opportunities include film-making networks, documentary websites and festivals.

We go through these in some detail in the 'Applying Theory to Practice' bonus chapter on the book's website, but the point we would make here is that, by this stage of your production career, you should be aiming to get your work out into the wider world and should feel confident enough to deal with any resulting criticism or, as we hope, to deliver your acceptance speech when your work wins an award!

Our top ten tips for documentary production

1. Always look around for good subject matter and compile an extensive list of possible documentary topics. There are hundreds of potential documentaries waiting to be made!

2. Conduct thorough research and analysis. Poor research will, in itself, lead to a poor production.

3. Watch lots of documentaries! Only then will you have an awareness of documentary styles and what makes a good or bad documentary.

4. Think about the kind of documentary that you *don't* want to make as much as the kind that you *do*. It will guide your final decision. Go with your gut feeling: if you think a subject will make a good documentary, then it probably will.

5. Even though you are making a documentary, always use a tripod unless the shot calls for a hand-held shot. Although there is a perception that documentaries rely on hand-held shots, even a cursory examination of them will show that this is a fallacy.

6. Always remember to have release forms signed on the day that you film people. It is difficult, and sometimes impossible, to obtain signatures after the event. Make sure that the participants record their details clearly.

7. Try to make the subjects of your video feel as relaxed and comfortable as possible. If they feel uncomfortable, they won't act naturally.

8. Always be prepared for the unexpected. Documentary production is notoriously fluid and often ends up a long way from where it started. It is a voyage of discovery: enjoy the journey!

9. Make sure that you obtain copyright clearance for all archive footage and music that you use in your documentary. If you don't, you won't be able to show your work publicly.

10. Your video is no good as a shelf-bender. Get it out there and let people see it!

9 The Drama Short

Introduction

The last few years have seen an explosion in the quantity of affordable video equipment available: Mini DV and HD cameras for production; powerful computers and editing software for post-production; broadband internet and dedicated websites for distribution. The reason that we mention this here is because this ease of access to equipment which allows for high-quality video production has led to a similar explosion in the number of videos being produced and distributed, especially short films. In this chapter, we shall focus on one type of video short: the drama short.

Before we go any further, we would provide the following definition: *a drama short is a piece of moving image which comprises a mixture of video, animation or stills, is made as close to industry-standard production values as possible, can be from ten seconds to twenty minutes long and of any genre but normally has a self-contained narrative and is primarily distributed or exhibited through film festivals, arthouse cinemas or short-film websites.*

Drama shorts have been used as a 'calling card' for people who wanted to enter the media industries but, with the proliferation of shorts, they no longer have the same impact. However, while a good student short will not guarantee you a job, people within the industry will take note of an outstanding short which is part of a wider portfolio or showreel. This is because producing a short can be as complex and challenging, and can require the same skills, as a much longer production: if you can manage to produce a great short you should be capable of working on a longer production. Equally importantly, you will learn more about the rigours of the production process when working on a short than on almost any other project you are likely to encounter as a student. The production of a short film, therefore, is an excellent opportunity to develop and test out all of the production skills that you have learnt to date. Indeed, it is for precisely this reason that this is often the video that students are most keen to produce. The definition above, therefore, does not include the vast majority of user-generated content seen on websites such as *MySpace, YouTube, Facebook* and

Bebo, much of which, owing to its mode of production and its frequently poor production values, we would characterize as home video, even if some of it is extremely good home video.

Given that producing a short is such a large undertaking and that it is likely to be your first experience of producing a drama, we would recommend that you attempt to produce a short later, rather than sooner, in your video career, as its success relies very much upon your mastery of the six essentials of video production that we outlined in Chapter 2:

1. ideas and the research process;
2. planning and management;
3. process and equipment;
4. reflection;
5. flexibility;
6. drive, determination and enthusiasm.

Tasks to do

1. If you haven't seen any or many shorts, then we suggest that you do so now! We recommend www.triggerstreet.com and www.bbc.co.uk/film-network along with the others websites listed in the bibliography.
2. Watch *at least* ten short films. We would suggest that you look at the following as a start:
   - *Who Killed Brown Owl* by Christine Molloy and Joe Lawlor (on the *Best vs Rest* DVD (www.shootingpeople.org);
   - *About a Girl* (www.bbc.co.uk/filmnetwork on the Cinema 16 DVD).
   For each of them, make notes on its duration, notable creative and technical aspects, narrative, overall style, use of dialogue and actors.
3. Is it possible to isolate some generic characteristics of short films generally? Is it possible to isolate subgenres of short film? What makes any of the shorts you saw different? How did they make you feel? How did they do that and why?

From watching even this small number of shorts, you should be aware that a *good* short has certain basic components:

- a story which is worth telling;
- convincing actors who deliver credible dialogue;
- appropriate locations, costumes and props;
- the imaginative use of cinematography and editing;

- the technically proficient use of sound in production and post-production;
- appropriate music.

This is achieved through an attention to detail in all aspects of the production process. It is these qualities that you need to have at the forefront of your mind throughout the process of producing your own short.

Your research at this stage should be detailed contextual research. As with title sequences and magazine programmes, drama shorts have not yet been the focus of sustained academic study and so specific resources are scarce. However, within television studies there is a body of writing about drama that you should begin to access at this point (see Creeber 2001 for a good introduction). To assist you in thinking about some of the issues relating to drama, you should consider the brief in relation to our key concepts of I CARLING.

Institution

Historically, short films have existed since the birth of film as a medium. You will remember from Chapter 8 that the first films produced by the Lumière brothers in France, but also by other film-makers such as Thomas Edison in the USA and Louis Le Prince in England, were of necessity short because of the limitations of the cameras used and the film stock available. However, as cameras rapidly became more sophisticated and capable of accepting larger reels of film and as editing technology became more advanced, film-makers realized that they could use the features of continuity editing which later became standard in Hollywood films – the compression of time, the instantaneous changing from one location to another, the camera changing angles, etc. – to create short narrative pieces: films such as *L'Arroseur arrosé* (*The Sprinkler Sprinkled*) by the Lumière brothers, for example, the narrative of which revolved around the by-now-standard joke of someone standing on a gardener's hose. One of the key figures in the development of narrative cinema was George Meliès. Space does not permit a full discussion here of the move to narrative cinema; see, for example, Cook (2001) for a much fuller discussion.

Very soon after this move, within ten to fifteen years, industrial modes of production, or what later became known as the Hollywood studio system, started to become dominant. The production of cinema film became concentrated within large studios which controlled all aspects of the production: from the writing of the films by salaried employees, through production in their own studios to distribution and marketing. One result of this move towards a studio system was that longer films started to be produced and feature films lasting about ninety minutes rapidly became the established norm. Even stars who had previously worked in short films – Buster Keaton, Charlie Chaplin and Laurel and Hardy – were, by the early 1930s, working in feature films, not shorts. The main reason for this was financial: it allowed a dedicated distribution and screening network under the strict control of studios such as Metro Goldwyn Mayer and Universal to be set up and to recoup the costs of the film as well as to make a profit. Whereas the earliest films, up to fifteen of them at a time, were shown at fairs and in theatres, these longer films were shown in the studio's own cinemas, thus creating a monopoly.

This move towards longer, narrative feature films and distribution networks controlled by major studios meant that the production of short films became increasingly marginalized. By that we mean that short films tended to be produced and distributed outside the main media institutions: namely, in film schools and universities, in artistic circles or by private individuals. The positive effect of production outside the major institutions was that the films were able to be much more experimental in terms of both form and content. Part of your research here, then, might involve you looking at short films produced from the 1920s onwards, especially experimental, avant-garde films.

Today, the production of short films encompasses many different types of institutional setting: from the no-budget short made by an individual film-maker to the publicly funded shorts made using grants and awards to shorts produced within major media institutions. Institutionally, some broadcasters are beginning to re-evaluate the value of the short film, both as content to fill broadcast or online space and as a proving ground for up-and-coming film-makers: in the UK, for example, the BBC has set up a dedicated short-film space on its website and occasionally shows the best films on its cable and satellite channels, while Channel 4 regularly shows *Four Docs* and *Three Minute Wonders* made for its websites.

Contexts of production

As with all other media, short films were, and still are, affected by the contexts (economic, political and social) in which they are produced. It is evident that they have been profoundly affected by the economic context in particular. We mentioned above that the production of short films was to a great extent marginalized by the studio system. What this meant in practice was that money was put into the production of feature films which would create and sustain large audiences and, as a result, provide the studios with large profits. While some cinema bills did have a secondary feature (or B movie), newsreels and short films, these were always seen as a warm-up for the main feature, so for many years the production of short films was almost exclusively carried out without the institutional might, and money, of the studios.

In practice, this meant that shorts tended to be shot on the lower-quality 16mm film, as opposed to the industry-standard 35mm film (and later video), that their budgets were significantly lower than those for studio productions and, as a result, the production values were lower. For many working within the area, this was exceptionally liberating and, rather than trying to ape the products of the studio system, they glorified in the freedom that such a space provided.

The production of short films is currently one of the most dynamic areas of media production. While there are still a large number of shorts being produced as 'art' pieces and installations which challenge the existing forms and content of video and push the frontiers of what can be achieved with the moving image, high-quality *narrative* drama shorts are becoming increasingly widespread. In the content-hungry new media marketplace that we explore in the bonus chapter – terrestrial, satellite, cable and internet television, mobile phones and PDAs and the proliferation of film festivals around the world – the drama short is now an accepted, separate and valid form of media production.

Audience

Given their production outside the mainstream media institutions, it is not surprising that shorts have also often been viewed outside the mainstream modes of distribution. Until fairly recently, the audience for shorts, especially the more esoteric and experimental shorts, would have been quite limited and would have been found within universities, film festivals and film-making groups. If we think of such an audience demographically, it is likely that the majority were young, educated, middle-class, and both male and female.

However, the fact that there is such a wide range of shorts – from the mainstream to the avant-garde – and such a wide range of distribution channels means that it is now difficult to generalize about the audience for contemporary short film. If you are to understand this relationship, you need to return to the questions about audience that we isolated in Chapter 1: how, what, when, where and why?

Representation

Given the breadth and scope of short films, from the most wildly avant-garde to the most generic of realist narratives, it is almost impossible to make anything other than the most general of points about representation within shorts.

One issue that you may wish to research and reflect upon, however, is in relation to the issue of stereotyping. We saw in previous chapters that representation is when something is shown not 'as it is' but in a partial and selective manner as a result of the conscious choices of the film-maker. One of the main problems for makers of short films is that they have to convey what may be extremely complicated and sophisticated situations *and* complex characters and the relationship between them. In such shorts, there is the possibility that, through lack of time, the characters and situations shown may appear stereotypical. For example, in both *Wasp* and *About a Girl*, it could be argued that the main characters were recognizable stereotypes of white, working-class British people at the beginning of the twenty-first century: feckless, blinded by celebrity, selfish. In the best short films, however, what may be perceived as stereotypes are built upon so that there is a complexity to the characters and their situations which takes the characters beyond stereotypes. As a video-maker you need to be very aware of this issue.

Language

Related to the discussion above is the notion of the film language of drama shorts. Once again, the huge range of shorts in terms of length, content and style mean that it is extremely difficult to make general points about their filmic language. By definition they are short and, as such, need to use the filmic grammar appropriate to their genre in an elegant and measured way.

Ideology

Again it is difficult, given the breadth of the short-film format, to make general points about the ideological positions of short films in general. What your research should allow you to do is to begin the process of carrying out research into whether certain ideological positions seem to be replicated within a range of shorts and, if so, how.

Narrative

The short film is a difficult form to work within as, by its nature, it is short! When producing a short you should give detailed consideration to the types of narrative structure which exist and work best within shorts. In order to do this, you must systematically analyse as wide a range of existing shorts as possible. To help you, we will start with the simplest and most likely narrative structure for shorts and move through to the most sophisticated (and unlikely).

You will remember that Bordwell and Thompson (1997: 90) defined narrative as being 'a chain of events in cause-effect relationship occurring in time and space'. The linear narrative is the most common type of filmic narrative within drama and can be characterized very simply as beginning, middle and end in that order. Tvetzan Todorov (1977) broke these stages down further into the following:

Equlibrium ➜ Disruption ➜ Recognition ➜ Attempt ➜ Equilibrium

The *parallel* narrative is another relatively common structure. This is where two narratives, which appear to be very separate, run throughout the film/programme, are brought together at or near the end of the film/programme and turn out to have some relationship:

Beginning   Narrative A ⎯⎯⎯⎯⎯⎯⎯⎯⎯⎯⎯⎯⎯⎯⎯⎯⎯⎯
                                                    ⟩ End
              Narrative B ⎯⎯⎯⎯⎯⎯⎯⎯⎯⎯⎯⎯⎯⎯⎯⎯⎯⎯

As there will, of necessity, be cross-cutting between the two narrative strands, this structure can be more accurately represented as:

Beginning ➜ A ➜ B ➜ A ➜ B ➜ A+B ➜ End

A third common type of narrative structure in shorts is the *interwoven* narrative. This is particularly common in soap operas. A film or programme using such a structure could have many possible narrative strands. A sample interwoven narrative with three strands (A, B and C) can be represented as:

Beginning ➜ A ➜ B ➜ C ➜ B ➜ A ➜ C ➜ A ➜ C ➜ B ➜ A +B+C ➜ End

Normally, there will be a clear relationship between the different narrative strands. It is perfectly possible, however, to have little apparent relationship between the strands. Whichever is the case, each strand will be worked through and, as with a parallel narrative, any relationship between the narrative strands may only become apparent at the end of the film/episode of the programme.

The flashback/flashforward narrative structure is relatively common within feature films but is not used as often in shorts as time does not allow for the relative complexity of such a structure. There are any number of different ways in which the narrative can move backwards or forward and a typical structure for a very simple one-strand narrative is:

End ➔ Beginning ➔ Middle ➔ End

Increasing levels of complexity can be introduced if more than one narrative strand is introduced or if the flashbacks and flashforwards are more frequent and less regular than shown above (for example, as in the film *Memento*). Bear in mind that using such a complex narrative structure requires you to be very skilful if you are not to lose your audience's attention.

When carrying out your research into existing shorts, you should think about which of these structures are used in the films you watch and which work best. Our position, as you will see in a moment, is that you must be aware at this stage that short films are not feature films. Using two or three characters and a relatively simple narrative structure is much more likely to make your short successful.

Genre

It is important to note that over the past few years there has been a rapid rise in the number and type of shorts being produced. Given that they may still function as 'calling cards' for people wanting to enter the media industries, shorts often mirror accepted film genres using the same codes and conventions as the genres they are working within. If you look, for example, at the categories of short film at www.triggerstreet.com, you will see that they include action, adventure, crime and historical films.

Ben Blaine, a producer and director of short films, hosted a short-film competition in 2004 for people subscribing to Shooting People, an industry networking forum and bulletin board. After the event, he provided feedback on his thoughts to all those who had subscribed and made the following useful points (2004: 1–2):

- Most of the entries were rigidly generic: 'a lot of horror films, a lot of comedy horror films, a lot of gangster films, a lot of comedy gangster films and a LOT of films about young men making films'. The problem with this is that 'by the time the filmmaker has included all the clichés that make the genre, they find that they have very little time for anything of their own'.
- Most of the entries could be categorized as follows: 'Micro-shorts, Arty Shorts, Comedy Shorts, Long and Serious Shorts'. Amusingly, we have

descriptions of 'micro-shorts' (up to twenty seconds in length), 'short shorts' (longer), 'Bermuda shorts' (even longer still!) and 'tartan shorts' which are, would you believe, produced in Scotland.

• Most of the films left him cold because 'no one seems to be doing anything very interesting' within the genres.

This does not mean that you should not do any of the above, just that if you are going to do so, you need to make sure that you are not just repeating what has already been done many times before and that you have an interesting take on your subject. As Blaine (2004: 1–2) notes: 'Always, for me at least, the really important distinction isn't whether something is a horror film or a serious drama but whether it works. Whether at the end of ten or fifteen minutes I feel like I have gained something.' The way to make sure that you do not fall into this trap is to be very aware of what is out there already and what possibilities the short-film format offers you. The only way to know this is through research. If you carry out your research properly, you should find that some of the most successful drama shorts are those which are *hybrid*: that is to say, they mix the codes from different genres in new and novel ways (Creeber 2001: 6). *Discful of Data*, for example, pays homage to the spaghetti western in some of its shot compositions (the ECUs of the eyes), the music (slide guitar) and the overall colour saturation, but it is also quite contemporary and, with its inclusion of a high-tech heist, recognizes other genres in its content.

Tasks to do

At this point, we would advise you to go to the website and have a look at the example of a fairly typical student drama short – *Discful of Data* – because this short will inform much of the later discussion in this chapter.

We would reiterate here that the above discussions are not meant to be exhaustive: it is up to you to use these brief discussions as the starting point for your own contextual research.

Pre-production

As ever, the first tip that we would give you when producing your short is to remember Cartwright's 70–30–10 rule: 70 per cent of your time should be spent on pre-production, 10 per cent on production and 30 per cent on post-production.

Thinking of ideas

Coming up with a range of ideas and narrowing it down

For the title sequence you had a programme to introduce and rigid generic conventions to copy or work within; for the magazine programme you were able to 'hang' your own content on to a widely accepted structure and for the documentary there were many accepted subgenres, each of which had its own specific conventions and likely content. This brief is more difficult because you have every film that you have ever seen or heard about to draw on for inspiration.This can be quite problematic, especially if, as many students do, you immediately come up with an idea to replicate a specific type of film that you like – the slasher movie, the zombie movie, the sci-fi movie – or, more specifically, aim to replicate in your short the narrative of a film that you know.

Our advice to you at this stage is that you should not complicate the process by thinking of specific genres or narratives but should keep it simple by thinking more generally about how drama narratives work. Although books and films may appear to have a huge number of different kinds of narrative, it is argued that there are, in fact, very few. Anita Russell (2000: 2) notes that only seven stories have ever been told in films and that 'each of these has a source, an original story upon which the others are based', such as a legend or an opera. These stories, which form the template for all filmic narratives, are named after their source and represent universal human themes. She lists them and offers an example of each:

- *Achilles*: the flawless (or almost flawless) person: for example, *Superman*
- *Cinderella*: the dream comes true: for example, *Pretty Woman*
- *Circe (Sir See)*: the chase: for example, *The Matrix*
- *Faust*: selling your soul to the devil may bring riches but eventually you belong to him: for example, *Bedazzled*
- *Orpheus*: the loss of something personal: for example, *The Sixth Sense*
- *Romeo and Juliet*: the love story: for example, *Titanic*
- *Tristan*: man loves woman but unfortunately one or both are already spoken for: for example, *Fatal Attraction*.

Clearly, you will be able to come up with more recent examples for each source but the point is that these seven narratives inform most of the narratives that we see and read. However, you can combine elements of the different types of narrative and present them in different ways. For example, *Romeo and Juliet* could be comedy, drama or horror.

For this brief, it is originality which makes a great short. Within these seven narratives, it is those things over which you have control, such as location, characters and storylines, which provide the originality. Some of you may have absolutely no ideas at this stage. Don't panic. You don't need to rely on a flash of inspiration: many of the best ideas are to be found around you and are waiting to be turned into a story *if you just look hard enough*. So, where do you look?

There are many potential dramas being enacted in front of your very eyes – on the bus, in the street, within your living room and at the next table in the café – so finding the germ of an idea for a plot is not as difficult as you might at first think. *Specifically for shorts*, good ideas often come from keeping your eyes and ears open: an article in a newspaper, especially the short 'fun-type' articles in many papers, a comment overheard on the bus, a joke, urban myths, something you saw on television or read in a book or comic book, a dream or an idea that you have been toying around with for a long while. The list of places to find potential stories is almost endless: it really depends on how focused you are and how hard you are prepared to work at coming up with ideas. Make the same walk that you made when you were generating ideas for the documentary chapter but this time look for ideas for a drama. If you are really struggling to come up with ideas, do what many good student scripts do: return to the seven basic narratives and then go out and find something that fits into one or more of them. It is important to remember also that an idea for a narrative or story does not have to be developed into something complex to be original: in fact, it is often best to keep it as simple as possible.

Assessing the feasibility of your ten best ideas

Whichever of the above routes that you use to come up with your ten ideas, there are fundamental reasons why some ideas might be selected to take forward to the next stage and others rejected. Consequently, and given the complexity of producing a drama short, it is *imperative* that you examine each of the ten ideas in relation to all of our standard limiters. Remember that at this stage you are using the process to reveal reasons why certain ideas should not go forward or are not capable of going forward.

This brief is slightly different to the others in the book in that while applying your limiters, you also need to be assessing whether or not each idea offers the possibility of:

- good narrative development;
- good characterization and character development;
- an imaginative use of the style and generic conventions of short film.

Carrying out research on each of your remaining ideas

For drama you need to take into account the usual considerations in terms of research and feasibility with which you have now become familiar from previous briefs. Although the process is the same as for all the other briefs in this book, the real difference in carrying out the research for the three remaining ideas is that a drama short is likely to involve much more depth over a broader range of areas than the previous briefs: more equipment, more props and costumes and more locations. A drama is a very complex project and so systematic organization is absolutely crucial:

- *Finance:* shorts have the capacity to be very expensive. Increasingly, short films are being made on 16mm or 35mm film. You may be lucky enough to have access to funding to create such a short but we are assuming that you don't, so it is likely that you will be working with DV, HD or Super 8. It *is* possible to produce a very good low-budget (or even no-budget) video short, especially if you have a great story and script, are good at blagging, have a clear idea of what you want to produce, are prepared to work very hard and have a reliable, technically proficient crew. Think about whether any of your ideas are too ambitious or not ambitious enough. At this early stage, the main items of expenditure that you need to consider are likely to be:
  - *Location:* locations can very often be used without charge but certain locations, such as a castle or private land, may charge a fee. Do any of your ideas require fee-paying locations?
  - *Props and costume hire*: sourcing and acquiring the *right* props, costumes and set dressing – rather than making do with anything that is readily available – in order to create the desired look and feel for the piece is key when producing a great short. They will all involve expense. Don't make the mistake of cutting corners: if you are going to do it, do it right or don't do it at all.
  - *Stock:* if using film, you will need to consider the cost of stock and of processing and transferring it to a form suitable for digital editing.
  - *Kit:* whatever the idea, aim high. Try to use the best kit possible. Do any of your ideas lend themselves to certain types of camera such as Super 8 or to support kit such as jibs, cranes or generators? This will incur costs if it is kit that your college or university does not already have.
  - *Accommodation:* you should consider who needs to be accommodated within easy reach of the shooting locations and for how long. Your actors and crew won't thank you if they have to travel long distances each day in order to get to work!

- *Actors:* you should think about paying your actors the minimum student Equity rates (which you can find at www.equity.org.uk) or, at the very least, reimbursing their expenses and buying them a gift at the end of the shoot. Increasingly, film-makers are offering actors what is known as deferred payment: that is, payment if the film makes any money through wider distribution.
- *Catering:* a film-maker on Shooting People (we are very sorry if you are reading this but we have forgotten your name!) recently touted for advice while making his first serious low-budget short film. He received hundreds of replies but was able to distil these replies into one useful piece of advice: 'pay nobody, feed everybody and save all your money for post-production'. Even as a student film-maker, you should try and heed the second part of this advice. It may seem like something that you should not have to deal with or budget for, but it is important always to ensure that everyone on set is fed and watered regularly. Don't forget that the size of crew, number of actors and number and length of shooting days will directly affect costs.

It is no good having a great idea if you don't have the budget to do it justice, so if at this stage it looks likely that raising funds is going to be a problem, you should save the great idea for the future when you have a bigger budget and choose another, more doable idea for the present.

- *Logistics:* although you have considered logistics for all of your previous briefs, the likely length of shoot, the potential number of locations and the numbers of people involved are likely to make the logistics for a drama short much more complex. Moving the people and the kit could be relatively easy for one of your three ideas and more difficult for the others, so you need to analyse the logistical requirements of each idea and give it a rating in terms of its level of complexity. For example, if shooting is scheduled for March and the idea suggests that you shoot in the Highlands of Scotland, this may cause logistical problems if you are based in the south of England. Similarly, if the short is to be shot in the snow, that too will have important logistical implications. Do you have the capacity to organize all the necessary logistics, especially if a shoot is likely to be particularly complex (lots of locations, lots of actors, lots of costumes, different start times)?
- *Health and Safety:* this is always of paramount importance and is sometimes ignored. Do your ideas ring any alarm bells in terms of risk, such as a car chase, filming at height or the use of pyrotechnics?
- *Technical resources:* most or all of your equipment will probably come from your college or university. However, some ideas may require specialist

equipment which is both difficult and expensive to access and requires training on the part of the crew. A good example of this is an idea which requires the use of a professional Steadicam or professional track and dolly.

- *Human resources:* as well as using actors, certain ideas may require a specially trained individual: a make-up and prosthetic artist, a fight or stunt co-ordinator, an animal handler, a qualified underwater camera operator, a helicopter pilot or a stunt driver, to name but a few. If you cannot afford to pay for them, are there alternatives? If you need an aerial shot of your town, for example, can you book a trial helicopter flight at your local airport and take a video camera up with you?

- *Experience and ability of the crew:* many of the shorts proposed by our students require them to use professional equipment and, more importantly, to use it properly and to its full potential. Does any member of your crew need further training with an expert in order to be able to use, for example, the latest HD camera? If you decide to shoot on a lower format, are you convinced that your camera operators are really proficient in the use of that equipment? You cannot afford to learn on the job: too much is at stake. This applies to all roles.

- *Time:* as with the previous briefs, you should have a timeline in mind for each idea and then establish whether you have sufficient time to produce each of the ideas. Some will require more time than others to produce: normally those with more locations, more actors, more kit (especially specialist kit such as a crane/jib). Many students grossly underestimate how long it will take to plan, film and edit an idea. Even the shortest of shorts can take much longer to produce than anticipated.

- *Output:* given the popularity of shorts, you might want to think about screening your production more widely than at local venues such as art centres, cafés and bars. Websites, festivals and competitions are increasingly targeted at drama shorts and mobile, or cell, phones now have the ability to download video, so discuss which of your ideas can be used and are suitable for each of the above. The duration, subject matter and language of some ideas may limit their ability to be screened more widely.

Deciding upon the final idea

Whichever idea you choose to take forward into production, it must be one that is realizable, that all members of the group are fully committed to and enthusiastic about and that is interesting and entertaining, both for you and, more importantly, for your potential audience.

Producing an outline

Figure 9.1 shows the outline for *Discful of Data*, which illustrates the structure and content for a drama short.

Given that there is often external funding available for the production of a short film, this may be the first outline that you have produced which could

---

Outline

Title of programme: Discful of Data

Duration: 15 minutes

Time slot: 8.30pm

Audience: Male/female 18–25 years

Screened: Channel 4 and festivals

Format: MiniDV

Resume: A mishmash of Leone-esque cool and big business. Taking on the original concept of Akira Kuwosawa's *Yojimbo*, this drama short uses the classic spaghetti western synopsis of the loner walking into town and pitting two opposing forces against each other. A contemporary twist on a well-respected genre, this short depicts the protagonists fighting to possess revolutionary new computer software in the barren backdrop of the Derbyshire Dales at the height of winter.

Suggested elements:

1. Two computer software developers arrange to meet at a quiet, out-of-the-way location; a cheap B&B run by its rather scruffy owner who acts as patron, waiter and receptionist.
2. The two men meet up, the interior of the B&B in a barren winter exterior. They are greeted by the owner who puts the valuable disc in his safe.
3. A mystery guest arrives and checks in, making three guests in total. The two other guests wonder who he is and why he is there … the man with no name. Distrust and paranoia pervade.
4. The fellow software developers conflict, the deal which is to combine their software is finally made and they celebrate their digital merger.
5. Unknown to them the man who has no name and the proprietor are working together and have swapped the master disc for a blank copy.
6. The software developers blame each other for the missing software and accuse one another of a double-cross.
7. The man with no name and the proprietor are seen leaving together with the revolutionary software disc.

Film days: 4 days

Estimated budget:	Accommodation	460
	Catering	300
	Actors	450
	Transport hire	120
	Fuel	50
	Props and costumes	50
Total		£1430

Figure 9.1   Outline for *Discful of Data*

fulfil its second purpose of selling your idea to a potential sponsor or funder and so you need to get it right: you need to find a 'hook' which will entice the funder to consider funding you and your project. This involves:

- selling the idea for the project as a whole by making it look exciting and attractive;
- being clear about what makes *this* short different from others;
- clearly outlining the narrative and/or character development;
- having a clear sense of your audience;
- having a realistic, albeit at this stage basically costed, budget.

Carrying out research

Once you have the one firm idea that you intend to take to production, you can start the real work: different elements of which need to be done simultaneously. Although we have written this chapter in a linear way (because that is all we can do in a book!), you need to be carrying out research for your idea at the same time as you are writing the various drafts of the storyboard and script. You cannot afford to wait for the final version of either before starting research: you simply won't have time. This may cause challenges, as you are now starting to look at the script in detail, which may cause you to have to change the focus and detail of your research. In turn, the detailed research may throw up problems relating to the script which need to be addressed. At this stage in your production career, however, you should know how to handle such challenges: it requires patience, good communication and time spent on solving problems:

- *Locations:* like any other video, a drama short relies on its audience believing what it is watching. This will only happen if you have done everything in your power to create the right look and feel. Central to this is your choice of locations. You should by now have a clear idea of the number and type of locations required and you need to research the specific locations required and the cost implications and set about obtaining permission to use them. Lack of detail to attention with regard to locations is often a failing in student dramas. As we saw in Chapter 3, more often than not this is because it is tempting to settle for locations simply because they are easily accessible or easily organized, rather than because they are the perfect choice for your drama short, which is crucial. So, if your video requires an office location, go and find one; if it needs a stately home, find that too! Never 'make do'. Your lounge will never be a substitute for the interior of a stately home (unless you are lucky enough to live in one!) However, be imaginative: if a stately home is not available, is there a local hotel, for example, which looks stately enough? If you need a 1950s interior, is there a museum locally or nationally which contains such a display and which will allow you to shoot there? This is where the magic of moving image can kick in: film at one exterior location and cut to the interior of another and, as long as the audience continues to believe, it will work. In order to make sure that this happens, never underestimate the length of time required for proper location-scouting! It may only take one phone call but it is more likely, given the complexity of a drama shoot, to take days or weeks.

- *Accommodation:* be thorough and practical in your research. Check out the costs of hiring different types of holiday accommodation during the low season, ask about group discount or look at sharing a room in a budget hotel or motel where you pay for the room, not for each person. Our own student crews often use youth hostels because they are relatively inexpensive and because it is often possible to book an entire hostel, which allows them to both live and film there uninterrupted.

- *Props and costumes:* when producing a drama short, it is possible that props and costumes may be run either by one person or by two people working together, hence our combining them here. The same general rules apply for both. The sooner you receive definite details from the scriptwriter the better, because you will then have some sense of what you are looking for in terms of suitable props and costumes. They need to be sourced as early as possible and this can be very time-consuming. Costumes would include everything worn by actors, from hats to shoes, while props fall into five main categories:

    1. *dressing props:* for example sofas, curtains and mirrors;
    2. *hand-held props:* for example a mobile phone, a newspaper or a mug of tea
    3. *hero props:* any object which is integral to the action in the scene, such as such as the phaser gun used by Captain Kirk on the Star Ship Enterprise;
    4. *stunt props:* for example a rubber brick or plastic knife;
    5. *mechanical props:* anything which moves, for example R2D2 in *Star Wars*, or which emits light.

Trees, food and plants are also considered to be props and may need to be sourced. While sourcing props and costumes has the potential to be very time-consuming, it can be much easier than you might at first think to acquire everything that you need, even the most bizarre of items. Once you have exhausted on-line auction websites, try your local charity shops, rummage, car boot or garage sales, house clearances, auction rooms, theatres, costume hire, showrooms and warehouses, friends and family, an advert or article in the local newspaper or on the radio station. It is amazing what people will do for a credit in the final video! If you don't ask, you don't get; if you do ask, the worst that can happen is that someone will say no. Don't forget, too, to make sure that you get the names of the people who help you out so that you can send them a thank-you letter or e-mail, that you include their names in the final credits and that you send them a copy of the finished video. As far as costumes are concerned, always try to measure the actors and organize a fitting prior to the shoot. Even if the costumes fit perfectly, you should allow time in the schedule for the actors to become accustomed to them and to feel comfortable wearing them, both physically and in terms of their role or character. This can pay real dividends: on a recent shoot in Prague, one of the British actors played the role of a Soviet soldier. After a day of wearing the costume he 'grew into' the part, moving and sounding much more like a Soviet soldier than a British actor. Much the same applies to certain props, especially if they are to be carried, used or handled by actors. Give yourselves and your actors time to familiarize yourselves with how the props are to be used. Whatever you have sourced and wherever you get it from, the main rule is that it must be convincing and must contribute positively to the overall look and feel. Remember that everything has a semiotic significance with important connotations. It is your responsibility to ensure that the *correct* preferred reading is stimulated. Get it wrong and all your hard work is wasted.

- *Kit:* there are certain decisions about kit which can be made relatively early. Key decisions are finalizing the format that you will use and the type of camera you will shoot with: are you going to shoot using a lower-end format such as DV or a higher-end format such as DigiBeta or HD? Higher-end cameras are more professional and provide more aesthetic and creative control through, for example, their ability to accept a wider range of lenses (which will allow you to increase and decrease the depth of field) and as a result of their sophisticated electronics: the ability to be able to alter the colour characteristics of the image through Gamma controls, for example. A visually defining factor for drama is the creative use of depth of field, so you can ensure that your work is more cinematic by using a selection of filters and lenses, and 35mm adapters. You know already that you will need lighting kits and sound equipment, so you can book these early. If shooting somewhere where you cannot hook up to power, you may now need to book a generator. This is also the time to book other specific equipment such as a track and dolly, jib or crane.
- *Actors:* again, you should at this stage have a relatively clear idea of the number and types of actors required and so you can now begin to

research how to enlist them. Beware of thinking that you can successfully act in your own productions or that you can use friends to take the roles. Although it may seem convenient to do this, it can cause problems throughout the production process and can affect the quality of the finished product. If your actors are not professional, or at least trained, they do not generally understand what is required of them and/or do not take the job seriously – you have probably seen films where a brilliant script has been mauled by bad actors. Try to attract actors who have some experience by offering them a piece of quality work which will be a valuable addition to their showreel and CV and will help them gain further work. While there is a strand of film-making which uses non-professional actors, the directors renowned for working in this way are generally extremely experienced in their craft and are able to spend their time getting the best out of their actors without worrying about the technical aspects of the production. At this stage of your career, we would suggest that you probably do not have the experience to think about both and would advise against it. Proper casting is, therefore, essential to the success of your short. By this we mean that you should go through the process of engaging professional or semi-professional actors who are right for the part. Advertise locally through theatres and in newspapers for professional actors. If your university or college has a drama course or department, then advertise and promote your call for actors there. Go and see the tutors and ask them to recommend reliable, hardworking and talented student actors who are suitable for the roles you need to fill. Be aware, however, that because they are young people, the roles they can fill may be quite limited and the number of students may be relatively small. If you cannot find the right people locally, try going further afield: for example, by putting a casting call in *PCR, Stage, Variety* and on Shooting People. This needs to be professional. Make sure that it follows the accepted format for casting calls (see, for example, www.shootingpeople.org/casting) and, once it has been written, have someone check it: if it does not make sense or contains spelling and grammar errors, it will immediately alert actors, directors and casting agents to your lack of professionalism. This is a common failing of student groups. When writing your casting call, make sure that you are clear who and what you want: if your script calls for a fifty-year-old woman who can juggle, then that is what you should ask for! It makes your life much easier and it allows the actors to do what they do best: act the role you want them to act.

- *Auditioning actors:* once the casting call is out and you are inundated by the CVs, headshots and showreels of hundreds of fifty-year-old jugglers, you need to whittle this down to a more a manageable number by sitting down as a team and working your way through the CVs to find the most suitable candidates. This is often, initially at least, based on whether the headshot suggests that they look right for the part and then on their previous experience, their location and their availability. Once you have decided who might be right for the part, organize a proper audition:

- Book two rooms: one as a green room where the actors can assemble, have refreshments and read the script; the other as a room with space for the camera, casting crew and actors.
- Invite the actors you like the look of, let them know what you want them to do when they come to the session (normally to read a part of the script for the production and possibly a monologue of their own choosing) and timetable them in. Make sure that you book video cameras to record the session so that you can concentrate on the actors in the session but remind yourselves later how they performed.
- The actors will often have travelled a significant distance and invested time and effort in preparing for the audition. Give them enough of your time to make them feel that it was worth it.
- Send them clear and detailed directions, the exact time of their audition and an emergency contact number.

It is impossible to advise on how to select actors. If you read anything written by professional casting directors, you will know that the way in which a decision is reached is often quite intangible. You will normally 'just know' who are the right actors for the roles on the basis of their personality and performance on the day of the audition. Once you have made your decisions, contact them to let them know that they have been chosen, together with an up-to-date copy of the script, a release form and, if it has been written, a provisional shooting schedule. Make sure that you keep them informed. Once they have been engaged, they are part of the team so give them the courtesy they deserve by phoning or e-mailing them regularly to update them on progress. Do remember to contact those who were not successful and to thank them.

- *Budget:* take a look at the budget for *Discful of Data* on the website. You will notice that it is detailed, clearly laid out and has an accurate final figure. What this suggests is that there cannot be any 'guesstimates'. It is essential, therefore, that you acquire a real sense of the importance of money at this stage: how much you are really likely to have, what you really need to spend money on and how much each of these things will really cost. A couple of phone calls or e-mails will normally allow you to obtain accurate prices for everything you need. Be astute and contact a number of suppliers to find the best price.

- *Raising the finance:* once you have an accurate breakdown of what you need to spend, you will have to raise the necessary finance. Be imaginative about where the money for your budget could come from but remember the basic rule: ask a large number of people for a relatively small sum; not a small number of people for a large sum. There are so many possibilities for raising the necessary money: donations from friends and family, donations of money or goods from local businesses and money raised by the group through, for example, organizing film screenings, DJ nights, sponsored events, gaming tournaments and bag-packing at local supermarkets. Don't forget to enquire within your own organization: there just might be pockets of money to fund certain types of project. The list is endless. If you think that your expenses will be considerable (if, for example, you want to hire HD cameras or to film abroad), it is a good idea to start fund-raising before you have even decided on your final idea because it can take a long time and a lot of hard work to raise the money. Those interested in providing you with support will inevitably want something back. Try to offer them something they want, such as advertising or promotion. If you intend to organize a screening of your finished drama for a reasonably large audience, you may just attract the attention of sponsors. Remember also that some funding comes with conditions and you need to make sure that you fulfil them.
- *Logistics:* detailed maps and local guides are essential, even if people are using satellite navigation, in order to ensure that everyone turns up at the right place at the right time. Isolated locations require particular attention. In remote areas place discreetly labelled directional markers on the side of the road to point people in the right direction.
- *Health and Safety:* every location will require a thorough recce and risk assessment. Multiple locations will need a systematic approach to documentation and attention to script directions. Make sure that your recce teams also research locations in terms of accommodation, route planning, including travel times, and local suppliers such as supermarkets and hardware stores, and that they take digital photographs for the production team to examine upon their return.
- *The experience and ability of the crew:* this is the time when you should re-evaluate the various skills that your team have both collectively and as individuals in specific relation to the allocated roles and the project overall. A skills audit for each crew member may be a good idea at this stage: how much experience do they have in the specific production roles? What is their previous experiences and what are their limitations? Do you have the right combination of skills within your team to produce a successful drama? Do you need to replace anyone in your current crew or acquire someone who has specific skills?

- *Catering:* once you have an outline shooting schedule, you can start researching and planning how you will feed everyone. For location shoots away you really do need to think of everything: breakfast, mid-morning break, lunch, afternoon break, dinner and late-night snacks (especially if you are night shooting). These will need to be costed, menus prepared and food sourced, prepared, cooked and served within the confines of the possibly changing shooting schedule. Make sure that you consider healthy eating, people's likes and dislikes and particular dietary requirements such as those for vegetarians and vegans.
- *Time:* the big one! This will be your largest and most complicated project to date and your plan must be as accurate as possible because of the complexities associated with the drama short: scripting, auditions, rehearsals, technical walkthroughs, multiple locations for filming, potentially complicated set-ups using lights and camera support equipment, endless takes and sufficient time for the three stages of editing. You must use all your professional experience now to ascertain how long it will take to complete each stage of the production process and still meet the deadline. Now is the time to draw up your detailed group project planner.
- *Output:* at this stage you need to know where you intend to screen your finished drama and what audience you have in mind.
- *Content research:* most people within the industry will isolate the story and resulting script as being the thing which makes or breaks a production. So, for shorts, as for any other drama, the story is everything. You may remember that in Chapter 7 we told you that the three-minute story is king in relation to magazine programmes. Well, for dramas, of whatever length, it is the script which is king. A poor script will inevitably produce a poor video, no matter how good the cast and crew: look at two-star film reviews in magazines and newspapers or online and you will notice that they often receive a low rating because potentially good actors are working with a poor script. Avoid making the same mistake by researching your idea. The script depends upon quality content research and this should continue to evolve as the script evolves. It involves looking at the story and thinking about all the information that you need to gather to give depth to the narrative. This research might be historical, political, geographical, cultural or political.

Producing a script

The script and storyboard have to start being developed as soon as the idea for the production is finalized. To restate the obvious, a script is the document which contains written descriptions of each scene, including the actions of the characters, where those actions take place and the dialogue. More often than not, the drama script is written by one person, so if you are working in a group you might want to let one person in the group write the first draft.

The best place to start when writing a script is to get down on paper the basic story (which you should have done for the outline). Many writers begin with a plot and have the events of the plot as the key thing in mind when writing the script: this is a *plot-driven* script. Others start with characters whose interactions and relationships are the main focus of the story: this is a *character-driven* script. As a scriptwriter, you have to think about which is more applicable to you and your idea. You must be clear about what type of script you want to write from the beginning as, without this clarity, the script will become muddy and confused.

As any scriptwriter, scriptwriting book or website will tell you, the secret of producing a great script, as opposed to a good one, is to know some of the 'rules' of scriptwriting and to go through a process of drafting and redrafting.

The rules of scriptwriting

When writing a drama script, the writer should have a clear idea of what the aims of the script are. These aims relate to two things: the hoped-for reactions of the audience to the video and the narrative structure. All films are written to produce reactions in the audience. These reactions are:

- *sensual*: they appeal to the visual and aural senses. Films with overt special effects appeal to the visual sense; snappy dialogue, as in *Friends*, and music appeal to the aural sense. Be careful if you intend to write a script which does only this as there is a danger of the story having no substance. It is this problem which is often seen as being a characteristic of postmodern film and television: namely, that it is all style and no substance.
- *emotional:* they aim to create certain emotional responses, such as fear or happiness, on the part of the audience. Don't forget, too, that the music score is one of the key elements in producing the required emotions.
- *intellectual*: they offer some sort of moral standpoint. Film and video which does only this risks being seen as didactic and 'preachy'.

The more successful short films attempt to produce all three reactions.

The primary aim of any script is to create a coherent narrative structure. By that we mean the selection and ordering of the elements at your disposal: characters, events, dialogue and locations. The linear narrative that you have already worked on in many of your videos is also totally appropriate for short films. In many ways it is ideal as it is relatively easy for the audience to follow.

However, we saw in the contextual research above that short films also offer the possibility of being more imaginative in their narrative structure. There are various other types of narrative structure that you can adopt in your short: flashback or flashforward, circular, parallel or interwoven. Be aware, though, that you do not have long to articulate your story. In a feature film you have the time to play around with narrative structures but also the time to guide your audience around them so that they understand them: in a short, if you try to be too adventurous and it is too difficult to follow, you may well find that the audience will give up trying to follow it.

Once you have made these key decisions about the type of script you wish to produce, you need to develop the idea into the first draft of the script. As with any script, numerous rewrites are essential. There is no limit to the number of times you may need to revisit the script, as we found out in writing this book. Write little and often and, if necessary, leave your script for a while and go back to it. This might stop you becoming angry or frustrated with the script! Don't leave it all to the last minute, but keep working away at it steadily, revising, sharing and reworking. This process of script development is, if done properly, very time-consuming, as it requires you to think about the following in detail:

- *Narrative:* you can use any of the different narrative structures that we looked at earlier. The linear narrative structure that we introduced in Chapter 1 works especially well in a short. In scriptwriting terms, you will often hear this referred to as the three-act structure. In a feature film, this is normally broken down as follows:
  - *Act One:* this presents the introduction to the situation, characters and the main premise of the film. At the end of the act, the first major twist in the plot occurs and opens it up. This act accounts for approximately a quarter of the screen time of most films.
  - *Act Two:* this is the act of confrontation. It focuses on the struggle of the main character who is forced to make some sort of choice at the end of the act and accounts for approximately half of the screen time of most films.
  - *Act Three:* this is the act of resolution. Once there is resolution, the story ends. This act accounts for approximately a quarter of the screen time of most films.

  From your own viewing of films and videos, you may already have noted that all narratives need some form of conflict. Many successful scripts and subsequent films have conflict as the basic theme of their story. Conflict creates tension, which in turn engages the viewers and their emotions. The move towards conflict resolution keeps the viewer watching and the eventual resolution of the conflict offers the viewer release. If we return to the film examples above, we will notice that they are all about characters and the problems or dilemmas that they must deal with. This process of working through the problem is what defines the drama in the story. Four different types of conflict are possible:

1. *Internal:* the individual versus the self.
2. *Personal:* the individual versus the individual.
3. *Social/environmental:* the individual versus society.
4. *The physical environment:* the individual versus nature.

- Drama shorts seem to be most effective if they are limited with regard to what takes place. By focusing on the unfolding of a single event, in a specific time and place, it is far easier for the writer to explore the drama of the situation and for the audience to empathize satisfactorily with the main character and his/her situation.

- *Characters:* the main point about characters, especially in a short film, is that they must be believable and must be able to live in the world that you are about to create in your narrative. This is what is called the *internal logic* of the story. You can ensure the internal logic of your story by writing a character profile of *each* of your principal and supporting characters. This is a relatively detailed description (one to two pages) of both the history (place of birth, type of family, education, etc.) and present circumstances of the character.

   Writing character profiles is fun but you can see how this might go on and on. However, writing these profiles is *vital* because once they have been written, the dialogue and, to some extent, the plots write themselves and are much more likely to contain internal logic. For example, if your character is driving along and a young girl throws a ball into the path of the car, a detailed character profile will enable you to know how the character will react: forgive her; smile and drive away; gently reprimand her, or shout and swear at her.

   This is *motivation*: the reason why someone does something. Each character must have a good reason for carrying out an action and the audience must believe that the character's behaviour is credible. If the audience can say, 'She would never have said that' or 'He would never have done that', there is a problem in relation to your character's motivation.

   There are two other points about characters to consider:

1. Longer dramas may allow for more than one major character but drama shorts seem to work best with only one major character on whom we are able to focus our attention and emotions. If you have

more than one or two main characters you run the risk of confusing the audience.

2. One of those characters should be what is called the *protagonist*, the main character (normally the 'goodie'): the other should be the *antagonist*, a secondary character trying to prevent the protagonist from achieving his/her goal (the 'baddie'). Antagonists may not receive our care and attention in the same way as do the protagonists but they must be suitable adversaries. Both must be capable of facing the challenges and conflicts which come their way and of holding the viewers' attention as they anticipate the outcome or resolution.

- *Dialogue:* this is the spoken part of the script. There are two main rules that you should adhere to, especially if this is the first script you have written:

    1. *Dialogue should be kept to the bare minimum:* the scripts of inexperienced scriptwriters are often much too wordy. Such scripts sound very unnatural when spoken. Listen to real conversations and you will discover that people tend to use as few words as possible. Much of what they are saying and how they are feeling is apparent in their faces, gestures and body language: very often it is what they are not saying which counts! This needs to be at the forefront of your mind as you labour to put words on to paper. Concentrate on describing in words what is seen rather than what is said: in the industry, this is known as *show not tell*.

    2. *Dialogue should be 'sayable':* the script should use everyday language not flowery, literary language. Don't try to be too clever. It won't work unless you have top actors.

- *Mise-en-scène:* if, as suggested above, narrative structures and the narrative stages are broadly similar in most narratives, one of the things which marks out one film from another is *mise-en-scène*. You will remember that the term refers generally to the overall look of a scene but specifically to the things which are put into the scene as a result of conscious decisions on the part of the director. This means that you need to understand exactly what the script is asking for in terms of locations, props and set dressing.

One final word of warning: be aware that when an audience sits down to watch a video it is prepared to suspend its disbelief (to forget that it is watching a constructed media text) but only up to a point: character, dialogue, plot and *mise-en-scène* must all be believable. This is the main task of scripting.

So, to sum up what makes a good narrative for a short film, we would ask you to bear Ken Dancyger's five suggestions in mind when producing your first short film:

1. Keep it simple. The plot should be simple and contain a maximum of three or four characters.
2. Be original. Within the strictures mentioned above, try to present your idea in as new and original a manner as possible.
3. One of the key mistakes that students make is that they often confuse story with style. A narrative must have all the narrative elements. So, for example …
4. Conflict should occur and be very visible.
5. Find the focus of your film and stick with it. (1997b: 59)

Once the script has been locked, organize a date and time for actors to do a read-through of the script with the key members of your production team. At this stage, you can sit around a table in a quiet, private room (studio, rehearsal room, etc.) and the actors can read the script aloud to see how it sounds and what changes need to be made to make it more believable and deliverable. Do give yourself time and space to do this: it won't be wasted. If you looked at the bonus chapter on the website, you will remember that the writers argued that this was the stage where the 'specialness' of each episode of *Friends* originated. Use the experience of your actors and listen to what they say. If they tell you that their character wouldn't say something, change it! If they say their words are too clunky, change them! Work *with* the actors to change the written word into the spoken word and to build upon the personalities and interactivity of the characters.

Before finalizing the shooting schedule, make sure that you also leave time for walkthroughs of the script, as this will save you no end of time at the shooting stage. A walkthrough is where the production team sets up an accurate reconstruction of a location and asks the actors to walk through it (hence its name!) while reading through the script. Professional productions will often use a bare room with tape on the floor as 'walls' and, for example, a desk as a cooker to make sure that everything in the location is in the right place. You should, as a result of your recces, know what your location will look like and what it will contain but, as we suggested in Chapter 1, you should take full measurements of the location and photos at the recce stage to remind yourself of the location. At its most basic level, the walkthrough allows the production team to know whether or not all the actors, crew and kit can be fitted into the available space. The director and director of photography (DoP) should, at this stage, be working out the shots, the lighting director should be deciding where lamps should go and the sound person should know where to position microphones. We have seen production teams set up in the real location only to discover that they cannot fit all the kit in. This is too late! Equally importantly, though, the walkthrough enables the director to synchronize the spoken words of the actors with the actions required of them by the script. It also allows the actors to know where they should be and what they should be saying at any given point, known as *script timings*. Use the walkthrough as an opportunity to shoot scenes or aspects of scenes, both as practice for the actual shoot but also so that they can be played back to see whether they can be improved. What this means is that scenes shot on location are not a rehearsal because they have already been walked through.

Producing a storyboard

Clearly, given the scale of the production, the main point about storyboarding for a drama short is that each individual shot should be represented in as much detail as possible and as close to the shot required in the final video as possible.

Given the job of work that each shot within your short has to do, it is vital that you plan each one well in advance of shooting it. As always, start by producing thumbnails of each shot. Make sure that your audience will be able to follow the action through the inclusion of a combination of different shots from different camera positions. Argue over, amend, adjust and finalize your shots at the thumbnail stage and then, but only then, produce the definitive storyboard.

When producing storyboards for drama you have absolute control over where the camera will be placed in relation to the action. The process of deciding the camera positions and the type of shot which will be acquired is known as *blocking*. Given that the drama must have a narrative, it is essential that careful consideration be given both to the individual shots but also to the shot before and the shot after, as this will ensure visual and narrative continuity.

As with previous videos, make sure that you cover your scene with simple shots so that you have a video. However, we will make the point again that drama shorts allow you the space fully to use your imagination, especially with regard to the camerawork. Each shot is an opportunity to enhance and supplement the narrative or, as in *Who Killed Brown Owl* – the short that we suggested you look at in the activity at the beginning of this chapter, can effectively structure the narrative. Jeremy Vineyard (1999) provides a host of complex and developing shots that you can use to make your video look much more professional and cinematic. Be careful, though, not to get carried away: not only do such shots take a lot of practice before you get them right, but they can make the audience think that you are being too clever.

It is at the stage of producing a storyboard that you need to think about the other key elements which will make up your short film: the sound design and graphics.

Film music

Music in film can take the form of a music soundtrack or a music score. The first thing we need to do is define what we mean by both terms. For our purposes, the soundtrack in a film is the music, either diegetic or non-diegetic, original or 'found', within a film narrative which either overtly or covertly supports the narrative and helps to create a specific mood in the audience. The music score, on the other hand, is the non-diegetic music, usually original, within a film narrative, which supports the narrative and helps to create a specific mood in the audience. These terms are explained in more detail as follows:

- *Diegetic or non-diegetic music:* in simple terms, diegetic music is 'music whose apparent source is the narrative world of the film' (Gorbman 1998: 44): that is, it is the music within the film which happens at the same time as the action and that the characters, as a result, will hear: for example, the music in a nightclub or on a radio. Non-diegetic music (or scoring) is music which has been added over the narrative at the post-production stage and which, as a result, is not heard by the characters but supplements and enhances the narrative.
- *Original or 'found' music:* music within a film can be original, as is the case with most scores, or can be 'found': that is, can use pre-existing music to create a sense of time and/or place.
- *Music within a film narrative:* music within films is used in three main places: over the opening credits, within the narrative itself and over the closing credits.
- *Music which is overt or covert:* music soundtracks tend to be more overt; music scores tend to be more covert
- *Music which supports the narrative:* as may be obvious, the music chosen can be used actively to support the narrative.
- *Music which helps to create a specific mood:* the use of specific instrumentation has a semiotic significance and, as a result, a direct effect on the emotions which are evoked in the audience with regard to the narrative. Lush orchestration, for example, has a completely different significance from hip-hop. So, in making creative decisions about what instrumentation and arrangements to use, 'the key is to try to create a suitable emotional context' (Dancyger 1997: 332). The type of instrumentation and arrangement also has another level of signification with regard to the film: epic instrumentation leads to a perception of 'epicness' while stripped-down instrumentation often leads to a perception of artiness.

Don't forget, too, that music can be used to good effect if it opposes the visuals: what is known as *counterpoint*. For example, in *A Clockwork Orange* the song 'Singing in the Rain', which is normally associated with a pleasurable musical, is used for a traumatic rape scene. Finally, the music can be so minimal as not to be music: for example, a synthesized drone.

Graphics

Generally, graphics are used at the beginning, in the form of titles, and at the end, in the form of credits. As with the title sequence brief, your graphics can be computer-generated in post-production or produced as part of the production stage. Whichever you choose, they also need to be storyboarded so that they can be discussed and agreed before the production stage. It is an obvious point but it is worthwhile conducting research on titles and credits within drama, especially drama shorts, to assist you in constructing your drama short. With such research you will develop a sense of the basic rules of screen design, which would include careful consideration about the size, colour, font, positioning, movement and duration of text. The images used as the background for text are also an important part of the overall meaning of the drama. If such shots are required, or if the titles or credits are particularly elaborate, you will need to plan time and possibly a separate team to work on them. Their production can, if necessary, be incorporated into the production schedule.

Producing a shot list and shooting order

As if things were not complicated enough, you now have to produce a shot list and shooting order. Simple descriptions of each shot, including the camera position, direction, movement and intention, will provide much needed clarity to your shoot, especially if you have a large number of locations and scenes to cover.

Use the shot list to work out your shooting order by grouping shots and scenes. It is important to think in a practical and logical way about the order of shots. For example, each scene can be broken down into its various camera positions so that the camera does not constantly have to be moved from one position to another and then back again. Shoot the whole scene as a master shot from one camera position, then again from another, and so on. Plan to film one after another all those scenes which take place in one location, if appropriate. This may mean changing the actors' costumes and altering the lighting from early morning to night, but will save a lot of set-up time. Check and discuss your shooting order carefully before locking it and distributing it.

Producing a shooting schedule

Key to being an organized team is that each member of the team should know what to do, when to do it and where. This is achieved by ensuring that the group proactively *manages* the production process. This is the function of the shooting schedule which, as you will remember, should list the locations, equipment, crews and talent being used for each day of shooting.

Whereas your previous productions were single-camera shoots, your drama may well have two crews: the first and second units. If you are fortunate enough to have access to sufficient kit, this method is very economical on time because one crew can shoot one scene while the other crew can either gather relatively simple visuals, such as exterior location shots and insert shots, or prepare for the next scene.

Student productions often fail even to consider scheduling the set-up time and rehearsal time for the actors. It is imperative that both be scheduled. The crew needs to set up properly and if the actors come to a shoot cold they will not have had time to get to know the other actors, to develop their character and to perfect their lines, as opposed to just having learnt them. If you neglect to schedule in such time, your production will almost inevitably suffer.

Production

As we have mentioned a number of times before, there are two main ways of organizing your production:

- *democratically*: all members of the group have an equal say about all decisions at each stage of the production process;
- *hierarchically*: each member of the group has specific roles and responsibilities.

Unless you are very lucky, the first of these is *absolutely* the worst way of producing a drama short. What happens in most groups which are organized democratically is that discussions go round and round with little chance of agreement or with everyone agreeing to go with the lowest common denominator. What can also happen is that groups split into factions and end up subverting the production, thus ruining the whole production and lowering everyone's marks.

Given the size of the production, it is far better to manage your production professionally: that is, hierarchically. You already know the reason why most, if not all, professional productions work in this way: it allows everyone in the crew to know who has responsibility for any task which needs completing.

Tasks to do

Go to the book's website and look at the interviews with the crew members for *Discful of Data*. While watching the interviews, listen carefully to what each of the crew says about what he/she learned from the project. Think about how what they are saying might relate to your own production and whether it alerts you to any areas which still require attention.

Roles and responsibilities

All of you are, by now, relatively seasoned video-makers and have probably already taken some or all of the roles within a video crew, so you may well have an idea of which role you want to take and, more importantly, are realistically able to cope with.

At this point you should visit the website. On it, you will find downloadable sheets which clearly outline all the roles and responsibilities for drama production, the key skills required for each role and the key tasks for each of the stages of production.

Two key roles that you may not have had in your crew before and which are specific to drama production are:

1. *Director of photography (DoP):* the DoP's role is to work closely with the director to ensure that everything is visually perfect and meets the intended style in terms of light, colour and camera movement both for individual shots and the drama as a whole.
2. *First assistant director (1st AD):* the 1st AD's job is to make sure that the location shoots progress smoothly and to be in charge of everything that happens in the space of the shoot: ensuring that the right people are on set in the right places, that all shots on the storyboard are actually shot and, more generally, taking work away from the director but never taking over from him/her.

We have based these outlines of the various roles and responsibilities on our experience of working with students while filming drama shorts on locations in various parts of the UK and Europe. Each job is realistically broken down into its various parts within the production process. We recognize that some roles are absent or merged with others and we make no apologies for this, as it faithfully reflects our experience over the years of how student drama shorts tend to function in terms of roles and responsibilities.

Editors should get out more!

With the advent of increasingly powerful laptops and time-saving logging software, you may consider taking your editor on location with you. While we are on location we often lock our editor in one of the rooms with a laptop, deck and the tapes and logging sheets from the day's filming. Given a couple of hours he/she is able to produce an assembly of a scene from the drama and play it to the director and crew either last thing at night or at the morning production meeting. This has the obvious advantage of giving an early indication to those watching of what the drama is beginning to look like and also saves time for the editor, who could log, capture and assembly-edit the entire drama while still on location!

Post-production

Editing the drama short is probably the most extensive and sophisticated job of editing that anyone in your group has yet carried out. It is for both of these reasons that we would suggest that only one person take on the role of editor.

The assembly

Logging

As with the other briefs in this book, logging can, and should, be done on location by either the PA or, if you have a larger crew, the camera assistant. All the shots taken during production will have been recorded on to log sheets which, to remind you, must include details such as tape number, scene, shot, take, start and end timecodes for each shot, and comments. It is more pertinent for the drama short, given the complexity of the production and the likely number of tapes.

Capturing/digitizing

Using the logging sheets, storyboards, scripts and any director's notes, you can now digitize or capture the appropriate takes of the most suitable material and store them in a separate bin for each scene.

Methodically record scene names, shot numbers and takes, the timecode and descriptive comments for each clip that you store in the bin. You need to be able to identify a bin or clip by its name alone and, ideally, you need to know exactly where that clip came from should you wish to redigitize it later. As shots are successfully digitized, tick them off on the storyboard; as entire scenes are completed, tick those off too. As you progress, you may wish to consider backing up your work on a separate hard drive at some point, just in case. Hard drives do crash!

The assembly 'merely' requires that you choose the appropriate clips and drop them on to the timeline in the correct order. This is actually quite a skilled process. Although you will be working from a storyboard, the manner of shooting means that you may well have numerous takes, angles and – if the lessons about filming for editing from the documentary chapter were heeded – shots which were not storyboarded.

Earlier in the book we likened the idea of video production to playing with a child's construction set because you have so many pieces at your disposal and so many ways to put them together, each way creating a completely different final video. You should, therefore, spend a long time both thinking about the possible order of the clips and, almost certainly, producing a number of different assembly cuts. Don't make the mistake of producing only one, as it is amazing how a number of totally different videos may be made from the same footage. As Lisa Gunning (2007: 141) notes, 'Editing is all about falling in love with sequences, smashing them up, making them perfect, throwing them away and then sometimes putting them back together again!' The ability to play with a scene is vital: the careful selection of material shot from different camera angles, the emotional high and low points, the important moments or turning points, the drama within the sequence all contribute to allowing each scene to evolve: this is 'the infuriating but rewarding process of assembling a scene' (Gunning 2007: 140).

Technical and creative quality control is essential at this stage. There is little point in including a soft shot: a shot which is poorly lit, poorly acted or badly framed. What may have looked appropriate during logging may not be suitable now, so be decisive and look for alternative shots when needed. You also need to be thinking about the narrative of each sequence, by considering the purpose of each sequence as well as the narrative structure of the drama as a whole.

One other point: it is very easy to get carried away at the stage where you see a film coming together but remember that there should not at this stage be any attempt to colour-correct, balance the sound or use any effects: just put the right clips in the right order on to the timeline for all the sequences.

The assembly screening

In the industry, it is likely to be only the editor and director who look at the video at this stage. By now, they should have a feel for the flow of the story and be able to assess it in terms of both visuals and dialogue.

Our experience with student drama tells us that now is also a good opportunity for the other members of the crew who have not been involved in the edit to see an early realization of the director's vision and the result of all their hard work. It will be unrefined, perhaps somewhat clunky, but it will represent the entire story from start to finish. It is a good idea to screen it to the group at this point so that the editor can gain feedback from the rest of the production team as well as from the director. This will help the editor enormously, especially if a decision has to be made about which of the cuts to continue working on.

You may wish to screen the assembly to people outside the crew, family and friends in order to ensure more honest and critical feedback. As always, note their comments and their emotional engagement with the drama: their faces may tell you which sequences work and which ones do not.

From the comments of those at the screening, it should become clearer to the director whether the visuals are successful in allowing the narrative to unfold and what needs to be done to improve each scene and the drama overall. The main questions which should be addressed, however, are whether it works as a drama short and how it can be improved.

The rough cut

Before jumping into the edit, we would recommend that you stop and do two things:

1. Reread the section on the rough cut in Chapter 5 to reacquaint yourself with some of the more basic editing techniques.
2. Think back to the contextual research that you carried out earlier in the production process. In looking in detail at as many short films as possible and reflecting upon them, you will start to see the types of technique which are specific to short films.

Now that the story has finally moved from scripts and storyboards to a moving image on a timeline, albeit only as an assembly, it is time to take into account the comments from the screening and further refine its telling through careful consideration of the visual narrative and key dialogue. Use these comments as your guide from now on.

It is likely that your assembly is far longer than you anticipated and individual scenes may appear to drag. You need, therefore, to go through each sequence or scene, cutting anything seen or said which does not contribute directly to the story. You should go through each scene several times, eliminating shots which do not fit while ensuring narrative and visual continuity and also returning to the unfolding story in its entirety. You should trim the dialogue, removing any unwanted sounds from the director or crew, and also the shots, where they are unnecessary or unduly long. You should eliminate anything which does not make a contribution to the story.

This stage, paradoxically, requires you to start adding to and amending some of the building blocks of your story to provide the essential material which is still missing: establishing shots for setting scenes and locations; the use of CUs to provide detail and emphasis; cutaways to assist with the general unfolding of the story, and transition effects to permit movement in time and space.

The key throughout is to concentrate on telling the story for each scene and for the video overall. Don't get too close to or too precious about shots, sequences or scenes. If they do not contribute to the story, lose them. If they slow the pace, trim them. You, the editor, make the decisions and justify them to the director. Work with what you have, never linger, move on and always tell the story. At this stage, therefore, you should also address the issue of rhythm and pace.

The need for rhythm and pace

Producing the rough cut affords you two further opportunities which are vital with regard to working on rhythm and pace:

1. Each scene's rhythm is determined by how it is cut, the duration of each shot and how these shots are strung together. It is the editor's role to recognize the purpose of each scene and to ensure the appropriate rhythm and pace for each. Shots of long duration and sequences with long dissolves between shots will have a slow pace (as in a love scene); fast-paced scenes will have a straight cut every couple of seconds (as in a chase).
2. When put together, the scenes and their individual rhythms will determine the overall rhythms of the entire drama short. Most dramas require variations of rhythm and pace which are associated with the unfolding events or action. This variation within a scene or between scenes could be compared to a well-designed roller-coaster ride which has emotive highs and lows: some anticipated, some not. A good ride contains a well-balanced mix of the two and, as suggested above, can still provide some surprises.

Recognizing the purpose of each scene and what it is trying to say, both emotively and in terms of the story, and studying the dialogue and action of each scene should help you with the above.

As an editor you need to immerse yourself in the flow, the dialogue and the visuals. Work at a fast pace, use your instinct, don't deliberate over an edit, do it and move on, continuing until the scene is finished. Only then should you go back over it, further refining it and moving on. It can be lonely work and very frustrating so it is often very useful to have the director with you: it is less lonely and can help with decision-making. Even if you argue with the director over an edit, a cut or the order of a scene, it can still result in a positive outcome.

Continuity

You must ensure continuity between each of the shots in your video: continuity of lighting, colour, sound and action, If you are having a continuity problem, sleight of hand is a good tool for the drama editor. If you are short of a CU or insert for one scene, borrow from another: as long as it matches, no one will notice. Be creative about overcoming problems – a pair of glasses are held in an actor's left hand but there is a cut to a CU of them in his right hand: use your digital know-how and simply flip the image so that the glasses now appear to be in the correct hand and continuity is restored. In the film *Titanic*, only one side of the ship was constructed, and the image was reversed in order to represent the other side of the ship: a simple and cost-effective method of apparently showing the ship from both sides.

One of the key methods of ensuring continuity between shots is to give careful consideration to the transitions between these shots:

- A cut is a change from one shot to another which does not rely on any form of effect and is used in the edit to change the camera view. *Straight cuts* are one of the most essential tools for the drama editor because they allow you to move simply between different camera positions in order to offer the very best way of telling the story. Investigate some drama shorts and note the number of edit effects used. You will see that cuts predominate.
- A cut can also be used to move to a different subject or narrative within the story. This is known as *cross-cutting*.
- *Dissolves* are the effect that you are most likely to use in drama and they can move the story in terms of time and place as well as heightening dramatic or emotional effect. The duration of the dissolve must be carefully considered as it directly affects the pace of the sequence: slower dissolves lead to a slower overall pace.
- Other effects, such as *wipes*, can also be useful but you need to use them with care and consideration.

In addition, you have the following techniques at your disposal:

- *Constructing shot continuity:* this is editing which supports continuity of action using what Dancyger calls 'a seamless cut' and will select shots which match the action and put them together in such a way that the logic of an event, such as an individual getting into a car, is viewed without the edits being noticed.

- *Ensuring adequate cover:* this is what all editors should hope for and is when the director has considered the edit during the shoot and offered sufficient camera coverage for each scene. This might mean simply shooting the action from different angles and using the full range of shots from LSs through to extreme CUs or, in the case of dialogue between two characters, providing a range of shots including POVs for each person, CUs and reaction shots.
- *Matching the action:* this technique is also known as cutting on action or match-cut and relies on cutting on a specific intentional movement such as reaching for a door bell which then permits a cut to a CU of the bell being pressed and a further edit of a reaction shot from someone within the house who hears the bell, and so on. This technique can also be useful for cutting dialogue, but is prompted by the conversation itself.
- *Maintaining screen direction:* 'Maintaining screen direction is critical if the film is to avoid confusion and keep the characters distinct. A strict left-to-right or right-to-left pattern must be maintained' (Dancyger 1997: 300). If an actor enters the frame and moves through it from left to right, it is the viewers' expectation that the actor will appear at the left-hand side of the frame in the next shot. This also applies if a character is moving diagonally across the screen, away from the camera for example. We recommend that you watch a chase sequence and observe this theory in action. Editing the movement of an actor can be assisted by careful consideration of movement at the storyboard stage.
- *Scene-setting:* it is often important for the viewer to be introduced to a scene and the content of the scene by the use of an LS or establishing shot, progressively moving through the shots to a CU. This can also be the last shot of a scene.
- *Matching tone:* consistency of lighting and colour during production is essential to the editor. Post-production tools such as colour-correction can help but often produce other problems when they are used and can be time-consuming. Matching tone between shots is important in order to maintain continuity, but is an almost impossible task for the editor if there are huge variations in lighting and colour.
- *Matching the flow over a cut:* everyday activities do not need to be shown in real time and do not require every aspect of the process to be shown. For example, not every action involved in the routine of a man preparing to leave home in the morning to go to work would need to be shown when editing a sequence. It is the editor's job to decide which visual

information is dramatically interesting and which is dramatically necessary. This selection will condense time while maintaining the continuity of, for example, eating breakfast as an integral element of the narrative.

- *Location change:* this is similar to matching flow inasmuch as the intention is to condense time while moving a character or characters from one location to another. This can be achieved by showing the departure from one location and the arrival at another, with some information – such as a shot of the travelling vehicle and surrounding backdrop – in between. It is worth pointing out that screen direction (discussed above) would need to be addressed in order to support the sequence.
- *Scene change:* this is normally achieved with a cut or dissolve, but there are a number of different ways of doing this:
  - Link two scenes together with the same sound.
  - Crab left to right out of one shot and then crab in exactly the same manner left to right in the next shot. The cut can be made as the camera reaches the edge of the set or a dark or plain object which is replicated at the start of the next shot, thus maintaining the same tone and hiding the edit.
  - Cut halfway through a tracking shot to another identical tracking shot in the next scene.
  - Follow a character who continues talking in the next scene, but is wearing different attire.
  - Focus attention on a prop such as a CU of a television screen at the end of one scene and then cut to a CU of another television screen in the next scene, pulling back and revealing that it is a different television in a different location.
- *Blocking shots:* if you shot to your storyboard, you should have a number of blocking shots available to you for each part of each scene. This is a joy for the editor because it means there is a choice of shots to cut to. Blocking shots should also include CUs cutaways and inserts: all those essential ingredients that the editor needs to put together the scene visually. Blocking shots can be used to cover continuity errors and actors' mistakes: when a dialogue line is finished off badly, for example, it is possible to cut round it by moving to another shot which picks up the dialogue.
- *Cutting on movement (also known as matching the action):* this is a standard technique in editing drama and, as the name suggests, involves making an edit when there is some movement or action in the shot. The visual continuity of the action is enhanced through cutting when a movement is taking place: a shot of someone opening a door in one room, for example, can be cut to a shot of the door being opened as seen from the other room.

Cutting on movement allows for a much fuller exploration of an event such as reaching for, and drinking, a glass of water, by exploiting the many blocking shots and subsequently adding visual value to the event as well as essential continuity. Cutting on movement can also be used between shots which may not be logically connected as a means of moving the action within time or space.

- *Dialogue overlaps:* these are a standard part of the editor's armoury of techniques and are widely used in all genres of drama. A dialogue overlap is where the first shot in a sequence contains the visuals and sound of one person speaking but is then cut to a second shot, this time using visuals only, of the other person in the conversation: what is known as a *reaction shot*. This type of edit is also referred to as a *split edit* or, less commonly, an *L-edit*. Overlapping dialogue and image both helps to represent normal patterns of speech more accurately and allows you to play around with the pace and the rhythm of your video

- *Additional dialogue:* at this stage, it may become apparent that you need additional lines of dialogue which were not recorded at the production stage and which are essential in order to explain the scene or the narrative. It is possible to add new lines of dialogue in post-production by asking your actor to deliver these additional lines either in the same location as before or, if that is not possible, in a room with a similar audio ambience. However, it will only be successful in the edit if you have shots of the actor turning away from the camera or off camera.

It is the editor's function to provide new life to the material. It is possible that in doing so the drama moves away from the original script and storyboards and becomes something else. Lisa Gunning (2007: 143) comments:

A film usually ends up being true to a script in its essence but it undoubtedly has a life of its own. The script may work beautifully, but once it is shot you can make the film do what you want it to; moving scenes around, cutting them down, adding to them, cheating them or even creating new ones by using additional dialogue recording (ADR) ... This is the job of an editor, to find solutions, play tricks, use cheats. As long as the end result seems intended.

So, now you've finished the rough cut!

Having spent many hours with the director furiously slaving over a hot screen, it is time to view the film in its entirety and pose some simple but painfully honest questions. The main one is does it work as a drama short? In order to answer this, you need to ask some further questions:

- Do any scenes require more attention with regard to inserts, cutaways, CUs or basic visual and sound effects such as transitions or overlaps?
- Do you need to shoot new footage or new dialogue?
- Do you need to reshoot anything?
- Do you need to restructure any of the edited scenes?
- Do you need to reconsider the overall structure of the piece?

By now you are a very long way from the early days of scripts and thumbnails. The production has taken on an independent life of its own, so put the scripts and storyboards away and concentrate on allowing the drama to become whatever it will be. Work only with what you know you have and with what you know that you can obtain if necessary.

If your drama becomes a bit of a drama (and they often do!) keep calm and work on restructuring. Remember that there are some things which cannot be improved upon, such as wooden acting. Be prepared to spend a lot more time in the edit suite with the director, working and reworking.

One piece of practical advice that we would stress at this point is always to save versions of the edit as you go, possibly at the end of each day, both as an EDL and by printing them to tape so that you have a number of stop-off points to return to if you should need to do so. Label them carefully to avoid any confusion. Finally, it is also worth noting that some of the remaining tasks such as the design and execution of a title sequence or credits can be undertaken by the assistant editor while the rough cut is being produced.

The final cut

Once you and the director feel that the structure and content, and therefore the story, are almost correct and require only minimal or subtle attention, you can move on to produce the final cut.

Visuals: grading and compositing

Once you have a 'picture lock', which is when the visuals are unlikely to undergo further alteration, you may need, or wish, to spend some time on grading. For drama especially, the two main reasons for this are equally important: to ensure that there is colour continuity between all the shots in the video and to add colour effects to the footage, which will further enhance the 'look' of the video. Depending on how good your footage is and the look you wish to produce in post-production, this can be quite a time-consuming business, but it can be the icing on the cake with regard to the visuals.

The first use of colour-correction is carried out in order to address problems created during production. It is important to remember that although filters can help, they cannot and should not be relied upon to resolve set-up problems: this needs to be done in pre-production, by matching up camera settings if using more than one camera and through the expert use of cameras and lighting during production.

The editors of shorts shot on DV are using grading increasingly frequently as an opportunity to use filters within the editing software. Alternatively, external software such as the Magic Bullet post-production packages After Effects and Shake offer a myriad of effects which can provide an added dimension to your drama. As with all effects, be selective and always justify your decision. For those of you using Final Cut Pro to edit, go to www.kenstone.net for good advice and a step-by-step guide to colour-correction and the use of filters. There are similar specific forums for all the other main non-linear edit systems, as well as more general advice forums. Some editors prefer to do this after they have locked both picture and sound.

Titles and credits

The titles and credits for drama can play a very crucial role in building up the expectations of the viewer: just think, for example, of the title sequences for the James Bond films. Unlike many other genres, titles and credits for drama can be built into the narrative or plot and, as such, can become part of the opening sequence.

For drama shorts you have a number of choices about how you create and use the title and credits for your production: from those which are very simple, such as a black background and white scrolling text, to very elaborate sequences. Credits and titles do need to take into account the end user and the context of how and where the short will be viewed. A short-short may by dint of its duration require a very short title sequence and credits, while a short designed for screening at festivals can perhaps afford to have more elaborate titles and credits. The best advice we can offer is to view other dramas and drama shorts and pick up ideas.

You may wish to use the title within the opening sequence and this should be storyboarded carefully prior to shooting, allowing space within the frame for the title itself. Credits can also be introduced at the start of the drama short and similarly built into the opening. Titles and credits are an interesting phenomenon inasmuch as they are a regular part of our normal viewing but we rarely analyse them, although we do occasionally admire them. We are reminded at this point of the credits for the film *Lemony Snicket's A Series of Unfortunate Events* (Brad Silberling, 2004). We were spellbound by the quality and execution of the graphic design of the credits for this film, which ran for several minutes and must have cost a fortune to produce. They were truly stunning, but we were the only people in the cinema to appreciate them as everyone else got up and left as soon as the credits started rolling. Our advice for drama shorts is, as usual, simple is best. Either build them into the shot footage or create them in post-production: either way they will need to be carefully considered in pre-production, storyboarded and executed.

The sound edit

Try watching a tense scene from a horror film without the sound. So much vital information is missing. Rather than being subordinate to the visuals, the sound effects and music can often stand in for the dialogue and the narrative. This is why paying attention to the sound in your drama is important, whatever the genre.

You should at this stage be paying close attention to sound: dialogue will certainly need to be further edited and balanced, wildtrack should be added, along with sound effects and Foley and, finally, the music should also be edited. All the sound will then need to be carefully and painstakingly mixed, or 'sweetened', so that it is in balance: that is, so that all the sound elements work together, rather than one drowning out another.

The sound mix

Mixing the sound for your drama is a job in itself. Your group may be lucky enough to have someone who can act as a sound designer to work with the editor. This can come as a blessed relief to the editor who has spent so much time on the visuals, and, more practically, it offers a new pair of ears. It will require a lot of hard work on the part of whoever carries out the sound edit.

In order to prepare for the sound mix, the editor and/or sound designer will need to 'spot' sound. This entails listing all the sounds which need to be added. This should be done scene by scene and you should be looking for:

- on-screen sounds such as footfalls and any other sound or noise which accompanies on-screen actions;
- off-screen sounds such as a radio playing, the sound of an ice cream van or children playing outside in the street;
- ambient sounds associated with the on-screen environment, such as birds singing or the sound of road traffic;
- unusual sounds such as the twang of a jaw harp in *A Fistful of Dollars*. These tend to be non-diegetic sounds which are not connected with any of the action except inasmuch they are incongruous and often add a rather surreal quality to the scene.

The best advice that we can offer is that you should look out and listen out for where sound should be: if there should be sound but there is none, then add it. Consider what it is that the audience is meant to be looking at and decide what sound should perhaps dominate in the mix: a wine glass being thrown and smashing against a wall, for example, or a kettle being filled with tap water. Although it may only be for a couple of seconds, these actions will shift the balance of the sound. The level of individual sounds is obviously very important and should be carefully set according to where the attention of the audience should be drawn. It is also important to identify any gaps in the sound. In the real world, there will always be numerous individual sounds which make up the sound around us but very rarely do we ever really listen to them. Again, it is vital to look and listen. Try to do that now. What can you hear around you? How many different and individual sounds can you make out and which ones dominate within the mix? Always think of sound in terms of layers – not just one sound, but a number of sounds – as that is how we hear our environments, as a perpetual mix of all kinds of sound.

The first area to tackle is fine-tuning the dialogue. To do this, you need to work scene by scene, watching each scene separately and listening carefully to what is said. You need to make sure that the sound levels between speakers are balanced, overlapping where necessary. It as at this point that camera perspective and dialogue should be addressed. This is the consideration of what connection needs to be made between the viewer and what is being heard in terms of dialogue. A conversation shot in LS or MS can be at a different level to a more intimate conversation shot in CU. These more subtle shifts in levels and balance can add much greater realism to edits in terms of vision and sound and ensure that scenes appear more natural. For example, a couple walk arm in arm and are seen in the distance, We can hear their conversation and the background sound which surrounds them. Cut to an MS or a CU of the couple as they continue to talk intimately. The dialogue is crisper, clearer and appears slightly louder and the ambient sounds of their surroundings are far less noticeable. This has the overall effect of drawing the viewer more intimately into the conversation. We already know that emotion can be heightened through the use of visual CUs or extreme CUs. A similar effect can be produced with sound, which can be given the equivalent of an extreme CU, or *lift*.

Once the dialogue has been fine-tuned, you can move on to the other sounds in the scene. We mentioned earlier that it is important to think about what the audience will be looking at, as this helps to determine what sounds are present and how they may be mixed. We already know that the camera can do this by what it shows us. Different camera perspectives will require different audio perspectives. For example, a couple are sitting in their car while it is pouring with rain. The camera cuts from an exterior shot of the vehicle to an interior shot. The couple sit quietly watching the rain and eventually a conversation starts. The content and levels of the mix would need to consider the rain in terms of the exterior and the interior, and the sounds of the couple when they start talking would need to blend in seamlessly throughout the scene. A couple (a different couple this time!) approach the exterior of a house where there is a noisy party. They enter the hall, looking into a room where loud music is playing, they say hello to people sitting on the stairs who are talking loudly because of the music and then they go up to the top floor and into an attic room where they close the door behind them and start to talk in hushed tones. Think about the sound design for this short scene. What would need to be heard and how should it be mixed?

When faced with many different sounds within a scene, it may be useful to consider the narrative intent of the scene. This may allow you to decide which sound will take precedence over the many other sounds. Consider, for example, a beautiful, natural landscape and a group of walkers enjoying the tranquillity. The ear-splitting scream of a fighter jet passing overhead blocks out all other sound until it has passed and we return to the sounds of nature.

Once you have all the audio (except the music) balanced and on the respective timelines, go through it again scene by scene using your 'special ears' to ensure that you cannot hear any sound edit, that the balance is correct between the various sounds and that each sound works to support the narrative correctly. If you can hear an edit or there is a gap in the sound, then you need to stop and correct it. Unlike when editing visuals, you should almost never use straight cuts as they sound very unnatural. Always listen for the transitions: if you can hear them, then they haven't worked and need addressing.

Music

The final, often ignored element of sound design is the music. It is part of the language of the short and must never be underestimated or left until the very last moment. Well-selected music can do much to enhance your short: poorly selected music can do much to damage it.

The final 'spotting', then, is for the music soundtracks. As we saw in Chapter 6, there are a number of ways of sourcing music: from paying for the work of an established artist to commissioning your own. Whichever route you decide to take, the position and role of the music is determined by its function and this can vary throughout: it can sit underneath the action, underpinning it; at other times it can move the story or the action from one scene to another; at other times it is at the forefront and leads the action in terms of audience expectations.

One other interesting point about sound is the decision about when *not* to have sound. Sometimes an absence of sound can be very effective. An example of this might be when you wish to convey the state of mind of a character who is very disturbed by offering a sound and visual POV. We see the busy city streets surrounding him but hear no traffic or people, which contributes to our understanding of his alienation and offers a surreal account of his world.

Most editing software will provide you with sufficient tools to produce a reasonably complex soundscape and subsequent sound edit. There is also an increasing amount of sound editing software such as Sony's Soundforge, Apple's Logic Pro and Adobe's Soundbooth CS4 which work alongside video edit packages. These allow for a more complex and detailed sound mix and should really only be used if you are lucky enough to have an individual who will work alongside the editor specifically as the sound editor.

And now the end is near ...

The end result of all of your hard work to date is a drama short that you have, as part of your group, devised, planned, shot and edited. As we said at the beginning of the chapter, it is probably the biggest project that you have ever undertaken and, as such, you can rightly be very proud of yourself.

The *real* end of the project, though, is that you have to screen your short publicly. So, even though you probably hate the sight of it by now, make sure that you have enough energy left to send it to festivals, upload it to a website or, at the very minimum, arrange a local screening. It is still amazing to us how many of our students do not do this, even when the finished piece is excellent, simply because they have run out of steam. It is such a shame, especially given the vast amount of time and energy which has been spent on the project.

Our top ten tips for drama shorts

1. Recognize the true scale of this project: it's BIG and, as such, will test your project-management skills to the full.
2. Don't run out of steam: you need to keep going right to the end. You need to use all six of the essential elements but it is the fifth and sixth elements which will get you through this project.
3. Spend as much time as possible thinking of good ideas for your short: without the 'nugget' of a good story, it is difficult to make a good video.
4. Draft, redraft and redraft your script again (and then probably again!) until it is *right*. The script is king!
5. Choose *decent* actors rather than those who are the easier to enlist. Give them the time and space to do their job while you concentrate on doing yours.

6. Make sure that you have considered every aspect of the video and that everything has been done to the best of your group's abilities.
7. Schedule breaks and feed and water everyone regularly.
8. Function as a team throughout. Understand what you are meant to do and do it well but also support other members of the crew at all times.
9. Enjoy yourself. There may be times when the words 'drama', 'short' and 'enjoy' don't seem to belong in the same sentence but if you do enjoy the experience, it will spur you on to bigger and better things.
10. Get your short 'out there' by any means possible. As a minimum, have a local screening. It really will finish off the production and, as it is a fun ending, means that you will stay friends with *most* of the crew.

Bibliography

General further reading

Allen, R. (ed.) (1992) *Channels of Discourse, Reassembled*, 2nd edn. London, Routledge.

Barthes, R. (1957) *Mythologies*. London, Verso.

Bignell, J. (1997) *Media Semiotics: An Introduction*. Manchester, Manchester University Press.

Bordwell, D. and Thompson, K. (1997) *Film Art: An Introduction,* 6th edn. New York, McGraw Hill.

Branston, G. and Stafford, R. (1996) *The Media Students Book*. London, Routledge.

Cartwright, S. (1996) *Pre-production Planning for Video, Film and Multimedia*. Oxford, Focal Press.

Casey, L. *et al.* (2002) *Television Studies: The Key Concepts*. London, Routledge.

Chater, K. (2002) *Research for Media Production*. Oxford, Focal Press.

Creeber, G. (ed.) (2001) *The Television Genre Book*. London, BFI.

Dancyger, K. (1997a) *The Technique of Film and Video Editing: Theory and Practice*. Oxford, Focal Press.

Dancyger, K. (1997b) *The World of Film and Video Production*. London, Harcourt Brace.

Dimbleby, N. *et al.* (1992) *Practical Media: A Guide to Production Techniques*. London, Hodder and Stoughton.

Fiske, J. (1990) *An Introduction to Communication Studies*, 2nd edn. London, Routledge.

Geraghty, C. and Lusted, D. (eds) (1997) *The Television Studies Book*. London, Arnold.

Gillespie, M. and Toynbee, J. (eds) (2006) *Analysing Media Texts*. Maidenhead, Open University Press.

Gitlin, T. (1994) *Inside Prime Time*. London, Routledge.

Glasgow University Media Group (1976) *Bad News*. London, Routledge.

Hesmondhalgh, D. (ed.) (2006) *Media Production*. Milton Keynes, Open University Press.

Hill, J. and Church Gibson, P. (1998) *The Oxford Guide to Film Studies*. Oxford, Oxford University Press.

Jameson, F. (1991) *Postmodernism, or the Cultural Logic of Late Capitalism*. London: Verso.

Jarvis, P. (1987) *Shooting on Location*. London, BBC Television Training.

Lapsley, R. and Westlake, M. (1988) *Film Theory: An Introduction*. Manchester, Manchester University Press.

Lopate, P. (1997) 'In Search of the Centaur: The Essay Film', in C. Warren (ed.) (1997).

Lyver, D. (2001) *Basics of the Video Production Diary*. Oxford, Focal Press.

Marshall, J. and Werndly, A. (2002) *The Language of Television*. London, Routledge.

Millerson, G. (1992) *Video Production Handbook*, 2nd edn. Oxford, Focal Press.

Millerson, G. (1997) *TV Scenic Design*, 2nd edn. Oxford, Focal Press.

Millerson, G. (1999) *Television Production,* 13th edn. Oxford, Focal Press.

Monaco, J. (1977) *How to Read a Film.* Oxford, Oxford University Press.

Neale, S. (1980) *Genre.* London, BFI.

Nelmes, J. (ed.) (1996) *An Introduction to Film Theory,* 3rd edn. London, Routledge.

O'Sullivan, T. *et al.* (1994) *Key Concepts in Communication and Cultural Studies,* 2nd edn. London, Routledge.

O'Sullivan. T. *et al.* (1997) *Studying the Media: An Introduction,* 2nd edn. London, Edward Arnold.

Saussure, F. de (1915; 1974) *A Course in General Linguistics.* La Salle, IL, Open Court.

Schirato, T. and Webb, J. (2004) *Understanding the Visual.* London, Sage.

Schön, D. (1987) *The Reflective Practitioner: How Professionals Think in Action.* Farnham, Ashgate.

Thompson, R. (1998) *Grammar of the Shot.* Oxford, Focal Press.

Todorov, T. (1977) *Poetics of Prose.* Ithaca, NY, Cornell University Press.

Vineyard, J. (1999) *Setting Up Your Shots: Great Camera Moves Every Filmmaker Should Know.* Studio City, CA, Michael Wiese Productions.

Ward, P. (2003) *Picture Composition for Film and Television.* Oxford, Focal Press.

Warren, C. (ed.) (1997) *Beyond Document: Essays on Nonfiction Film.* Hanover, NH, Wesleyan Press.

Watts, H. (1997) *On Camera: Essential Know-How for Programme-Makers.* London, Aavo.

Wayne, M. (1997) *Theorising Video Practice.* London, Laurence and Wishart.

General online resources

www.aber.ac.uk – a treasure trove of theory. Useful section on semiotics.

www.bfi.org.uk – the website of the British Film Institute. A key resource for finding out information held by the British Film Institute with useful links to other websites.

www.brainstorming.co.uk – a website devoted to brainstorming.

www.channel101.com – a US-based internet television station. Well worth checking out.

www.imdb.com – the internet movie database with extensive information about almost any film you can think of. A superb resource.

www.mcps.co.uk – the place to obtain copyright clearance for music for your videos.

www.royalty-free.tv – specialist video and film music website.

www.screenonline.org.uk/tv/index.html – part of the British Film Institute's wonderful website. The website should be bookmarked or added to your favourites!

www.shootingpeople.org – the UK industry bulletin board for those working, or wishing to work, in the industry. You pay a subscription fee but get loads in return: daily bulletins, access to work, access to resources. *Well* worth the money!

www.skillset.org – the UK skills council for film and television. Some extremely good resources and up-to-date information about production in the UK.

Digit magazine (www.digit.co.uk)

Showreel magazine (www.showreel.org)

Vertigo magazine (www.vertigo.com)

Title sequences

Nelmes, J. (1996) (ed.) *An Introduction to Film Theory*, 3rd edn. London, Routledge.

Twitchen, R. and Birkett, J. (1983) *Starters: Teaching Television Title Sequences*. London, BFI.

www.bbc.co.uk/cult/classic/titles/index.shtml – a good range of different sequences with examples of well-known, and less well-known, title sequences from the BBC archives.

www.tvtropes.org/pmwiki/pmwiki.php/Main/TitleSequence

Magazine programmes

Bermingham, A. *et al.* (1994) *The Video Studio*. Oxford, Focal Press.

Bonner, F. (2003) *Ordinary Television*. London, Sage.

Ellis, J. (1992) *Visible Fictions: Cinema, Television and Video*. London, Routledge.

Gauntlett, D. and Hill, A. (1996) *TV Living: Television, Culture and Everyday Life*. London, Routledge.

Hobson, D. (1980) *Crossroads: Drama of a Soap Opera*. London, Methuen.

Lull, J. (1990) *Inside Family Viewing: Ethnographic Research on Television's Audiences*. London. Routledge.

Morley, D. (1980) *The Nationwide Audience: Structure and Decoding*. London, BFI.

Radway, J. (1987) *Reading the Romance*. London, Verso.

www.aber.ac.uk/media/Modules/TF33120/morleynw.html – a very nice and detailed discussion of David Morley's *Nationwide Audience* study by Daniel Chandler of Aberystwyth University. Well worth checking out.

www.channel4.com/richardandjudy – UK daily early-afternoon magazine programme

www.itv.com/thismorning – UK daily morning magazine programme

Documentaries

Austin, T. and de Jong, W. (eds) (2008) *Rethinking Documentary: New Perspectives and Practices*. Maidenhead, Open University Press.

Barthes, R. (1977) *Image – Music – Text*. London, Fontana.

Beattie, K. (2004) *Documentary Screens: Nonfiction Film and Television*. Basingstoke, Palgrave Macmillan.

Bernard, S. C. (2004) *Documentary Storytelling for Video and Filmmakers*. Oxford, Focal Press.

Bruzzi, S. (2000) *New Documentary: A Critical Introduction*. London, Routledge.

Casey, B. *et al.* (2002) *Television Studies: The Key Concepts*. London, Routledge.

Cook, D. (2004) *A History of Narrative Film*. London, W. W. Norton.

Corner, J. (1996) *The Art of Record: A Critical Introduction to Documentary*. Manchester, Manchester University Press.

Creeber, G. (ed.) (2001) *The Television Genre Book*. London, BFI.

Forsyth, H. (1966) *Grierson on Documentary*. London, Faber and Faber.

Goldsmith, D. (2003) *The Documentary Makers: Interviews with 15 of the Best in the Business.* Mies, Switzerland, Rotovision.

Hall, S. (1980) 'Encoding/Decoding', in S. Hall, D. Hobson, A. Lowe and P. Willis (eds), *Culture, Media Language.* London, Hutchinson.

Kilborn, R. and Izod, J. (1997) *An Introduction to Television Documentary: Confronting Reality.* Manchester, Manchester University Press.

Nelmes, J. (ed.) (1996) *An Introduction to Film Studies,* 3rd edn. London, Routledge.

Nichols, B. (2000) *Introduction to Documentary.* Bloomington, Indiana University Press.

Petric, V. (1987) *Constructivism in Film: The Man with the Movie Camera – A Cinematic Analysis.* Cambridge, Cambridge University Press.

Rabiger, M. (2004) *Directing the Documentary,* 4th edn. Oxford, Focal Press.

Wells, P. (2001) 'The Documentary Form: Personal and Social "Realities" ', in J. Nelmes (ed.) (1996).

Winston, B. (1995) *Claiming the Real: The Documentary Film Revisited.* London, BFI.

www.channel4.com/fourdocs – the Channel Four documentary website with a very useful historical timeline.

www.sidf.co.uk – the Sheffield International Documentary Festival website.

Studies in Documentary Film. Intellect Journals (www.intellectbooks.com).

Drama shorts

Blaine, B. (2004) 'UK Screenwriters Network: Issue 1099' at www.shootingpeople.org. Accessed 14 December 2004.

Cook, D. (2004) *A History of Narrative Film,* 4th edn. New York, W. W. Norton and Co.

Dancyger, K. (1997) *The Technique of Film and Video Editing.* Oxford, Focal Press.

Gorbman, C. (1998) 'Film Music', in J. Hill and P. Church Gibson (1998).

Grove, E. (2001) *Write and Sell the Hot Screenplay.* Oxford, Focal Press.

Gunning, L. (2007) *Getting Your Short Film Funded, Made and Seen.* London, Shooting People.

Gurskis, D. (2007) *The Short Screenplay: Your Short Film from Concept to Production.* Boston, MA, Thomson Course Technology.

Nelmes, J. (ed.) (1996) *An Introduction to Film Studie,* 3rd edn. London, Routledge.

Nelson, R. (1997) *TV Drama in Transition: Forms, Values and Cultural Change.* London, Macmillan.

Rea, P. and Irving, D. (2001) *Producing and Directing the Short Film and Video.* Oxford, Focal Press.

Russell, A. (2000) *Screenplay.* London, Film Education.

www.atomfilms.co.uk

www.bbc.co.uk/filmnetwork

www.filmsound.org

www.minifilms/history.com

www.reelshorts.com
www.scripttoscreen.co.uk
www.shootingshorts.com
www.studentfilms.com
www.triggerstreet.com

Index

Index compiled by Frank Pert